A NEW SPIRIT OF CAPITALISM

THE TRILATERAL COMMISSION

A New Spirit
of Capitalism

*Toward More Sustainable
and Inclusive Economies*

*A REPORT TO THE TRILATERAL TASK FORCE
ON GLOBAL CAPITALISM IN TRANSITION*

Co-Chairs
CARL BILDT, KELLY GRIER, TAKESHI NIINAMI

Research Director
EDOARDO CAMPANELLA

Senior Advisor
ANDREW ERDMANN

HURST & COMPANY, LONDON

First published in the United Kingdom in 2022 by
C. Hurst & Co. (Publishers) Ltd., New Wing, Somerset House,
Strand, London, WC2R 1LA
© The Trilateral Commission, 2022 All rights reserved.
Printed in Great Britain by Bell and Bain Ltd, Glasgow

The right of The Trilateral Commission to be identified as the
author of this publication is asserted by it in accordance with the
Copyright, Designs and Patents Act, 1988.

A Cataloguing-in-Publication data record for this book
is available from the British Library.

ISBN: 9781787387942

This book is printed using paper from registered sustainable
and managed sources.

www.hurstpublishers.com

The royalties from this book will be donated to humanitarian and
economic relief projects to support the people of Ukraine.

CONTENTS

LIST OF EXHIBITS

LIST OF BOXES

FOREWORD

Capitalism has been the greatest engine of prosperity and well-being in world history. While the focus on capitalism is often associated with material well-being, it is the system that has contributed to delivering hundreds of millions of people from famine and abject poverty, improving health outcomes, and reducing infant mortality, to extend lifespans across the globe. Throughout history, no other system has come close to delivering such benefits to such a wide group of people.

Yet, as this report to the members of the Trilateral Task Force on Global Capitalism in Transition makes clear, despite these manifest benefits, observers across the political spectrum now question whether capitalism is up to the challenges of the twenty-first century. To some extent, capitalism—or rather the prosperity it created—has contributed to some of these challenges. Industrial economic development, while the basis for much growth, has damaged the environment and climate and, if left unchecked, risks existential damage to our societies. Similarly, capitalism has unleashed enormous innovation, which has provided vast improvements in the lives of many—the digital revolution being among these gamechangers. But while the digital revolution holds tremendous potential to help address many challenges faced by society, it is also disrupting entire industries and their workforces and risks concentrating power in the hands of the few. Both the green transition and the digital revolution could exacerbate inequality that, along with other social and cultural forces, has contributed to the erosion of capitalism's legitimacy and fed political backlashes in parts of Europe, Latin America, and the United States. Policymakers, activists, entrepreneurs, CEOs, and others are asking, "Can a system whose byproducts have exacerbated some of society's ills also be the system that enables us to address the largest challenges and opportunities of our age?"

We stand at a crossroads, and the decisions we make about the future of capitalism will have a profound impact on the rest of the twenty-first century.

This is not the first time that the core institutions of advanced democracies have confronted this sort of uncertainty. In many respects, *A New Spirit of Capitalism* is a follow-on to the Trilateral Commission's seminal report, *The Crisis of Democracy*. Published in 1975, that work addressed the existential crisis afflicting Western democracies as the unrest of the 1960s settled into the stagflation of the 1970s. At that time, the future of democracy itself appeared unclear. Many leaders of industrialized economies were pessimistic. Willy Brandt, a former German chancellor, predicted darkly "Western Europe has only 20 or 30 more years of democracy left in it; after that it will slide, engineless and rudderless, under the surrounding sea of dictatorship." In Japan, Prime Minister Takeo Miki warned after taking office in 1974 that "Japanese democracy will collapse" unless it carried out major reforms. And in the United States, President Richard Nixon, who left office under a cloud of corruption, became the first and only president in U.S. history to resign. The Commission forcefully entered the debate about the future of democracy through its report, an effort led by three distinguished authors—Michel Crozier, Samuel P. Huntington, and Joji Watanuki.[1]

In a similar vein, the Trilateral Commission now joins the discussion about the future of capitalism. In recent years, numerous critics have stepped forward with ambitious proposals to reform, or even replace, the current capitalist system.[2] This report to the Task Force on Global Capitalism in Transition is an effort to provide members of the Task Force with a well-developed framework for how capitalism might evolve. *A New Spirit of Capitalism* seeks offer a roadmap for making capitalism more equitable and sustainable. The Trilateral Commission's perspective is unique, arising from its distinctive global membership. The Commission's members are comfortable confronting difficult challenges and developing practical solutions. As with democracy in the 1970s, they remain convinced that there is no better alternative to capitalism's market-based model for our economies and societies. But the challenges with today's capitalism cannot be denied. We need to face them directly.

A New Spirit of Capitalism is offered to help us understand the historical context of our current challenges. The study reveals that we are now in the middle of a historic transition to the fifth stage in capitalism's evolution since the seventeenth century. Many of today's challenges have deep roots in that history, which also informs the solutions this report to the Task Force proposes.

The report charts a path forward to a more equitable and sustainable capitalism. In doing so, it challenges us to prioritize the pursuit of equality of opportunity for all the world's citizens. Its proposed "Social Compact with the Next Generations" is bold and thought provoking. Its shift to a long-term perspective holds great promise. We do not expect that *A New Spirit of Capitalism* will be the final word on the subject, but rather we hope that it will stimulate discussion, debate, and, ultimately, decisions.

This project was made possible by a generous grant from the Hewlett Foundation, the support of two highly committed members of the Trilateral Commission, David Rubenstein and Michael Klein, as well as contributions by numerous other members. The royalties from this book will be donated to humanitarian and economic relief projects to support the people of Ukraine.

On behalf of the whole Trilateral Community, we extend our thanks to Carl Bildt, Kelly Grier, and Takeshi Niinami for their incisive leadership of the Task Force on Global Capitalism in Transition as well as to the Research Director, Edoardo Campanella, for his outstanding intellectual and managerial stewardship of the project, including carrying out the research and drafting the study. We are also grateful for the exceptional work of Andrew Erdmann, who served as senior advisor to the study. This study is in part a testimony to Andrew's guidance, intellectual firepower, and standard for excellence. We also thank all Task Force Members and participants in the Task Force's workshops for their time and commitment. Finally, we wish to recognize Jean-Claude Trichet for having chaired the European chapter of the Trilateral Commission for almost a decade with passion, wisdom, and dedication. We thank him for having embraced this project with his usual enthusiasm from the beginning.

We look forward to the discussion and debate we anticipate this study will spark.

The Trilateral Commission Co-Chairs
Meghan O'Sullivan, Akihiko Tanaka, Axel A. Weber

PREFACE

In the spring of 2021, the leaders of the Trilateral Commission asked us to co-chair the Task Force on Global Capitalism in Transition. Our task was daunting and humbling: to convene a group of distinguished business leaders, scholars, and former policymakers from around the world to develop recommendations that will move us to a more equitable and sustainable model of capitalism.

The time was right for this effort. Despite capitalism's manifest positive impact on prosperity and well-being, many people are frustrated by its role in some profound challenges. Foremost among these are capitalism's contributions to environmental degradation leading to climate change, disruptions triggered by the digital revolution, and rising inequalities in our countries. In light of these issues, putting capitalism on a better path represents a defining challenge of our time.

We are grateful to Meghan O'Sullivan, Jean Claude Trichet, Akihiko Tanaka, and Axel A. Weber for the honor of chairing the Task Force. This report to the Task Force—*A New Spirit of Capitalism*—represents the culmination of over fifteen months of research, dialogue, and reflection, with more than 50 people from some 20 countries contributing to it.

Thanks to its unique Trilateral perspective, coupled with the diversity of views and backgrounds of the people involved in the project, *A New Spirit of Capitalism* goes beyond a monolithic understanding of capitalism. Too often, conversations about its future tend to consider it as sort of homogenous socio-economic system, whose features vary little from one place to another. Certainly, the main elements characterizing modern capitalism remain the same regardless of national context. *Profit* is the goal of private investors and entrepreneurs. *Markets* are the main mechanism to allocate resources. *Capital* is deployed with the expectation of future return. And *decentralized decision making*, largely by individuals and firms, shapes resource allocation.

Nevertheless, there is no single or ideal model of capitalism. Consider the vast differences among China, France, Germany, India, Japan, South Korea, Sweden, the United Kingdom, and the United States. The differences in approach between more democratic capitalist systems and more politically authoritarian ones are touched upon throughout this report. The Chinese model of state bureaucratic capitalism stands out as a challenging extreme to Trilateral countries' models. Each country has adapted capitalism to its own unique context and circumstance. Each system has its strengths and its weaknesses.

Our year of intense and wide-ranging conversations reinforced the conviction that capitalism remains the most powerful engine to advance economic prosperity and human well-being. But the market alone is not enough. A new balance needs to be reached between the economic institutions that generate wealth and the political institutions that regulate them. The green transition, the digital revolution, and rising inequalities pose difficult trade-offs in terms of growth, efficiency, and stability. Depending on its own features, each capitalist model will solve these conundrums differently, adjusting and reacting in its own way to the same systemic challenges.

Behind this variety lies a basic insight that we too often neglect. Capitalism is not just about products and profits, materials and markets. It is not a machine governed by timeless mechanical laws. Capitalism is also about institutions—and ideas. It is, first and foremost, a cultural system.[3] "We shape our buildings, and afterwards our buildings shape us," said Winston Churchill. So too with capitalism. Our ideas, beliefs, and values provide the architecture for how capitalism works, and then how capitalism operates shapes our lives.

PREFACE

The recognition that capitalism is rooted in shared ideas, values, and norms is nothing new. It was a profound insight from the sociologist Max Weber, who famously spoke of a "spirit" of an age, over a century ago.[4] That is why, following his work with modesty, this report to our Task Force calls for "a new spirit of capitalism"—a new code of behavior that is tailored to our twenty-first century era's aspirations, challenges, and opportunities.

We were conscious this study took shape during profound transition and uncertainty. In addition to their tragic human costs, the lingering COVID-19 pandemic and the Russian invasion of Ukraine have together disrupted global supply chains, forced reassessments of energy and food security, and heightened market volatility. While it is too soon to forecast precisely their long-term impact, the unprecedented sanctions placed on Russia in response to its invasion of Ukraine mark a further and likely lasting fragmentation of international trade, investment, and data flows. Cold War analogies are common again. Complicating matters, the world now confronts the risks of severe inflation not seen in decades.

This is one reason why this report begins with a survey of capitalism's history. This approach helps put in perspective our moment's uncertainties and highlight the long-term factors driving capitalism's development. In considering capitalism's long run, we are reminded of not just its dynamism—the "creative destruction" identified by political economist Joseph Schumpeter—but also its adaptability. We see how it has evolved through distinct stages. We are today living through another great transition in capitalism's history. The spirit of this "Fifth Stage" of capitalism will depend on how well it adapts to help respond to the challenges posed by climate change, the digital revolution, and inequality.

To guide that response, this report calls for a new *"Social Compact with the Next Generations."* It challenges us to commit not just to our citizens today but to our citizens of tomorrow. Each person should have an equal opportunity for a good life. Such an approach can be summed up easily. In every decision—from the halls of government to the board room to the shopfloor—we should ask ourselves: Is the decision I am about to make right for the next generations?

This new social compact will require bold action. Such change needs to match the scale, scope, and pace that defined earlier transitions in capitalism's long history. The report to the Task Force proposes, therefore, three goals as a foundation:

- *Every person should live and work in a net-zero world by 2050.*
- *Every person should have access to full benefits of the digital revolution.*
- *Every person should have equal opportunity to achieve their potential.*

The report argues that these three goals are essential. Without them, the world that we seek will be at risk.

We appreciate different countries will approach the task in different ways. We also appreciate the need to work together across state-market boundaries in new ways. Therefore, the report does not offer one-size-fits-all solutions to today's problems, but rather a menu of policy options for how governments, business enterprises, and nonprofits can make progress toward these goals while preserving the flexibility of each capitalist system to adapt to its own unique context. The focus of the report's recommendations is on three broad themes: how to build shared understanding and direction; what investments to prioritize; and what "rules of the road" will keep us heading in the right direction.

As befitting this Trilateral Commission effort, each chapter is capped off with a proposed recommendation for how advanced democracies can collaborate to achieve the three guiding goals and thereby help make capitalism more sustainable and equitable:

- *For Green: Establish a "Climate Club" among advanced economies.*
- *For Digital: Establish an alliance of "techno-democracies."*
- *For Inequality: Ensure quality life-long learning accessible to every person by the end of the decade.*

A New Spirit of Capitalism reflects a true Trilateral perspective— diverse and experienced, visionary and practical. This report reflects the breadth of the topic and the diversity of the Task Force members' perspectives. We welcomed this diversity and accepted that the Task Force members would not agree on every point when considering this report. Likewise with this report itself, participation in the Task Force should not imply a consensus or endorsement of every point of this study. We did share, however, an aspiration for this document to be a starting point, not an endpoint. We hope it helps stimulate constructive discussion, debate, and above all, decision.

On behalf of the Trilateral Commission, we would like to express our gratitude to those who invested their time, talent, and energy to make this project a success. We would like to thank the members of the Task Force on Global Capitalism in Transition who participated over a year in this collaborative endeavor. We also want to thank the thought-leaders from around the world who shared their perspectives during our virtual meetings. Together, the intellect and experience of this diverse group proved crucial to shaping this report. Lastly, we want to convey our deep appreciation to the project's Research Director, Edoardo Campanella, for his exceptional intellectual leadership and tireless efforts to organize the Task Force, identify topics of discussion, carry out the research, and produce this report.

Task Force on Global Capitalism in Transition Co-Chairs
Carl Bildt, Kelly Grier, Takeshi Niinami

ACKNOWLEDGEMENTS

The analysis and recommendations that appear in this report represent the outcome of a long intellectual journey. The Trilateral Task Force on Global Capitalism in Transition met eight times between spring 2021 and spring 2022. The process was fully virtual due to the COVID-19 pandemic, a historic first for the Trilateral Commission.

Each of the eight sessions was devoted to the discussion of specific aspects of the future of capitalism. The first meeting was to determine the scope of the research project. Out of it, the group agreed to consider for this effort China as an extreme form of capitalism rather than an antithetical economic system. Furthermore, integrating China into this research was essential given China's massive economy and its role in influencing capitalism's development globally. Such an approach thus allowed the identification of sources of tension but also areas for potential cooperation along the wide capitalism spectrum. The following six meetings dealt with, respectively, the green transition, the digital revolution, income inequalities, the changing balance between the state and the market, the role of purpose-driven firms, and possible reforms to the global governance. The final meeting was devoted to refining the Report's recommendations. In addition, the whole Trilateral Commission was convened for a three-day virtual conference in November 2021 to discuss the key topics of the Report.

The discussions within the Task Force greatly benefited from the insights of its members. At each meeting, we had the additional honor of being joined by a number of internationally renowned thought leaders. I would like to warmly thank Maria Chiara Carrozza, Mike Froman, Arunabha Ghosh, Rebecca Henderson, Keyu Jin, Mariana Mazzucato, Branko Milanović, Dambisa Moyo, Henry Paulson, Jr., Raghuram Rajan, Yasuyuki Sawada, Marietje Schaake, Eric Schmidt, Anne-Marie Slaughter, Rohini Srivathsa, Joseph Stiglitz, Susan Thornton, Laurence Tubiana, and Luigi Zingales. All Task Force meetings took place under Chatham House Rule. I also want to thank Peter Hall, who shared his invaluable perspectives.

This report to the Task Force on Global Capitalism in Transition also benefited from two pro-bono knowledge partnerships. The first, with the McKinsey Global Institute, was facilitated by Task Force member James Manyika and saw the involvement of Michael Chui, Jose Pablo Garcia, Mekala Krishnan, Anu Madgavkar, and Kevin Russell. The second, with Ernst & Young, was mediated by Task Force Co-Chair Kelly Grier through Nita Bhat. I wish to thank all the people involved for their time and insights. The material received contributed to the report, while the Task Force retained full autonomy in how it was used. I wish also to thank Michael Dwyer, the managing director of Hurst Publishers, whose commitment to the project made possible an impossible publishing timeline.

At the Trilateral Commission, I extend a big thank you for their engagement and support to the regional chairs Meghan O'Sullivan, Jean-Claude Trichet, Akihiko Tanaka, and Axel A. Weber; to the regional directors Richard Fontaine, Hideko Katsumata, and Paolo Magri; to Cassandra Favart and Francesco Rocchetti, as well as to Chris Miller, who was part of this endeavor in its early stages. Andrew Erdmann, in his role of senior advisor, made essential contributions to the report, made sure that the project remained on track, and was a source of invaluable and constant counselling. Katie Salam was the dedicated and essential editor of the manuscript. ISPI, with Nicola Missaglia and Sara Cerutti, provided invaluable help with the graphics. Gray Bender, Daniel Gottfried, Michaela Lee, Amelia Pedrone, and Zach Wehrli provided excellent research assistance. I am personally grateful also to the

ACKNOWLEDGEMENTS

Mossavar-Rahmani Center for Business and Government at the Harvard Kennedy School for having hosted me to partly conduct this research during my senior fellowship that was kindly supported by UniCredit Bank.

Research Director
Trilateral Task Force on Global Capitalism in Transition
Edoardo Campanella

1

CAPITALISM'S FIFTH STAGE

Capitalism has delivered unmatched benefits to humanity. It now stands unchallenged as the world's dominant economic system. Many look to it to help solve the defining challenges of our age. This report offers a way forward to a more equitable and sustainable capitalism. Understanding capitalism's history helps us chart our course to this goal.

I. Capitalism between its successes and "crisis"

Capitalism is the greatest enabler of prosperity and well-being in the history of humanity. It enabled the sharp rise in living standards of the past 200 years, and it created not only vast wealth and income but also helped solve human problems and spread those solutions widely.

People now live longer, better, and healthier lives. They enjoy significant quantities of leisure time and enjoy goods and services that were once the prerogative of an elite. The difference between capitalism and its alternative is self-evident.[1] Whereas China faced economic ruin under Mao, Deng Xiaoping's "reform and opening up" ushered in years of rapid growth. South Korea is far wealthier than its socialist neighbor. With only a few exceptions, namely a handful of isolated, command economies like North Korea and Cuba, capitalism now rules the world. Even China, still Communist in name, has an economy more capitalist than not (*See Box 1.1*).

Today, observers may take its global victory for granted, but they should not. Its triumph represents a radical departure from most of human history (*Exhibit 1.1*). For millennia, growth was slow, halting, and sometimes reversed itself. Only with the acceleration of the First Industrial Revolution did some parts of the world start to enjoy sustained growth that gradually spread everywhere. Capitalism delivered in the past two centuries economic growth unmatched in the entirety of human history.

The numbers are staggering. In the millennium before 1700, scholars estimate that income per capita grew at an imperceptible rate of .11% per year. That meant per capita income doubled only every 630 years. By comparison, the United Kingdom's GDP per person was 10 times larger in 1989 than in 1820. Germany's was 15 times larger, the United States' 18 times, and Japan's 25 times.[2]

Exhibit 1.1

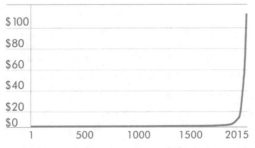

Global wealth exploded in the last 200 years

Total output of the world economy;
expressed in 2011 prices in trillions of dollars

Source: Our World in Data based on World Bank & Maddison (2017),
The Trilateral Commission

THE TRILATERAL COMMISSION

Meanwhile, since adopting market reforms in the late 1970s and then integrating into the international economic system in the 1990s, China has experienced growth unlike anything seen in history. Its per capita income is over 45 times larger today than it was when those reforms started.[3]

Rapid economic development touched almost everyone. Consider perhaps the most basic measure of wellbeing: life expectancy. It has risen everywhere in the world since capitalism's acceleration in the 1800s, doubling overall (*Exhibit 1.2*). In the premodern era, people around the world could expect to live about 30 years on average. Now they can enjoy lives over twice that length.

Yet there is a perceived negative side to capitalism's ledger, too, which has generated for some a sense of "crisis."[4] Following the Cold War, the accelerating velocity of global flows of trade, finance, data, and people reshaped the economic order inside countries and internationally as well. This was the era of the so-called "Washington Consensus." Some communities "won"; others "lost." The global financial meltdown of 2008–09 further exacerbated these dynamics. Prominent voices describe capital-

Exhibit 1.2

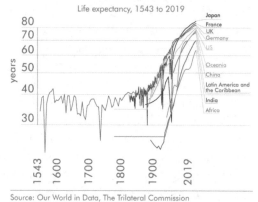

Life expectancy doubled
in the last 200 years

Life expectancy, 1543 to 2019

Source: Our World in Data, The Trilateral Commission

THE TRILATERAL COMMISSION

ism in "crisis."[5] They argue that it does not deliver for many individuals, societies, countries, and even the global community writ large.

Many now judge capitalism by how well it helps address the defining challenges of our age. First, climate change, which is largely a consequence of industrialization and the spread of middle class lifestyles enabled by capitalism, calls into question the long-term feasibility of the system.[6] The recent increase in extreme weather events—from drought and wildfires in the American West to flooding across Europe to unprecedented high temperatures in the Arctic to destructive hurricanes and typhoons—now pose undeniable threats to communities on every continent and represent a global existential crisis. Just 100 companies and state-owned entities were the source of more than 70 percent of the world's greenhouse gas emissions between 1988 and 2015.[7]

Second, there is the digital revolution, which both offers tremendous opportunities and potential solutions to help address other challenges like climate change but also risks compounding some of capitalism's problems. Over the last several years, a handful of private companies have accelerated the digital revolution and transformed how we work and live our lives. But their "move fast and break things" approach in pursuit of profit has also had social and political downsides.[8]

Finally, unless they are addressed, environmental degradation and the digital revolution risk contributing to a third challenge, rising inequality. Left unchecked, rising inequality can merge with other social and political issues to undermine the legitimacy of the current socio-economic model. "In 2020, the world's 2,153 billionaires," notes Oxfam, possessed "more wealth than the 4.6 billion people who made up 60% of the world population."[9]

No wonder, then, that skepticism of capitalism is rife. According to a global public opinion poll released by the Edelman Foundation in 2020, 56% of those interviewed agreed "capitalism does more harm than good" and 74% considered it an unjust system. In a survey of OECD countries, more than 60% reported they thought their country would be worse off for future generations.[10] Younger generations appear most skeptical of the current system.[11] In the United States, for instance, a majority—54%—of people aged 18 to 24 expressed an unfavorable view of capitalism while only 42% had a positive view in a 2021 Axios survey.[12] Similar generational patterns appear in the United Kingdom.[13]

Such skepticism has already helped fuel political shifts in many countries. Populist movements on both right and left have reshaped politics in places as diverse as Brazil, France, Great Britain, Hungary, Poland, and the United States. Since 2018, a majority of registered Democrats in the United States have rated "socialism" more favorably than "capitalism."[14] Leading economists like Thomas Piketty have proposed "participatory socialism" as an alternative to capitalism.[15] In Japan, new Prime Minister Kishida Fumio called for a "new form of capitalism."[16] Even China—the largest beneficiary of global capitalism over the past two decades—launched a campaign in 2021 to curb "the disorderly expansion of capital."[17]

If one chart can capture the major tensions in modern capitalism, it is the "Elephant Chart"[18] (*Exhibit 1.3*). Originally developed by Christoph Lakner and Branko Milanović at the World Bank, it shows

Exhibit 1.3

An elephant tells much of capitalism's recent story

Growth in mean equivalized real income for each percentile of the world population (1988-2008)*

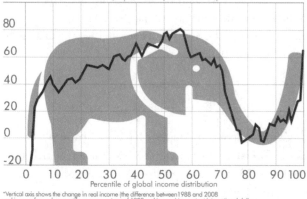

Percentile of global income distribution

*Vertical axis shows the change in real income (the difference between 1988 and 2008 real income for each percentile as a percentage of 1988 real income) in constant international dollars

Source: Corlett (2016), based on data from Milanović and Lakner (2013), The Trilateral Commission

THE TRILATERAL COMMISSION

how much a person's income grew between 1988 and 2008 based on their relative percentile income within world's economy.

Three parts of the chart are worth noting. The hump at the 50th to 70th percentiles of wealth was driven mainly by massive Chinese economic growth that lifted hundreds of millions out of poverty and led to explosive growth in the middle class. The dip in the 70th to 95th percentiles represents largely the stagnation in incomes among workers in wealthy economies like the United States. The elephant's trunk shows how the world's wealthiest 1% got much richer in this same era, driving inequality within many countries. All in all, Lakner and Milanović's chart confirms an adage: where you stand [on capitalism] depends a lot on where you sit [on the curve].[19]

Tensions over capitalism, of course, aren't new; they've defined its history from the start, inevitable byproducts of what the great twentieth century economist Joseph Schumpeter called capitalism's relentless dynamic of "creative destruction."[20] The economic system often moves with disorienting speed to challenge established interests, erode traditions, and upend familiar rhythms of life. Inevitably, some win and some do not.

But the wise elephant reveals, however, the basis for an acute upswing in discomfort with capitalism. Such tensions need to be addressed, lest they weaken the system and deny its vast benefits to people around the world. And that leads to a question: How can capitalism evolve to become more equitable and sustainable and address the major challenges of our era?

Box 1.1: Is China really capitalist?

The Chinese economy defies easy classifications. The very idea of a socialist-market system—a concept which Beijing coined in 1992 in occasion of the 14th Congress of the Chinese Communist Party—looks like a contradiction in terms. The original aspiration was to combine the perceived superiority of socialism with the practical flexibility and performance of a market economy.

China famously launched major economic reforms under Deng Xiaoping in the late 1970s, including the embrace of many capitalist-market principles. Deng's "crossing the river by feeling the stones" approach to reform led to historical growth into the twenty-first century. Despite a top-down, state-centric mode of governance, the market component of China's system gained increasing prominence. Recently, most capital ownership was in private hands and nearly all prices for consumer goods were set by market supply and demand. Even with all its peculiarities, the Chinese economy arguably meets criteria for a capitalist system, at least in key sectors of its economy, including: production largely organized for profit; market-based allocations, and also wage-based labor; largely privately owned capital; and a significant decentralization of decision making among entrepreneurs and firms.[21] Furthermore, the Chinese economy is integrated into the globalized capitalist system.

For these reasons, this study considers China as defining the "state-bureaucratic" end of the spectrum of capitalist systems. It also acknowledges that applying "capitalism" to today's China is increasingly debatable.

To be sure, there are indications that the Chinese state has begun to "strike back" and move the economy further away from capitalism.[22] Since the rise of President Xi Jinping, Beijing moved to retrench to greater state-direction to the detriment of more market-based reforms. In January 2021, President Xi declared that "China has entered a new stage of development," the goal of which is to build China into a "modern socialist power." By the summer of 2021, the Communist Party authorities were committed to working to curb "the disorderly expansion of capital." The sum impact of this sort of retrenchment may move China once again fully off the edge of the capitalist spectrum.

II. The advantages of a Trilateral perspective

In 2021, the Trilateral Commission convened the Task Force on Global Capitalism in Transition to answer the questions about capitalism's future. This report to the Task Force, *A New Spirit of Capitalism*, is the culmination of that effort, which spanned 18 months and involved a diverse array of experts from across the world and across disciplines, coming together to debate and set an agenda for purposeful reform. (*See Appendices for the list of Task Force members as well as the workshop topics and invited speakers*).

The report's approach is rigorous but practical. It is interdisciplinary—integrating history, economic theory, and data—and also global in perspective.[23] At the same time, the report's scope is selective. It concentrates on how healthy the forest is, not on the status of individual trees. It also looks to the broad patterns in the development of capitalism since the 1600s to help diagnose today's problems and offer a workable set of prescriptions for the future. As such, we hope this report will stand as a helpful reference, in addition to offering its recommendations to stimulate discussion and debate.

Throughout *A New Spirit of Capitalism*, we define today's capitalism as having five main features.[24] First, profit seeking is the goal of private investors. The search for profit propels innovation, for example through the pursuit of economies of scale and scope, division of labor, market expansion, new organizational and management models, and so on. Second, markets are the main mechanism through which resources are "commodified" and allocated. Those resources include labor, legally free to earn wages. Third, capital, mostly private, is deployed with expectation of future return. Fourth, decision making is mainly decentralized and coordination among private entrepreneurs and firms occurs in largely autonomous ways, often enabled by a predictable legal regime. Finally, modern capitalism is forward-looking, with "a psychological orientation toward the pursuit of future wealth and prosperity," as the historian Thomas McCraw wrote in the introduction to *Creating Modern Capitalism*.[25] Capitalism is ultimately grounded in faith in the future.

Among the economies that count as capitalist under this rubric, there is a great deal of diversity. Indeed, as a "cultural system" as well as an economic one, to use historian Joyce Appleby's term, capitalism is always embedded in and shaped by a nation's specific context.[26] Political systems matter, as do prevailing economic ideas, industrial composition and level of development, institutions, and culture (*Exhibit 1.4*). (*See also Box 1.2 for a description of capitalism's many forms.*)

The practical upshot of all this variety is that, even facing the same challenges, each country will chart a unique course as its national governments, firms, and consumers interact. The transition in global capitalism will not be uniform, and no single approach will be perfect. Starting points will differ, and so will the end-points. But such variety also represents strength, and it is something the Trilateral Commission was well-placed to appreciate given its diverse membership.

The challenges capitalist systems have ahead of them are manifold, but the Trilateral Commission identified three that deserve particular attention. All three are defining challenges for our era. If we "get them right," then our future and our children's futures

Exhibit 1.4

The capitalism spectrum today

Varieties of capitalism span from more democratic & inclusive to more authoritarian & extractive

		Democratic and Inclusive Models		Australia
Utopian pure free market systems	Liberal democratic capitalism			Canada
				New Zealand
		Economic	Political	United Kingdom
		Secure property rights	Democratic pluralism	United States
		Open markets	Voting rights	
Capitalism Spectrum	Social democratic capitalism	Balanced labor relations	Checks & balances	Continental
		Consumer protections	Free media	Europe
		Robust regulation	Individual rights	Japan
		Antitrust enforcement	Impartial judiciary	South Korea
			Minority rights	
	Competitive authoritarianism	Authoritarian and Extractive Models		Egypt
				Russia
				Singapore
		Economic	Political	Turkey
Non-capitalist economic systems (ex. Cuba, North Korea)		Weak property rights	Oligopoly or single-party rules	
		Crony capitalism	System of elites and	
	State bureaucratic capitalism	Anticompetitive monopolies	interests groups	
		Extractive labor	Suppression of	China
		Disregard for externalities	expression	
			Patronage networks	

Source: Buzan and Lawson (2014), Acemoglu and Robinson (2012), Henderson (2020), The Trilateral Commission

THE TRILATERAL COMMISSION

in the twenty-first century will be much brighter. If not, we risk global setbacks to not only our economies, but our societies and polities as well. And, for each of these three challenges, modern capitalism has simultaneously played a role in exacerbating them and yet it is also best placed to address them.

First, the report looks to climate change, specifically how to accelerate the greening of our economies. Second, it takes on the digital revolution, and how to ensure individual and corporate access to these technologies so that everyone can thrive in the modern economy. And finally, there are inequalities, particularly within countries, and how to promote equality of opportunity while preventing today's winners from locking in their advantaged positions.

To prevent misunderstanding, it helps to say here what the report will not do. The report does not attempt to provide a comprehensive examination of every dimension related to each of the three major problems. Furthermore, it may mention, but not explore in depth, a host of important related topics. For instance, the report does not focus on globalization—the international flow of goods and services, people, resources, data, and finance—and its implications. It does not explore in depth specific negotiations or the development of important international organizations. Nor does it investigate topics such as the potential impact of cryptocurrencies on finance. (The endnotes help guide interested readers to additional resources.) While some nuance may be lost, much is gained by this approach. Namely, by focusing on economic fundamentals, we can also focus on fundamental solutions.

Box 1.2: The varieties of capitalism[27]

Market economies come in many varieties. At the highest level, what differentiates different types of capitalism is the extent and intent of the role played by the state—i.e., whether they are authoritarian or democratic. This approach moves beyond traditional classifications used by some academics who tend to focus on the degree of market regulation or the features of a social welfare safety net, thereby downgrading the role of the state itself as an economic player.[28]

In this project, we found it helpful to distinguish among four systems as archetypes for the varieties of capitalism today (*see also Exhibit 1.4*):[29]

Liberal democratic capitalism: Through an emphasis on individualism and healthy competition, this system is characterized by limited state engagement in the market and deference to private owner and shareholder interests. These systems often have higher concentrations of power and higher inequalities, but also greater innovation, entrepreneurship, and social mobility.[30] The United States, the United Kingdom, and other Anglophone countries epitomize this archetype.

Social democratic capitalism: In this system, the state attempts to manage more deliberately than liberal democratic systems the social contract between markets and communities. State policies aim to mitigate the market's more severe

---

impacts through extensive social welfare safety nets and more intrusive regulation, with the state making itself responsible for protecting not only civil liberties but also social cohesion and equity.[31] Social democratic capitalism can be seen in continental Europe, parts of South America, and across Asia including India, Japan, and South Korea.

Competitive authoritarian capitalism: Competitive authoritarian states formally allow competitive elections but take measures necessary to ensure that the competition is only nominal.[32] When it comes to the economy, the state leverages its institutions (often a dominant political party) and ideology (often nationalism), combined with other restrictions on civil liberties, to control its market. This type of capitalism, which is extremely heterogenous both in terms of political settings and economic performance, is present in countries as diverse as Iran, Kenya, Malaysia, Pakistan, Russia, Tanzania, Singapore, and Venezuela.

State bureaucratic capitalism: This archetype is at the outer boundaries of capitalism with the system sitting at the intersection of state socialism and capitalism. In this form, political and economic boundaries are almost indistinguishable. The state, controlled by a ruling party, maintains a high degree of control over the economy often through direct ownership of strategic industries, especially finance, and a willingness to intervene. While allowing entrepreneurs and large corporations to develop specific markets, like the high-technology sector, the state retains ultimate influence through tight regulation and ability to set policies without the checks and balances of transparency, firm property rights, and divided government power. China's state-led development from the late 1970s into the twenty-first century is the leading example of this model.

The more political approaches—competitive authoritarian and state bureaucratic—also demonstrate the weak link between democracy and capitalism. Even though the market expansion of the last thirty years has taken place alongside a rapid process of democratization, democracy is not a prerequisite for capitalism to flourish. The principles of the two do not necessarily reinforce one another. Where capitalism allows for inequality, democracy is supposed to be in principle egalitarian.[33]

At the moment, capitalist economies roughly outnumber democracies by a 2:1 ratio. That figure could be even higher if one took out of consideration those illiberal democracies where elections remain in theory free and competitive, but civil rights are violated in practice on a regular basis.[34] Democracy usually coexists with capitalism, but the opposite is not always true.

III. Our starting point: How did we get here?

The history of capitalism is the best starting point for comprehending the realities of today's challenges. It highlights that the work we face today is not entirely new but, rather, the legacy of capitalism's earlier stages. This is particularly true in periods of transition and uncertainty, like ours as the world emerges from the COVID-19 pandemic with its social and economic disruptions to renewed geopolitical conflict accelerated by Russia's invasion of Ukraine.

Climate change, for one, is a result of the world's dependence on fossil fuels after the First Industrial Revolution and from changes in lifestyle and diet driven by capitalism's global success. The digital revolution is the kind of innovation that capitalism is best poised to spur, but the learning process is sometimes long and painful. And as for inequality, capitalism fundamentally accepts it as a byproduct of the functioning of a competitive market economy. That said, the recent acceleration of inequality in many countries was not inevitable, but rather linked to the combination of unique local histories and contexts sometimes along with earlier policies that promoted privatization, deregulation, and labor market reforms and decline of organized labor in many places across the world.

Historical perspective should inoculate against headlines proclaiming some "unprecedented" or "unique" challenge today. Of course, much is novel. But considering that history reminds us we

Exhibit 1.5

The rise of the West
and the rebalance to Asia

Distribution of GDP among major economies

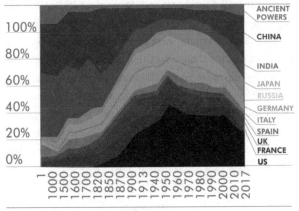

Source: Maddison Database, The Trilateral Commission

THE TRILATERAL COMMISSION

have navigated tricky problems before, and in doing so, have reformed how capitalism works. Those changes have, at times, been difficult and rarely linear, but they have created the most productive economic system. Now, as we sit on another transition in capitalism's evolution, thinking historically will frame the challenges and potential solutions most effectively.

The broad sweep of capitalism's history is captured in a simple graphic depicting the shifts in major economies' output over the past two millennia (*see Exhibit 1.5*). Before the opening chapter of capitalism's history around 1600, Asian economies dominated the world's economic production. In the following 300 years, the leading capitalist economies based in Europe and America flipped the script; by the twentieth century, they dominated the global economy. In the past three decades, accelerating capitalist-led growth in China and India then rebalanced the global economy once more.

This macro-level picture fits rather neatly with four distinct eras of capitalist practice.[35] Academics may debate start and end dates, since capitalism moved at different paces in different places, and innovative technologies often took decades after their invention to achieve their full potential. Indeed, capitalism's history is defined by successive changes and evolutions, not singular events or inventions. Nevertheless, there is a pattern to how the stages rose and then fell, and it will sound familiar to readers today.

First, at some point, tensions build within the dominant model—sometimes arising out of a failure to provide equitable outcomes, sometimes thanks to the introduction of new technologies and modes of production, sometimes because of a shock to the system like a war or an economic downturn. In crafting a new approach to address these tensions and new ways of working, businesses and industries grow and adapt while the balance of power between the state and the market adjusts. And that new alignment eventually marks a new era (*Exhibit 1.6*).

Exhibit 1.6

Stages in capitalism's evolution

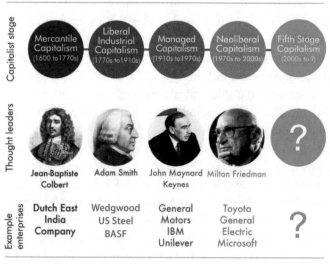

Source: The Trilateral Commission

THE TRILATERAL COMMISSION

Mercantile Capitalism: 1600s–1770s

Capitalism's first era, from the 1600s to the 1770s, was defined by struggles for power among European states. In the first part of this period, Europe was rocked by the Thirty Years War, out of whose horrors the nation state arose in the mid-1600s. For well over a century thereafter, European states continued to wage war on one another with brutal regularity.[36] "War made the state, and the state made war," sociologist Charles Tilly quipped.[37]

In the context of this great power conflict, Mercantile Capitalism reigned supreme. Traders enjoyed lucrative, state-ensured monopolies on goods shipped from distant lands to their own local markets. This system placed the economy squarely at the service of the state.

At the start of this era, France was the most powerful state. The economic reform program pursued by Jean-Baptiste Colbert, King Louis XIV of France's minister of state in the mid-1600s, epitomized the approaches at the start of this era. The French state built roads and canals and invested in manufacturing, military power, and navies. It sponsored scientific research through new academies. It also tightly regulated economic activity by enacting tariffs to protect domestic industry, restricting skilled labor's mobility, protecting intellectual property, promoting trade with colonies, and chartering monopolies for industry and trade. All this was designed to strengthen state power for the glory of the King.

Wind, water, and muscle powered this age, as they had for centuries before. Europeans innovated by developing tri-masted oceangoing ships that could carry cannon. This mobile firepower extended their commercial and military reach around the world.[38] Trade networks expanded, especially in the Atlantic, linking colonies back to the colonial power. Labor migrated westward to the Americas—free, indentured, and enslaved.

In this context, the Dutch innovated and accelerated the transition to full-blown Mercantile *Capitalism*. In 1602, the Dutch established the world's first publicly owned joint stock company, the Dutch United East India Company (or VOC for *Vereenigde Oostindische Compagnie*). Over 200 citizens purchased shares with limited liability and regular dividends. Soon the Dutch also pioneered the first official stock exchange, securities market, and other modern banking practices. Capital and credit now mobilized. The words "share" and "shareholder" emerged. Investments proliferated for the growing middle classes. So too speculation and financial panics. The state consolidated public debt. The Dutch became the wealthiest people in Europe.[39]

This system was certainly capitalist, as it relied upon heavy investment of capital in expectations of large profits. But it was far from a free market. Profits were contingent on monopolies and the exclusion of competitors, and not on the rationalization of production through gains in productivity.

England's "Glorious Revolution" of 1689 was an early marker that this stage of capitalism would not last. It had established checks on state power and foundational individual rights for Englishmen, including protections of private property. Agricultural reforms boosted productivity and expanded the workforce for manufactures. London became a metropole. Its financial markets blossomed, as did a culture of scientific inquiry, experimentation, and tinkering. England was also blessed with geologic good luck—a seemingly limitless supply of easily accessible coal. By the middle of the century, the first steam engines began to pump water out of England's mines.

Technological progress empowered entrepreneurs. Meanwhile, into the eighteenth century, the high level of indebtedness of many European rulers weakened their ability to control the market. Economies started to be regulated by supply-demand dynamics with limited government interference. A new legal order began to emerge, enshrining the supremacy of the contract and private property, clearly dividing the public power of the state and the private power of capital.[40] The era of Liberal Industrial Capitalism was taking shape, soon marked by a step change in the West's economic growth as it overtook other regions.

Liberal Industrial Capitalism: 1770s–1910s

The publication in 1776 of Adam Smith's *An Inquiry into the Nature and Causes of the Wealth of Nations* marks a convenient milestone.

Recognized as the first work in economics, Smith critiqued the corrupt state monopolies and the intrusiveness of the state in business. He joined others in suggesting the then-radical notion that individual pursuit of self-interest could serve a higher social purpose. The powerful metaphor of the "invisible hand," mentioned but once in his magnum opus, would become an enduring legacy. It would go on to inform liberal or *laissez-faire* economic policy and stimulate critiques like those from John Stuart Mill and Karl Marx in the nineteenth century.

The inspiration for Smith's opus came from what was happening around him in England. The first steps of the world's Industrial Revolutions had started before *Wealth of Nations*, but it truly accelerated in the decades after Smith published his treatise.[41] And it would not have been possible without the second phase of capitalism, in which the economy was unshackled from the state's direction.

It is hard to convey the scale, scope, and pace of changes in those days. Coal replaced steam, beginning humanity's addiction to fossil fuels. Demand for natural resources (to which were soon added oil) came to shape foreign and domestic policy. Manufacturing moved from mass labor-saving industries like cotton and textiles into capital-intensive and technically demanding industries like steel, chemicals, and machinery. Craftsmanship gave way to interchangeable parts, both manufactured and human. Entrepreneurs innovated new forms of management, starting with factories and ending with corporations, sprawling trusts, and the "org chart."[42]

Time and space compressed. Transportation raced on land, coal and then oil-powered engines ships trawled the seas. Communications approached instantaneous with the telegraph and then telephone and wireless radio. The mechanical clock and an invention called "time zones" delivered new notions of punctuality. All this made it possible to wrap global trading networks and supply chains around the whole world—sometimes by force. It also enabled transnational learning and adaptation as countries raced to keep pace. First among non-Western economies, for instance, Japan adapted liberally from both Europe and America, and combined them with its own commercial traditions, during the Meiji Restoration's reforms.

The private economic sphere did have relative independence from the state compared to eras before, but governments still played a critical role in shaping the economic environment. They invested in infrastructure, ranging from turnpikes to railroads to canals. They upended the earlier system of private property rights by ending slavery. Their spread of compulsory education of children proved one of the most consequential investments ever. Literacy and numeracy rose. Modern universities were established, often with state support, as with the U.S. land grant colleges. Engineering and technical education took off especially in Germany and America. The democratic franchise extended over time, and with it came burgeoning labor movements and the first state-sponsored social welfare movements, hinting at further reforms to come in capitalism's next phase.

After nearly a century without a major war in Europe, the world had never been more connected. Different countries had evolved different varieties of capitalism—ranging from the more owner-based model in the United Kingdom to the more competitive American model to Germany's more cooperative capitalism to Japan's more state-led model. The United States and Germany had surpassed Great Britain in economic production by 1910.

Some believed global trade networks made conflict unthinkable. But it turned out that it was not. The transition to capitalism's third stage came more violently than anyone could have anticipated.

Managed Capitalism: 1910s–1970s

Liberal Industrial Capitalism fell as an early casualty of World War I. Managed Capitalism stepped into the breach, at first more by necessity than by design.

As hopes for a quick war faded, the belligerent governments in Europe asserted greater control over their economies to sustain their war efforts. Mass conscription proved the most obvious and intrusive example. But governments also rationed food (except in the United States), seized control of infrastructure, and took either direct control of industrial production or else influenced it from the sidelines. At the same time, as governments struggled to manage modern wars and modern economies, a new challenge arose: the specter of radical alternatives to capitalism threatened by the Russian Revolution of 1917.

In the next two decades, wartime mobilization soon gave way to the Great Depression, during which governments eventually came to accept the need to prevent unrest by speeding economic recovery. If capitalism had already been managed before, government influence went into overdrive. No longer could economic cycles be left to the market alone. The risks proved too high, as the collapse of many capitalist systems to Communism on the left and fascism on the right proved.

And so, a new mode of economic thought eventually came to prevail: Keynesianism, developed by the English economist and investor John Maynard Keynes. His ideas brought "the state back in" to tame the business cycle by managing demand and reducing the economic insecurity of the least well-off.[43] Indeed, post-Great Depression and in the face of rising Communism, citizens in capitalist societies, too, increasingly looked to their governments not only to provide the most basic of emergency support but to offer greater protections and services through complex social welfare systems, health services, consumer protections, new investment in educational opportunities, and more. This was the era of establishing Social Security in the United States and the National Health Service in the United Kingdom.

As the welfare state was emerging, modes of production changed, too. Modern industrial enterprises, with tens of thousands of employees and scores of divisions spread geographically, required new approaches to management. "Mass" became an adjective for the World War II and postwar era. Mass enterprises integrated mass manufacturing and distribution with mass marketing campaigns over mass communications channels to stimulate mass consumerism. Organized labor grew and extended its influence alongside the growth of these industrial enterprises and the state. The value of management and technical acumen increased, and so salaried and, increasingly, credentialled managers emerged as leaders. General Motors under the leadership of Alfred P. Sloan and his team of managers—many of them graduates of institutions like the Massachusetts Institute of Technology—embodied these trends.[44]

Mass applied at another level, too. Beyond the nation-state, advanced democracies established a sprawling architecture to manage the international economy and prevent the economic disruptions that fed the Great Depression. Keynes was one of the principal architects of the Bretton Woods reforms, which started during World War II and accelerated through the 1950s. The eventual results were the World Bank and International Monetary Fund; the Marshall Plan for the reconstruction of Europe; the European Coal and Steel Community and then the Common Market to integrate European economies; and the General Agreement on Trades and Tariffs to open trade and avoid destructive "beggar thy neighbor" trade policies.

In the context of both the World Wars, managing economic output had proved an existential necessity. As the Cold War took off, though, lines between war and peace among great powers blurred. Nationalization or direction of major industries in many countries never receded. Wage and price controls hit. Conscription too remained.

Governments again invested in expanding educational opportunities and promoting technical acumen. They ranged from the postwar "red brick" universities and polytechnics in the United Kingdom to Germany's "dual educational" system with its distinctive apprenticeship model to the "GI Bill" and massive investments in higher education during the Cold War in the United States. In the era of Sputnik and the Space Race, scientific research and engineering talent were mobilized toward state ends just as during World War II.

Through the prosperity of the 1950s and into the 1960s, Managed Capitalism appeared secure. The Apollo 11 moon landing in July 1969, however, marked its apogee. Soon the combination of social and political unrest and the rigidity of the "managed" systems began to erode confidence in core institutions, including democracy itself. Stagflation, oil shocks, and the end of the Bretton Woods monetary system proved their undoing.

CAPITALISM'S FIFTH STAGE

Neoliberal Capitalism: 1970s to 2000s

When government-managed economies reached their limits with the stagflation of the 1970s, critics of Keynesianism were suddenly everywhere. Milton Friedman and colleagues from the so-called "Chicago School" of economics shaped the intellectual foundations for a new "neoliberal" model of capitalism. Deregulation, market liberalization, privatization, globalization, and free trade provided its pillars. Explicit skepticism of the potential for constructive government action permeated its approach.

Market reforms under U.S. President Ronald Reagan and British Prime Minister Margaret Thatcher in the 1980s both embodied and helped accelerate the shifts in state-market relations. They also challenged the power of organized labor. Left-leaning parties in both countries moved toward the center and accepted, in U.S. President Bill Clinton's phrase, that "the era of big government is over." Instead, the "Washington Consensus" appeared here to stay.

That approach, which involved deregulation of the private sector, inspired market reforms in regions as diverse as Scandinavia, Russia, East and South Asia, and Latin America in the aftermath of the Cold War. The results proved mixed. Cycles of financial crisis in emerging economies suggested underlying weakness. The Japanese economy entered a long stagnation. Social welfare states around the world weakened as inequality within countries rose. But the pace of globalization—often involving outsourcing to countries with lower labor costs—continued to accelerate into the twenty-first century.

On the corporate front, new ideas attacking the foundations of Managed Capitalism also gained traction. Among them, two took top billing. The first was introduced in a 1970 *New York Times* essay, in which Friedman famously argued that corporate leaders had primary responsibility to provide value to their shareholders, not other social benefits.[45] Then in 1976 the *Journal of Financial Economics* published an article by Michael C. Jenson and William H. Meckling. In 56 pages of dense economic analysis in "Theory of the Firm: Managerial Behavior, Agency Costs and Ownership Structure," the authors attacked managerial capitalism head on:

they argued professional managers' objectives were not aligned with the shareholders'.[46] The article would become "the most-cited business article of all time."[47]

Shareholder value would continue to dominate well into the twenty-first century, shaping corporate governance and strategy, especially among large multinationals, at the expense of social benefits like equality and the environment.[48] It combined with new financial products and the growth of investment banking to "financialize" much of the global economy. Financial engineering to deliver quarterly results shaped many leaders' incentives and thus their corporate strategies. General Motors and General Electric, for instance, soon had their own separate credit and financing businesses.

New graduate business talent shifted away from manufacturing toward finance, consulting, and high tech industries—"knowledge, work," and the related information technologies services that became the hallmark of this era of capitalism. Businesses worth trillions of dollars made their marks in software, social media, search and digital advertising, and digital entertainment and gaming. Computing power transformed business practices and everyday life, reshaping every economy. At the start of the twenty-first century, the retail shopping experience was being transformed by big data analytics behind "loyalty programs" and online shopping. Science-based products in biomedical and pharmaceutical innovations delivered growth to shareholders and transformed lives.

At the same time, it is an exaggeration to see this era as a "post-industrial" economy. Manufacturing remained the foundation for many advanced economies. Firms continued to innovate the manufacturing process itself. The Toyota Production System perfected a management philosophy for continuous improvement starting on the factory floor that made Toyota the largest car manufacturer in the world. In Germany, the *Mittelstand* supported precision manufacturing and high-end exports.

China's truly unprecedented rise, however, proved the most significant development of the Neoliberal era. (*See Box 1.1 on the question of whether China is a capitalist economy.*) Beijing seized the opportunities presented by neoliberal-inspired reforms in other countries—such as open trade, pressure to outsource to low-cost country labor, and desire to sell to the world's most populated country—while preserving a high-degree of state-bureaucratic control. China emerged in the early decades of the twenty-first century as a global innovation leader (*See Exhibit 1.7*). China's unique recipe delivered unprecedented economic growth, helped created a new middle class, and led to historic rebalancing of global economic power.

Toward the "Fifth Stage" of capitalism

Besides Managed Capitalism, the arrival of which was accelerated by World War I, past transitions between eras of capitalism have unfolded over a few decades. And in every case, the shift followed a similar pattern. Capitalism drives innovation and growth. It

Exhibit 1.7

Trends in patents

Applications in the
world's top five offices, 1883-2020

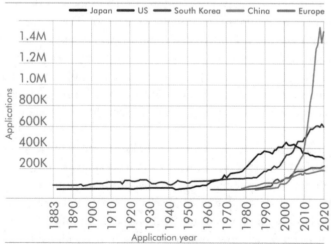

Source: WIPO, Intellectual Property Indicators, The Trilateral Commission

interacts with and shapes political, social, and cultural dynamics. Tensions arise when a capitalist system does not deliver results or when its second-order, unintended consequences erode confidence in its legitimacy. The existing model is then challenged, new ideas explored, and reforms sought. The new form of capitalism typically addresses its predecessor's perceived failings. The balance between the state and market adjusts once more.[49]

We are now living through another great transition.

Today's capitalism confronts challenges including rising inequality, climate change, and the digital revolution that are great and in large part legacies of a now fading era. Neoliberal Capitalism's roots were never particularly deep in many countries. And even where they were, as in the United States and parts of Europe, brewing problems started to bubble over.

Even before the Global Financial Crisis of 2008–09, the excesses of unchecked shareholder capitalism were manifest: what once seemed like a virtuous drive to maximize returns on investment for everyone came to seem like a race to the bottom. The wealthy got increasingly wealthy, workers' wages stagnated, the environment suffered, and parts of many countries were left behind. Those problems got harder to ignore once that first bubble popped.

In Europe, the euro crisis and mass migration from the Middle East gave populists the continent over a boost. That wave crested with Brexit. In the United States, meanwhile, populism has found a home in both major political parties. And it isn't just politics that have changed. Even corporate leaders in fora like the United States' Business Roundtable and the World Economic Forum have pledged to adopt a broader "stakeholder" approach to managing their enterprises.[50]

Another blow to Neoliberal Capitalism came in the form of the COVID-19 pandemic, which exposed weaknesses in globalization's relentless pursuit of lowest cost production; the crisis highlighted instead the value of supply chain security and resilience, and of collaboration between state and business. And if that were not enough, the world now confronts geopolitical tensions at levels not seen since the Cold War. The international sanctions campaign launched in response to the Russia's invasion of Ukraine shows how governments can still mobilize their country's economic power to serve strategic objectives.

The decline of Neoliberal Capitalism is now paving the way for a new transition. Although it is far too soon to tell what the "Fifth Stage" of capitalism will eventually be called, or who its defining thinkers and firms will be, the decisions we make today will shape the story our grandchildren will tell. To influence capitalism's future trajectory, it is worth recalling a few themes from its past. Five "lessons," informed by the history recounted in this report, are key.

First, history has proved Schumpeter's observation that "stabilized capitalism is a contradiction in terms" correct.[51] Capitalism is always evolving. The pursuit of profit is a powerful engine of innovation. And people's psychologies—their "animal spirits," to adopt Keynes' phrase—drive markets in often unpredictable ways. Capitalism is thus a force that may be channeled, but never fully controlled.

Second, past eras confronted changes of a similar magnitude to those we face today. We should thus be cautious when a headline proclaims something "unprecedented." Likewise, we must be humble when we try to imagine the scale, scope, and pace of future development. Before the first Industrial Revolution, time discipline—clocks and watches—was unimaginable.[52] Today, the precise future of work and life is similarly so.

Third, capitalism's development has historically been shaped by three broad categories of forces:

- **Shared understanding and direction:** Each era of capitalism is shaped by a particular viewpoint of how the world works and what matters, which defines in turn what is possible, informs priorities, bounds conduct, motivates action, and, therefore, helps align stakeholders around common purposes. These comprise the "spirit" of the age, an idea that famously attracted the pioneering sociologist Max Weber's attention more than a century ago (*See Box 1.3*).[53] *This report seeks to help define the core elements of a new "spirit" for the next era of capitalism.*
- **Investments:** Capitalism is driven by investments of time, creativity, and resources to develop and scale innovations to deliver future profits. These investments come in different

27

forms, and can take place at the individual, firm, nonprofit, industry, government, or even international levels. *This report seeks to identify priority investments needed to deliver on the promise of the new era of capitalism.*

- **Rules of the road:** Capitalism's evolution is inevitably shaped in dialogue with the state and politics, which create the rules that enable and even accelerate capitalism. Such rules include formal legal regimes of property rights, contracts, statutes, regulations, treaties, and other agreements. They also include more informal arrangements that incentivize entrepreneurs, investors, and firms. *This report seeks to identify the "rules of the road" that could help tackle the common challenges and seize the shared opportunities of this new era of capitalism.*

Fourth, history underscores "what matters" in how we design solutions for our era of capitalism.

- **Time horizon matters:** From the vantage point of history, we see that what we now call "revolutions" in capitalism were really "evolutions" that unfolded over decades. Even today's greatest innovations are the legacy of investments in higher education institutions and research made decades ago. *This report thus adopts a true long-term time horizon to shape capitalism for this new era. This work is of the next two to three decades, not the next two to three fiscal quarters.*

- **Ideas matter:** Keynes correctly concluded in his own study of economic history: "Practical men, who believe themselves to be quite exempt from any intellectual influences, are usually slaves of some defunct economist."[54] Consider the impact of Keynes himself, along with that of Smith and Friedman. Marx too. *Therefore, we need to continue to invest in developing insights to guide practical men and women of action in board rooms, executive suites, and legislative halls. We need to define the "spirit" of this age of capitalism.*

- **Interactions matter:** Capitalism's velocity and trajectory is never foreordained. It emerges from the complex interplay of entrepreneurs, enterprises, and economic systems.[55] Central to the story of capitalism is the oscillating pendulum-like balance between the state and the market. *This report will work toward bringing together multiple perspectives and capabilities to address challenges and seize opportunities.*

- **Variety matters:** Styles of capitalism in different nations shape one another through their interactions, which define how capitalism works across borders at the binational, regional, and global levels. *This report will eschew any reductive "one size fits all" prescriptions, and instead seeks to develop policies that recognize the differences among the world's capitalisms.*

Fifth, the history of capitalism provides a major caution: There is no inexorable natural law leading capitalism to find the "right" balance. Success is not inevitable. Instead, we craft capitalism to fit our norms and needs. And in the end, we get the capitalism we have the will and wherewithal to build.

Box 1.3: The spirit of capitalism

In *The Protestant Ethic and the Spirit of Capitalism*, the sociologist Max Weber challenged the then prevailing materialism of Karl Marx and his followers to emphasize the importance of beliefs and values to shaping and propelling capitalism.

Weber famously linked the rise of Western capitalism to the appearance of new norms of economic behavior that were rooted in Calvinist ideas of predestination. For Calvinists, where some individuals are in a state of grace and destined to salvation, others are damned regardless of their good deeds during their earthly life. Falling in one group or another is God's immutable and preordained choice. While no person can know his or her fate in advance or alter it, the accumulation of material wealth could be seen as empirical evidence of divine grace, up to the point of it becoming a moral obligation to pursue it in accordance with the Puritan principles of sobriety, self-discipline, honesty, precision, and hard work.

In this worldview, profit and wealth were no longer condemned, as Catholicism had done for centuries. And so, according to Weber's account, Protestantism provided not

---

only the motivations for capitalist entrepreneurs but also for workers, who imbibed the virtues of specialization, rationality, and industriousness.

The spirit of the original capitalism, therefore, was thus rooted in a religious ideology—one that justified engagement with the rational, market economic system. A bit like Adam Smith's invisible hand, this religiously inspired self-interest was supposed to benefit the whole society through the unco-ordinated actions of its members. Sometimes it could fail to temper the impulses that greed tends to fuel, leading to sys-temic crises.

In the end, Weber argued for the "cultural significance" of capitalism but also remained somewhat ambivalent about the limited power of rational market behavior to fulfill all of people's needs.[56]

While scholars continue to debate Weber's interpreta-tion over a century later, few question its essential insight that ideas, beliefs, and values matter as much to capitalism's evolution as material factors such as technology or business operations.

IV. Toward a more inclusive and sustainable capitalism

So what does our new capitalism look like? Instead of a glib label, we offer here preliminary principles for the spirit of capitalism that we should embrace for our age. These are rooted in the his-tory of capitalism's development as well as the Task Force mem-bers' dialogue about future challenges and opportunities. They include: pursuing equal opportunity in practice not just theory; delivering high quality growth not just high-volume growth; pri-oritizing long-term impact over short-term financial results; pro-tecting the interests of relevant stakeholders not just shareholders; and appreciating diverse histories, cultures, and needs while pur-suing cooperative solutions.

These principles are intended to provide the starting point, not the endpoint, for the development of capitalism's next stage. We anticipate that these design principles will evolve. New ones will be added, and all will need to be adapted to different contexts. In that sense, we hope that these principles will follow the logic of what the management scholar Clay Christensen called "nested systems." In these, the same underlying logic and dynamics operate at each level and scale to the next, from individual, to team, to firm, to nation, and beyond.[57]

Nested principles are necessary to support the type of enduring change we seek. The world will move toward a more equitable and sustainable capitalism only when each level in the system abides by the same mutually supportive structures and values.[58] These include an agreed understanding of what to do and why—that is, shared perspectives of challenges and opportunities, potential solutions, and urgency. We will also need standard models that guide our ways of working, our processes, incentives, measures of success, business and operating practices, and formal collaborations. And we will need common skills and capabilities to get the job done. And, finally, we will need exemplars—examples of places and organizations where things go right to inform and inspire ourselves and others.

The following substantive chapters—which focus on climate change, the digital revolution, and inequality—contribute to each of the above needs. The chapters share a consistent structure to help guide the reader. They begin with a survey of the topic's historical development and an explanation of why the topic is a top priority for global capitalism. That sets the stage for an exploration of the current context, its challenges, and opportunities. Each concludes with proposed recommendations to guide decision-makers in building shared understanding, investing in high impact priorities, and creating "rules of the road" to help Fifth Stage Capitalism fulfill its promise. Each chapter's recommendations close with a Trilateral one focused on how the advanced economies and democracies can collaborate to advance this agenda. The report then concludes by synthesizing key insights into the core elements of a new spirit of capitalism.

2

GETTING TO NET ZERO

Climate change is a defining challenge of the twenty-first century, set to shape our future and that of coming generations. Although it springs in large part from our capitalist-driven prosperity, the market—working in coordination with governments and other stakeholders—represents the best way to address it.

I. HOW WE GOT HERE

I.1. A slow-moving catastrophe

Climate change is one of the biggest challenges facing humanity in the twenty-first century. It not only threatens to exacerbate inequalities between and within countries, but also pits this generation against future ones. Consider this estimate: according to the World Health Organization, climate change is expected to cause 250,000 additional deaths per year from diarrhea, malnutrition, malaria, and stress.[1] But those will be unevenly spread across the world, with some feeling the brunt more than others depending on where they live and how wealthy they are. Indeed, the costs will fall disproportionately on those least able to manage the stress. Climate justice, then, calls for addressing climate change in a fair and even way.

Today's climate crisis was primarily caused by the rise of fossil-fueled economies and related greenhouse gas emissions (*Exhibit 2.1*). The emissions started to increase more than two centuries ago in England with the First Industrial Revolution and have accelerated with the pace of economic development ever since. While the twentieth century's socialist industrialization campaigns contributed, the vast majority of emissions resulted from the very success of the capitalist systems accelerating growth and changing standards of living around the world. These days, carbon dioxide accounts for roughly three-quarters of the human-generated global warming effect. Methane, nitrous oxide, and hydrofluorocarbons have contributed as well.[2]

Global capitalism confronts in climate change not only a singular challenge, but also the defining opportunity for its Fifth Stage. Tackling climate change requires nothing less than change on the

35

Exhibit 2.1

The jump

Global atmospheric CO2 concentration
(parts per million)

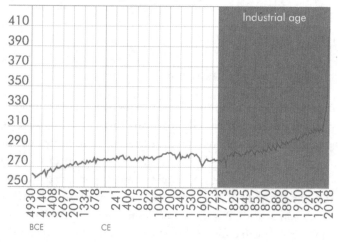

Source: Our World in Data, The Trilateral Commission

THE TRILATERAL COMMISSION

scale, scope, and pace in our economic activities on par with the original shift that created modern industrial enterprises and our original dependence upon fossil fuels two centuries ago. Perhaps ironic to some, the relentless innovation engine of capitalism offers today the best hope to address the climate change legacies from past capitalist innovations.

The core challenge is addressing the buildup of greenhouse gases. They come from a variety of human activities.[3] Burning coal, oil, and natural gas for power, electricity, heat, and transportation produces carbon dioxide and nitrous oxide. Cutting down forests reduces the ability of the planet to absorb carbon dioxide out of the atmosphere, adding to the greenhouse effect. Food production also plays a role. With a growing global middle class has come shifts in lifestyles and diets—including the increased consumption of meat. Cows and sheep produce large amounts of methane during their digestion. These gases act like glass in a greenhouse, trapping the sun's heat on earth.

The total pool of greenhouse gases in the atmosphere—not just emissions today—determines how far climate change will go. Indeed, carbon dioxide emissions from over a hundred years ago still contribute to the planet's warming today. Scientists estimate that, overall, humanity has pumped out about 2,500 billion tons of carbon dioxide since 1850. The United States is the world's leading contributor to that total, with a share of approximately 20 percent. China is second, with about 12 percent, a result of its massive scale and unprecedented economic development in the past 40 years.[4]

Scientists further estimate that, to keep global warming below 1.5° Celsius above preindustrial levels, we can only emit another 400–500 gigatons of carbon.[5] That's equivalent to about 11 years of emissions at the 2019 level.[6]

And even if we stay under that mark, we will still have to mitigate major disruptions. Human-induced global warming has already reached 1°, and that figure is increasing by approximately 0.2° per decade.[7] Eight of the top ten hottest years of the past 2,000 years have occurred in the last decade alone.[8]

There is growing evidence that the steady rise in global surface temperatures is already boosting the number, frequency, and duration of natural hazards.[9] Rising surface temperatures are connected to the likelihood and severity of droughts and wildfires in hot, arid regions. Equally, warmer seas generate more water vapor that evaporates into the atmosphere, fueling hurricanes, typhoons, and torrential rain that can cause severe flooding. Some of these processes were painfully visible in 2021, from extreme floods in China, Germany, and Belgium to an unprecedented summer heatwave in the United States, wildfires in California, and landslides in Brazil.[10]

Increased heatwaves, droughts, and floods are already exceeding plant and animal tolerances, driving mass mortality in several species of tree and coral.[11] At 1.5° warming, coral reefs are projected to decline by 70–90 percent. Nearly 14 percent of all people would face a severe heat wave at least once every five years (a percentage that rises to 37 under 2° of warming).

If temperatures increase over 2°, things will get far worse—and in unpredictable ways, as individual climate disasters set off other catastrophes. At a 4° rise, which is not viewed as a plausible scenario today, coastal cities may permanently flood, food and water insecurity would proliferate, ecosystems would become irreparably damaged, and even more frequent and extreme weather events would rock the world.[12] The modeling by the Intergovernmental Panel on Climate Change (IPCC) conveys graphically the global impact of these different scenarios (*Exhibit 2.2*).

Changes in the geophysical world will have deep consequences in the geopolitical one. Warming will most likely exacerbate social unrest even in affluent economies. It will lead to mass migrations from the fastest warming regions (according to the Red Cross, there were already around 25 million climate-related displacements worldwide in 2020).[13] And it will ramp up tensions between

Exhibit 2.2

The cost of inaction

Annual mean temperature change (°C) relative to 1850-1900

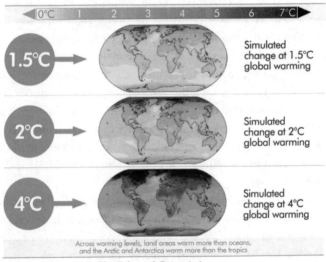

Across warming levels, land areas warm more than oceans, and the Arctic and Antarctica warm more than the tropics

Source: IPCC (2021), The Trilateral Commission

THE TRILATERAL COMMISSION

rich and poor countries, which are often located in regions that will see the greatest impacts from warming.

Global warming will also increasingly become a source of financial instability. Flooding and wildfires cause expensive damage. And routine crises could produce major repricing events.[14] In Florida, for example, McKinsey reports "that losses from flooding could devalue exposed homes by $30 billion to $80 billion, or about 15 to 35 percent, by 2050."[15] Eventually, episodes of sharp risk reassessment might pave the way to a systemic financial crisis.

"The cumulative scientific evidence is unequivocal," the IPCC thus concludes. "Climate change is a threat to human well-being and planetary health."[16] To limit warming to 1.5°, rapid and large-scale reductions in greenhouse gas emissions are necessary. According to IPCC estimates, global greenhouse gas emissions must be cut in half by 2030 and the world should reach net zero emissions by mid-century to keep the planet within its relatively small remaining carbon budget.[17]

This is the challenge that market-based solutions must meet.

I.2. Progress hard to come by

The majority of citizens around the world now support some kind of climate action. A recent survey from the European Commission showed that 93 precent of citizens in Europe see global warming as a serious problem.[18] Another study by the European Investment Bank reported that almost three-quarters of Chinese respondents named climate change as society's biggest challenge.[19] Almost 70 percent of Americans believe that protecting the environment should be a top priority for the political establishment; about the same amount support a carbon tax, which is also embraced by a bipartisan consensus of economists and an increasingly large portion of the business community.[20]

However, scientific understanding and public awareness of the problem has not yet been matched by a willingness to reimagine the way our economies and societies function. International climate cooperation has moved gradually and in small steps.[21] The United Nations Framework Convention on Climate Change entered into force in 1994. In 1997, it birthed the Kyoto Protocol, which required a limited number of developed countries to cap or reduce their greenhouse gas emissions up to 2020. After some failed attempts, in 2016, the Paris Agreement entered into force, asking action from all countries to work to keep the increase in global temperatures below 2°. To move toward a consensus approach led to a reliance on pledges and voluntary but non-binding commitments. Not surprisingly, therefore, real progress remained inconsistent and driven by local economic and political factors.

More recent developments confirm the challenges of international cooperation on climate change. For example, in November 2021, the United Nations Climate Change Conference (COP26) met in Glasgow intending to reaffirm the goal of limiting global warming to 1.5°. However, policy announcements fell short of what is needed to deliver that goal. For example, under pressure from China and India, targets for ending the use of coal were kept unambitious (e.g., "phasing down" instead of "phasing out"). Resistance to strong limits on methane emissions likewise hindered COP26's progress.

Recently, several countries have deliberately decided to scale back or eliminate zero-carbon nuclear power from their energy mix, thereby extending and even expanding their reliance upon fossil fuels. And renewable energy, while increasingly affordable, is still a small portion of total energy consumption. Coal, oil, and natural gas still supply more than 80 precent of the world's primary energy.[22]

Geopolitical tensions complicate matters further. Russia's invasion of Ukraine, for instance, may slow green transitions around the world, at least in the short term. Many European governments are considering ways to increase their energy security in the near term, which may involve replacing cleaner natural gas (from Russia) with greater reliance on coal. In the longer term, though, the increased tensions with Russia may push European countries to accelerate plans to switch to green energy such as wind and solar power. Some are also revisiting nuclear power.[23]

In parallel with policy deliberations at national and international levels, businesses have started to adapt, often moving ahead of policy negotiations. Across industries, but especially in those involving long-term capital investments, the continued uncertainty surrounding regulations and carbon pricing complicates their investment strategies. Consequently, many businesses, including former skeptics, now favor more consistent and definitive carbon pricing schemes, even if they may add costs to their business because they would reduce fundamental uncertainties too.[24] And many firms already build into their own financial planning assumptions about the future regulatory frameworks to address climate change.[25]

Furthermore, many businesses have begun to adapt their strategies and operations to improve their competitiveness in the green era. Naturally, innovators in developing and commercializing green technologies such as renewable energy, battery storage, and electric vehicles come to mind. (*For future developments, see Section II.1.3.*) Their investments have driven down the costs of these technologies so that they are often cost competitive with fossil fuel alternatives. For instance, electricity from utility-scale solar photovoltaics declined 89% between 2009 and 2019, while electricity from onshore wind declined 70 precent.[26] The rapid expansion of electric vehicles and the public commitment by major automobile manufacturers to phase out the internal combustion engine will mark a revolution in ground transportation.[27] Other more "traditional" businesses are also redesigning core processes from the ground up to improve sustainability and profitability simultaneously. Starting in 2018, the World Economic Forum established its Global Lighthouse Network (GLN) to showcase those businesses pioneering "Fourth Industrial Revolution" manufacturing to deliver superior business and sustainability impact. (*See Box 2.1 for an example*).[28]

Urgent though addressing the climate change may be, it should be no surprise that progress has been halting. Achieving net zero involves nothing less than transforming how capitalist enterprises work. The challenge is so difficult precisely because the use of fossil fuels has been woven into the fabric of capitalist development since England first started using coal at scale in the eighteenth century. Fossil fuel literally propelled industrialization and, therefore, capitalism. And it continues to do so today. Heating, light, transportation, supply chains, goods, and agriculture all depend, one way or another, on fossil fuels.

Box 2.1: A Fourth Industrial Revolution: "Sustainability Lighthouse" Shines in Malaysia

Industrial activity generates the most greenhouse gas emissions of any sector in the global economy, accounting for roughly one-third of emissions (*See Exhibit 2.7*). Consequently, how well and how fast businesses can innovate their operations will play a critical role in the green transition.

Many firms are already leading the way to realize the potential of Fourth Industrial Revolution operations—that is integrating Artificial Intelligence, networks of sensors through the Industrial Internet of Things (IIoT), advanced analytics, robotics and autonomous manufacturing, and connected supply chains to reimagine manufacturing.[29]

The World Economic Forum's Global Lighthouse Network (GLN) recognizes the exemplary firms and factories leading these innovations.[30] The GLN serves as a platform for sharing of best practices, learning, facilitating collaboration, scaling innovations, setting benchmarks, and celebrating success. By early 2022, over 100 facilities around the world had earned a "Lighthouse" designation—meaning that they serve as examples to guide others—including six as "Sustainability Lighthouses" that demonstrated, in particular, how new industrial operations can contribute to the green transition. "Lighthouses are," as the WEF notes, "defying the conventional wisdom that environmental responsibility is inherently at odds with productivity and, by extension, profitability."[31]

Western Digital, the American hard disk drive and data storage company, has earned a number of Lighthouse designations. Its factory in Penang, Malaysia earned a "Sustainability Lighthouse" designation in 2022.[32]

This smart factory had expanded its volume over 40 percent year over four years, and simultaneously delivered

---

dramatic improvements in its sustainability. The facility reduced its energy consumption by over 40 percent its use of water 45 percent, and its waste by 16 percent. Overall, the Penang facility lowered its greenhouse gas emissions around 40 percent.

Western Digital achieved these combined business and sustainability results by integrating the best of the digital revolution (*Chapter 3*) into its operations. At the heart of the change lies a network of more than 1,000 IIoT sensors monitoring some 500 pieces of equipment and 15 utility systems, all then linked to an advanced analytics plant monitoring system. Automation improved by machine learning helps deliver greater efficiencies. [33]

The Western Digital "Sustainable Lighthouse" in Penang, and other Lighthouses around the world, help illuminate paths for other businesses to redesign their operations to deliver sustainable impact and profitability.

The precise changes that are needed can be debated; numerous scenarios and models offer potential paths to net zero economies by 2050. On the optimistic side, most models suggest that closing the gap is possible, while, on the pessimistic side, they note that we are not on course yet.

According to the Climate Action Tracker, for example, even if all the commitments to net zero announced in 2021 were implemented, the world would still be at risk of a 1.8° temperature increase by 2100. [34] The International Energy Agency (IEA), meanwhile, paints a dramatic picture of what's needed to reach net zero. For starters: no new investment in new fossil fuel supply projects. [35] "By 2035," the IEA continues, there can be "no sales of new internal combustion engine passenger cars, and by 2040, the global electricity sector has already reached net-zero emissions."

In the near term, according to the IEA, "the path to net zero emissions is narrow: staying on it requires immediate and massive deployment of all available clean and efficient energy technologies." For the next ten to twenty years, most reductions in emissions would come from those technologies. After that, a larger share would have to come from new technologies that are in the demonstration or prototype phase, such as next-generation carbon capture technologies, electric trucks, and hydrogen-based steel production.[36]

Innovation will not be the only key to success. Perhaps even more important will be how humanity manages and works together. Some industries will be disrupted, and others accelerated or created. Millions of new jobs will be needed, and millions of workers will need upskilling and support (*See Chapter 3*). The total investments needed are staggering—measured not in millions or billions, but in additional trillions of dollars each year. According to IEA, the green transition "will require $3.5 trillion in energy-sector investments on average each year until 2050," which is around twice the current level of investment.[37] Other estimates are even higher.[38]

I.2.1 A matter of perspectives

Although the green transition will touch the whole world, its costs and benefits will not be spread evenly across countries or within them. Such differences inevitably complicate finding common solutions. Again, where you stand often depends on where you sit.

One major difference in perspective arises from countries' geographies. Hundreds of millions of Asians, for example, live along the coast, thus making them more exposed to floods, storms, heatwaves, and droughts.

Another difference arises from countries' level of economic development. This is captured in the so-called environmental "Kuznets curve"—named after the economist Simon Kuznets— which depicts the relationship between environmental degradation and income per capita as an upside-down U.[39] In the early stages of economic growth, both environmental degradation and pollution increase. After a certain level of income per capita, though, the trend reverses. High income levels lead to environmental progress due to greater energy efficiencies and greater attention to the environment after basic needs are met.

In practice, of course, the level of attention to environmental matters varies greatly even among affluent capitalist societies,[40] but the historical data from major economies since 1970 largely support Kuznets' idea (*Exhibit 2.3*). In the United States, Europe, and Japan, carbon emissions per capita are already on a downward path. India and China, whose income per capita still lags advanced economies, are on an ascending path.

The practical upshot is that nations at the bottom or the middle of the curve, where emissions per capita may still be growing, argue that it is the responsibility of the most developed economies to take the lead and compensate for their past development. Consider China's stand at the COP26 conference. The country is today the world's greatest global emitter of greenhouse gases in absolute terms. Nonetheless, in defending its position that coal should be "phased down" rather than "phased out," Chinese representatives argued that developed countries should be the first to

Exhibit 2.3

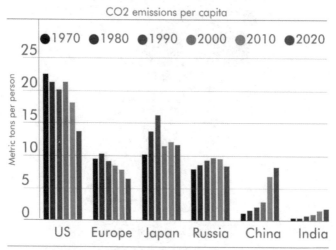

Level of development and carbon emissions

Source: Our World in Data, The Trilateral Commission

THE TRILATERAL COMMISSION

stop using coal, and that they should also provide financial aid to developing countries to adopt green technologies.[41]

A last difference in perspective arises from the varying structure of countries' economies (*Exhibit 2.4*).[42] For one, decarbonizing an economy involves massive investments in new physical assets and in upgrades to existing ones. Developing countries, according to a 2022 McKinsey report, tend to have "higher shares of jobs, GDP, and capital stock in sectors that are more exposed to the transition—which is to say, sectors with emissions-intensive operations, products, and supply chains." Relative to developed economies, they also tend to have higher exposure to more extreme physical risks. In addition, countries whose economies are reliant on fossil fuel production have a lot to lose if those fuels are abandoned. For Qatar, Russia, Saudi Arabia, and others, revenues from fossil fuels

Exhibit 2.4

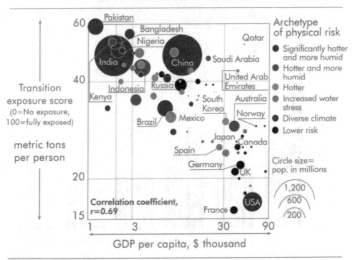

An uneven transition

Archetype of physical risk through exposure vs GDP per capita by country (logarithmic scale)

Source: McKinsey Global Institute, The Trilateral Commission

THE TRILATERAL COMMISSION

are often used to fund generous welfare programs and build domestic consensus.

By contrast, countries with higher GDPs per capita tend to be less exposed to green transition challenges. Such economies tend to have larger service sectors, which are usually less carbon intensive. For them, in many cases, the real difficulty is represented by the lack of domestically available cleaner energy sources.

Lastly, the green transition will likely impose especially heavy costs on low-income households, in advanced and developing economies alike, requiring the adoption of compensatory measures to make it politically and socially acceptable (*Box 2.2*). During the green transition, for example, the cost of electricity would likely rise substantially, even by about 25 percent between 2020 and 2040.[43]

Box 2.2: Green inequality

A poorly managed green transition risks exacerbating inequality (*Chapter 4*), which, in turn, could erode the political support needed to carry out the transition. As the OECD noted in 2021, "not only does environmental degradation tend to be concentrated among vulnerable groups and households, but the benefits and costs of environmental policies are also likely to be unevenly distributed."[44]

The so-called "yellow vest" protests in France in 2018, triggered by high fuel taxes that fell disproportionately on middle class families living in rural areas, show how politically explosive the nexus can be between inequality and climate change mitigation policies.

While carbon pricing in some form will be central to the green transition, affordability cannot be ignored. Higher energy costs put a disproportionate burden on low-income households, which must spend a greater share of their income on such essentials as transport and power. Such households may have to make difficult trade-offs that reduce their well-being. Similarly, higher taxes on road transport fuels affect rural residents more than urban dwellers because the former tend to rely more on private cars and have limited access to viable public transport alternatives.

Green policies can also have important distributional implications for jobs at the sectoral or regional levels, affecting employment levels in carbon-intensive industries. According to one estimate, a green transition could directly and indirectly create 200 million jobs but end 185 million by 2050.[45]

Different countries will find solutions tailored to their specific needs. In general, a fair green transition should involve steps to protect the most vulnerable, smooth labor transitions, and address systemic inequalities.

I.2.2 Multiple market failures

The level of development is not the only factor that complicates efforts to address climate change. In fact, the very nature of greenhouse gas emissions makes this a difficult challenge.

Greenhouse gases, no matter where they are emitted, are a global problem.[46] In that way, they are part of two market failures identified by economists.[47] The first is the traditional "tragedy of the commons." The atmosphere can be seen as a global common into which individuals, firms, and nations release pollution, creating a "public bad" that affects everyone, without anyone taking individual responsibility for it.

The second tragedy is the "tragedy of the horizons," whereby today's population reaps the benefits of releasing greenhouse gases, but the costs are incurred by future generations. The normal business cycle is measured in just a few years; the political cycle in two, four, or five; regulators and central banks often look ahead two or three. Those horizons are much shorter than what is needed to bridge the gap between action now and potentially catastrophic impacts of climate change decades in the future. Solving the "tragedy of the horizons" involves turning "our future hindsight into our current foresight."[48]

Another issue is that the broad range of measures that are required to cut emissions have significant "public good" characteristics. This suggests that markets will not sufficiently provide them without substantial government intervention. And while some countries might act with determination, others might simply free ride to avoid the adjustment costs associated with climate mitigation.

Any serious attempt to address it will require major innovation. These include not only new technologies and new infrastructures such as carbon capture technologies and hydrogen-based manufacturing of steel, but also policy and regulatory innovation, such as new environmental standards or the redefinition of urban planning and land use. The challenge of developing, securing political support, and then implementing meaningful carbon pricing regimes remains a top innovation challenge as well. (*See Section II.1.1 on efforts to devise international approaches to carbon pricing.*) Yet even a well-designed green transition might be frustrated by additional market failures along the way that require stronger public-private partnerships to mitigate global warming (*Box 2.3*).[49]

Box 2.3: Dealing with multiple market failures

The tragedy of the commons and the tragedy of the horizons are not the only forms of market failures slowing the green transition.[50]

Other market failures involve, for example, mitigation measures aimed at minimizing the possible impacts of climate change. The development and commercialization of the technologies necessary to move the world towards net zero could be subject to positive "knowledge spillovers" that lead to underinvestment.[51] Firms that invent new technologies might not be able to prevent others from benefiting from their work—for instance, when patents expire. In such situations, therefore, they would not reap the full benefits of their innovation. Such situations may reduce incentives to invest in research, thereby leading firms to invest less than what would be optimal from a societal perspective.

As a 2019 IMF report pointed out, "there may also be positive network effects, with benefits to society from the adoption of a single standard, such as one plug that works for charging all electric vehicles." Thus, governments can encourage technology diffusion with tax credits to lower the cost of new equipment. At the same time, uncertainty might misdirect investments to activities that are not beneficial for the environment, for example as a result of "greenwashing."[52] Alternatively, market participants might simply fail to price certain externalities because they are "tail events" that fall outside the historical distribution of outcomes. Consider, for instance, an unexpected natural disaster linked to climate change that destroys or damages manufacturing capacity in a major industrial area.

There are also potentially significant market failures associated with climate adaptation policies, whose goal is to reduce those negative effects of climate change that are not reversible or preventable.[53] In some cases, markets might simply not exist. In places where the risk of climate variability is steadily increasing, for instance, insurance companies might be unwilling to insure individuals and physical assets against climate-related risks. In other cases, the absence of clear property rights could complicate matters, which is another form of tragedy of the commons.

In the face of these market failures, governments and companies will have to develop active plans for getting to net zero. Financial and other institutions can help set standards, develop rules, coordinate, and give voice to vulnerable workers and communities. (*See III.2 Recommendations.*)

II. WHERE WE ARE TODAY

II.1. Move toward net zero as an opportunity

The universality of the green transition means that all stakeholders, from governments to firms to consumers, will need to play a role in moving it forward. As noted above, the costs will not be spread evenly. Some will find them more difficult to pay than others, economically and politically; and, as we have experienced already, "free riding" might induce some nations to under-deliver, triggering others to pull back their commitments.

Yet countries also have opportunities. The transition will bring great potential for growth, especially to those with the right human, technological, and natural capital. This is especially important for advanced economies that, unlike many developing countries, do not have access to low-cost clean energy resources, such as solar power, or are not geologically well situated to store the carbon dioxide that needs to be removed from the atmosphere. So too businesses. Those that creatively adapt, innovate, and invest will have opportunities to improve not only sustainability but also their bottom lines.

Practically speaking, achieving net zero will then involve solving a series of discrete problems rather than a single Gordian Knot. To be sure, there are difficult interdependencies to consider. Nonetheless, meaningful progress can be made toward the overarching goal by pushing forward on multiple fronts simultaneously. While working toward more effective global coordination of climate change policies, decentralized initiatives by nations, regions, cities, businesses, researchers, and nonprofits will move us forward.

To solve the green transition conundrum, we need to turn the puzzle on its head in some respects. Its vast overall scale and scope can be tackled by attacking it through many much smaller innovations and initiatives—just the kind the capitalist system generates with the right incentives. And the costs of the net-zero transition can be reframed as investments in a more advanced economy and a better environmental future.[54]

II.1.1 International cooperation

The green transition requires new forms of international cooperation to bridge the gaps in ambitions and abilities. While the European Union, the United States, Japan, and Australia, to cite a few, are committed to achieving carbon neutrality by 2050, China and Russia are eyeing 2060 to get to net zero emissions, and India pledges to get there by 2070.

From an economics standpoint, there is one obvious element to any program to solve the green transition challenge, namely, a price on carbon that would let capitalist markets work. By setting a price, firms, entrepreneurs, and researchers will be pulled into the market to innovate and put economies on a sustainable path. More than 3,600 economists, including several Nobel laureates, have signed a statement saying carbon taxes are the most "cost-effective lever to reduce carbon emissions" as it forces polluters to internalize their negative externality by giving a price to carbon, encouraging firms to develop, invest in and scale clean, low-carbon technologies.[55] Although every estimate can be debated in detail, the High-Level Commission on Carbon Prices conveys the order of magnitude of the prices needed to achieve net zero with its estimate that carbon would have to hit $50–$100 per metric ton by 2030 to reduce emissions in line with the Paris Agreement.[56] Other research, including scenarios outlined by the Network for Greening the Financial System's "Net Zero 2050," estimate carbon prices could be between $100 and $200 per metric ton in 2050.[57] The average explicit carbon price among G20 economies was roughly $4 per metric ton in 2021, within a wide range ($0 to $30+).[58]

In theory, such proposals are logical and sound. In reality, as described above, proposals to establish carbon pricing regimes globally, regionally, and also nationally in many places have run headlong into the tragedies of the commons and horizons. Oftentimes, leaders and many of their constituents have asked: Why pay today—economically and politically—to help the future? Why should we sacrifice if we do not know if others will too? Thus, the halting, fragmented progress on using arguably the most impactful market-based solution to the green transition.

The upshot is that today there are only about 60 pricing schemes now implemented at the regional, national, and subnational levels. This means that there is a plethora of voluntary and mandatory markets with incompatible standards that price carbon imperfectly and inadequately. While the European Union has a continent-wide cap-and-trade system for carbon dioxide emissions, in the United States, only California has one (*Exhibit 2.5*). (*For an overview of the Canadian model, see Box 2.4*)

Exhibit 2.5

Carbon pricing regimes

Schemes around the world, 2021

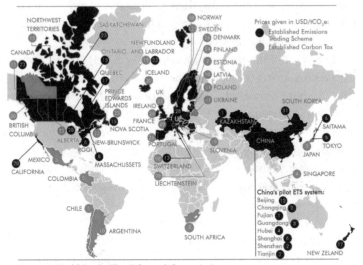

Source: World Bank, The Trilateral Commission

THE TRILATERAL COMMISSION

And any carbon pricing regime would only be one piece of the puzzle. Think, for example, about the lack of a common green taxonomy—that is, a shared framework for classifying investments as environmentally sustainable. This is not just a matter of regulatory monitoring, but also of transparency for consumers. Insufficient standardization, the proliferation of various Environmental, Social, and Governance (ESG) ratings for firms and investment funds, and data inconsistencies create confusion about what can be considered a green investment or a brown one, inhibiting growth in green initiatives.[59] Europe is currently setting the agenda for many of these issues, and it is also providing solutions, for instance, when it comes to the establishment of a green taxonomy.

In the long term, more stringent and universal environmental regulations can become drivers of economic growth and competitiveness by promoting improvements in efficiency, which will come with cost savings and could foster innovation.[60] Companies will differentiate themselves from competitors by reimagining their business models and reshaping business ecosystems. Agricultural certifications, for example, have helped farms adapt to climate change while also boosting their productivity and net income. Likewise, the need to redesign products to meet new standards opens new business opportunities.[61]

However, in the short and medium term, regulatory asymmetries across jurisdictions harm the competitiveness of those firms that are more regulated, both in domestic and international markets. In a 2018 paper, the OECD noted that "companies in countries with higher costs [could] lose market share to competitors in countries producing pollution intensive exports more cheaply." Over time, pollution-intensive industries, and manufacturing employment, could gravitate to the countries with relatively lax policies—so-called pollution havens.[62]

In turn, divergent regulations could lead to a race to the bottom or to environmental protectionism in the form of carbon tariffs. The Carbon Border Adjustment Mechanism (CBAM) proposed by the European Union as part of its Green New Deal aims to avoid such an outcome. The thinking is as follows: facing tougher emissions standards at home, companies based in Europe might move the most polluting parts of their production somewhere with fewer rules. Or European products could be replaced with cheaper imports. Both outcomes would frustrate the EU's efforts to slow emissions—while also reducing European competitiveness. The CBAM would thus impose a levy to equalize the price of carbon emissions between domestic products and imports. Some criticize the CBAM as protectionist first, green second;[63] it will pass costs along to major exporters to Europe such as China, Russia, and Turkey. So this move for a regional solution to potential "carbon leakage" may acerbate other trade issues.

Environmental protectionism is taking other shapes, too.[64] In order to reduce dependence on imports and build job-generating green industries within its own borders, India, for example, is imposing customs duties and tariffs on Chinese solar panels. Washington, likewise, has explored a tax credit to promote the manufacture of electric vehicles in the United States. In the midst of ongoing global supply chain disruptions, we are also seeing governments consider a variety of direct and indirect incentives—from tax relief to direct economic development support—to attract investments in critical industries related to the green transition, foremost among them semiconductors.

Other nations are looking to build international influence by spreading their own green standards abroad. Given their early activism in trading low-carbon hydrogen and ammonia, Australia, Chile, Japan, and Saudi Arabia may be able to set international standards for these, giving themselves an edge. Similarly, defining the standards for data technologies, such as digital tools that optimize electric grids or manage consumer demand, will give an advantage in exporting compatible domestic systems and in mining data from them.[65]

The fragmented efforts to forge international cooperation speaks to the challenges in climate policy faced by the democratic capitalist countries. A key source of asymmetry in these international efforts is not just countries' different stages of development, as outlined above, but also the type of capitalism—more democratic or authoritarian—in any given country.[66]

At least in theory, authoritarian environmentalism is supposed to produce a centralized response to environmental threats, while bringing in both state and social actors.[67] Indeed, despite its staggering pollution and colossal appetite for resources, observed Yifei Li and Judith Shaprio in 2020, "China is expanding its use of renewable energy, creating state parks, planting massive numbers of trees, and curbing the global trade in endangered species."[68] But Beijing pursues its environmental goals in an authoritarian fashion through forced inspections and closures, sudden bans, and the like.

To be sure, Beijing's interventions have been relatively successful. It is a leader in renewables, batteries, and electric vehicles.[69] Beijing's goal, as expert Barbara Finamore has written, is to "transform its economic model from one based on highly-polluting, energy-intensive manufacturing to a high-tech system based on the production of goods and services at the top of the value chain." Yet China, she continues, "faces a myriad of challenges in scaling up these technologies and accelerating its transition away from fossil fuels."[70]

Democratic governments, meanwhile, have a far more limited power to intrude into the life of their citizens and the business activities of their firms. The best response for democracies remains, therefore, to find ways to mobilize the ingenuity and dynamism of the market through the right set of incentives and to integrate them into partnerships with the public and nonprofit sectors. While competing with China on other geopolitical fronts, the advanced democracies will also need to seek potential common cause with China in specific areas to help accelerate the green transition.

Box 2.4: The Canadian carbon price model

Canada's carbon price system, which was introduced in 2019, is widely regarded as one of the world's most advanced. It could become the blueprint for a truly global agreement thanks to its great flexibility.[71]

The carbon price is federally mandated, but provinces enjoy a high degree of freedom in the way they choose to meet it. They are, in fact, "encouraged to create their own carbon pricing systems in line with their unique priorities," as reporter Marisa Coulton recently wrote for *Foreign Policy*.

Some use emissions trading systems where others have carbon taxes. "If a province chooses not to implement its own system or presents a plan that does not meet the minimum," explains Coulton, "the default carbon pricing plan, known as the 'federal carbon backstop,' kicks in." The pricing system covers 70 percent of polluting activities and revenues from the Canadian carbon tax rebate largely go back to households.

If similar models are adapted by other countries and internationally, this would allow countries to adopt carbon pricing systems (a carbon tax vs. an emission trading system) that are consistent with their local conditions, leading to more efficiency.[72]

II.1.2 Funding the transition

Better regulatory coordination will not be enough to get the world to net-zero if the public and private sectors do not also mobilize sufficient funding. And that will require updating how the financial system works.

For now, insurance companies have already started considering climate change in their risk models. And some of the largest banks have stopped lending to high-carbon industries. Financial markets, too, are starting to price in the transition to a net-zero economy.[73]

But this work will need to go further. When it comes to specific products, over the last ten years, progress in green and sustainable finance has been impressive. Just a decade ago, for example, green bonds were almost non-existent and were a prerogative of large multilateral organizations like the World Bank or the European Investment Bank. Now, they are becoming widespread. The green debt market has recorded growth of over 50 percent in the last six years. Whereas green debt had reached a total volume of about $100 billion at the end of 2015, in 2021 it topped $600 billion.[74] But it is still far away from the $5 trillion in annual green investment that is needed by 2025. And that market needs to be broader still, with more diversity of participants and products in the green and sustainability spaces.

Central banks and financial supervisors, meanwhile, need to incorporate climate risk into their stress-testing frameworks. Progress here has been slow so far, though there are lately signs of an acceleration. What is still missing is the global harmonization of climate stress tests to give a fuller picture of vulnerability around the world.[75]

Given the scale and existential nature of the net-zero challenge, the dialogue has begun about what additional roles central banks might play to accelerate the green transition. This is controversial. For reasons of law, policy, and practice, many central bankers are understandably loath to jeopardize their focus on the preeminent goal of monetary stability and, with it, "market neutrality" and deliberate avoidance of influencing allocation decisions to specific sectors or industries. Such reservations are reasonable. The question now, however, is whether the green transition is so exceptional that it requires reconsideration of these established practices. Several central banks have slowly opened the doors to forms of green monetary policies (e.g., accounting for the carbon intensity of assets in monetary policy). However, we still lack appropriate intellectual, operational, and legal frameworks for central banks to consider additional means to help the green transition or the misallocation of resources.[76]

Alongside financial institutions and central banks, national governments themselves should also play a role in catalyzing resources for the green transition. They can choose from a "wide range of financing measures to support the transformation of energy and industrial systems, improve energy efficiency, tackle environmental pollution, and protect and replenish natural capital," according to EY, including "loans and grants for green investments in sustainable agriculture, renewable or low-carbon energy sources, energy-efficient buildings, public walkways and cycleways, and electric vehicle infrastructure."[77]

One model for such spending is the European Green Deal's Investment Plan, which aims to deploy at least $1 trillion of investments by mobilizing public investment and unlocking private funds through EU financial instruments, notably InvestEU.[78] The U.S. Infrastructure Investment and Jobs Act provided a roughly similar amount for investments targeting sustainability.[79] But many countries in the world missed the opportunity to leverage their COVID-related fiscal stimulus to accelerate their green transitions. According to the Global Recovery Observatory at Oxford University, "zero recovery spending is considered green in six countries—Indonesia, Malaysia, Philippines, Thailand, Singapore, and Vietnam."[80]

As far as developing countries are concerned, the World Bank estimates that they will "need to invest around 4.5 percent of GDP to achieve infrastructure-related Sustainable Development Goals (SDGs) and to stay on track to limit climate change" to 2°.[81] Yet, the current climate-related financing is under 1.5 percent of what's likely needed. It is important, then, to build pipelines of investable projects to mobilize private capital. Advanced economies can facilitate the transition in these regions by finding ways to diffuse green technologies in ways that protect legitimate intellectual property concerns that are critical to sustaining innovation, for example, through joint ventures or other ways of sharing best practices more broadly. They can also coordinate facilitating access to financial capital through both multilateral institutions and private banks.

II.1.3 Spurring innovation

Technology will play a fundamental role in speeding up the green transition. Many of the necessary innovations in each of these sectors already exist and now need to be diffused and scaled up such as energy efficient technologies for buildings and household appliances, $CO2$ removal technologies or electric vehicles.[82] This process can be eased thanks to the development of enabling innovations such as artificial intelligence, the Internet of Things and blockchain technologies. According to McKinsey, "climate technologies that are already mature could, if deployed widely, deliver about 60 percent of the emissions abatement that will be needed to stabilize the climate by 2050."[83]

And there are five broad groups of promising technology development to prioritize to help close this technology innovation gap in the coming decade: electrification, agriculture, power grid, green hydrogen (defined as hydrogen produced by splitting water into hydrogen and oxygen using renewable electricity), and carbon capture (*Exhibit 2.6*).[84]

Promoting the development of new technologies is not enough to put the green or digital transition on the right track. Countries need to institutionalize ways to spread the diffusion of new technologies (*Chapter 3*). The European Institute of Innovation and Technology's Knowledge and Innovation Community, for example, is the EU's largest public-private partnership working on the transition to net-zero economy. With a number of centers, the initiative offers educational programs, supports research and development, and fosters entrepreneurship.[85]

Another example is SINCERE (Strengthening International Cooperation on Climate Change Research), a project by the

Exhibit 2.6

Green technologies to watch

ELECTRIFICATION	AGRICULTURE	POWER GRID	HYDROGEN	CARBON CAPTURE
Electric-vehicle batteries	Zero-emissions farm equipment	Long-duration storage	Low-cost production	Pre- and post-combustion capture technologies
Battery-control software	Meat alternatives	Advanced controls	Road-transport fuel	
Efficient building system	Methane Inhibitors	Software and communications	Ammonia production	Direct air capture
Industrial electrification	Anaerobic manure processing	Vehicle-to-grid integration	Steel production	Bioenergy with carbon capture and storage
		Next-generation nuclear	Aviation fuel	Biochar
		High efficiency materials		CO_2-enriched concrete

Source: McKinsey Sustainability, The Trilateral Commission

THE TRILATERAL COMMISSION

European Union, which aims to strengthen climate cooperation in Europe. SINCERE will bring together business, finance, research, and policy centers to expand the EU Joint Programme Initiative on Climate to include Eastern European member countries. It also aims to set up two flagship partnerships with Africa and Latin America.[86]

The diffusion of a technology will also create economies of scale that will help bring down its costs, further facilitating its adoption through a virtuous positive feedback loop. Over the past decade, for example, some green technologies became almost 90 percent cheaper, including electric-vehicle batteries, LED lights, and other hardware.[87]

History shows repeatedly that technological breakthroughs by themselves do not drive change; rather, organizations, businesses, and systems need to innovate as well to realize the potential of such technologies. So too with green technologies.

While national governments have a special role to play, cities are already in the frontlines of driving this sort of innovation in both climate change mitigation and reduction. Cities will have a disproportionate impact on whether the global green transition succeeds because in the twenty-first century the majority of the world's population lives in urban areas for the first time in human history. They are the major centers of economic activity. Consequently, they consume about two-thirds of global energy while generating three-quarters of global greenhouse-gas emissions.[88] In practice, the innovations that will integrate new green approaches to living and working will be defined and implemented largely by cities. An encouraging note is that greenhouse gas emissions in cities can be reduced nearly 90 percent by 2050 through the use of existing technologies.[89] Already cities are experimenting with different approaches to public and electric transportation, housing and building retrofitting, green spaces, renewable energy, and carbon capture, as well as taking steps to mitigate climate change impacts today.[90] (*See Box 2.5 for the example of Singapore's innovative approach.*)

Box 2.5: Cities lead the way to a greener future: Singapore

Singapore is at the forefront of cities formulating comprehensive strategies to manage climate change. In February 2021, Singapore released the Green Plan 2030, its latest initiative focused on achieving net-zero emissions, increasing sustainability, and building resilience to manage challenges exacerbated by climate change.[91]

Spearheaded by the Singaporean ministries of Education, National Development, Transport, Sustainability and the Environment, and Trade and Industry, this strategy sets ambitious goals by 2030, including targeting 60,000 EV charging points, achieving 75 percent mass public transport share during peak periods, and limiting all-new auto registrations to clean energy models.[92] Many of these efforts were underway in 2022, including the formulation of critical coastal protection plans. The government is also developing a coastal-inland flood model to enable it to game out what extreme rainfall inland and weather events on the coast would bring.[93]

This holistic effort builds on Singapore's track record of innovative ideas, from aquaculture to smart transportation. The Singapore Food Agency's (SFA) Marine Aquaculture Center (MAC), for instance, plays a vital role in facilitating interdisciplinary R&D in aquaculture initiatives. This includes an effort to create the world's first vertical seafood production system designed to mitigate the effects of carbon-intensive shrimp farming.[94]

Singapore has also been lauded for its Intelligent Transport System (ITS), which uses smart transportation technologies like GPS-enabled taxis, highly-integrated public transportation infrastructure, and the world's first Electronic Road Pricing Systems to ease traffic congestion and decrease greenhouse gas emissions.[95] Today, Singapore is one of the world's least congested major cities.[96]

II.1.4 The transition, sector by sector

The green transition is not one challenge. Rather, it will require a variety of transitions tailored to different economic sectors, each of which uses fossil fuels in a different way. The challenge is very different, for example, in industry than in agriculture, requiring different solutions (*Exhibit 2.7*).

Industry, the historic driver of capitalist development, claims the largest share of emissions, roughly one-third of the global total. This category includes cement, chemical, iron, and steel production; mining; and the oil and gas industries. And while industry produces a roughly even mix of carbon dioxide and methane, other sectors have a different balance, with different impacts on climate change. Power and transport, for example, produce only carbon dioxide.

The diversity across economic categories reveals the complexity of the coming sector-by-sector transition. Consider power generation. The biggest driver of carbon content in many products and services is the power generated to create them. The power sector is already huge and will likely have to grow even bigger as more things—cars, factories, and the like—are electrified. If the power system is not decarbonized, then none of the downstream uses of electricity will be able to live up to their own decarbonization potential.

To start to decarbonize the power sector, we will have to reduce rapidly coal and gas-fired power generation. Renewables (solar and

Exhibit 2.7

Different sectors, different challenges

Anthropogenic greenhouse-gas (GHG) emissions per sector and type of gas

■ Carbon dioxide (CO_2)　■ Methane (CH_4)　■ Other GHGs[1]

	Metric gigatons of CO_2 equivalent (GtCO_2e[2]) in 2016, by source, %			Total GHGs, metric gigatons	Share of total GHG emissions
Industry[3]	45	46	9	25	33%
Agriculture/ livestock	6	80	14	15	20%
Power	100			12	17%
Transport	100			8	10%
Waste[4]	98		2	6	8%
Net deforestation	100			6	7%
Buildings	100			3	4%

[1]Includes emissions from hydrofluorocarbons, perfluorocarbons, and sulfur hexafluoride.　[2]Non-CO2 emissions converted into CO2e using 20-year global-warming-potential values from IPCC Assessment Report 5.　[3]Includes cement, chemical production, iron and steel, mining, oil and gas, and low- to medium- temperature and high-temperature industries, among others.　[4]Includes food waste, biological treatment of solid waste, incineration and open burning of waste, solid-waste disposal, and wastewater treatment and discharge.

Source: McKinsey Global Institute, The Trilateral Commission

THE TRILATERAL COMMISSION

wind), sustainably sourced bioenergy (biokerosene, biogas, and biodiesel), and green hydrogen will need to play an important role in the transition as well.

As that happens, though, the industrial sector will have to adapt to accommodate changing needs, such as the increased demand for solar panels and wind turbines. And the shift from central power plants with consistent output to renewable energy (which is variable) presents a challenge for the grid, which was designed for consistent power. All sectors, too, will have to reassess the role of zero-carbon nuclear energy.

The great challenge posed by green electrification is that, in the short-term, it might boost energy prices beyond levels that are affordable, especially for low-income households. Some form of compensatory measures will be necessary. But the transition will be costly and challenging for firms as well, as it might lead to asset stranding, as McKinsey has pointed out, "whereby existing physical assets are either underutilized or retired before the end of their useful life." According to McKinsey, in power alone, for example, some $2.1 trillion worth of assets could be stranded by 2050. This implies that also for firms, especially in the sectors that are more exposed to this kind of transformation, governments should think about some form of compensation.[97]

Cement provides an example to illustrate the types of challenges each industry will have to address during the green transition. Cement will remain vital to our economies throughout the green transition: large parts of the building and transportation sectors are literally built with cement and that will not change. Today, however, cement accounts for 4.5% of global greenhouse gas emissions because it is very energy intensive to make. Here, the most appropriate transition may be the use of alternative fuels in the production process. One option is Refuse Derived Fuels, where burning of garbage substitutes for fossil fuel. Reduce, reuse, recycle, and other techniques across the production cycle likewise promise to reduce the cement industry's carbon footprint.[98]

While similar bespoke transitions will be needed across different sectors, there are nonetheless broader patterns to note.[99] Decarbonization will require new industries focused on carbon capture at the point where that carbon is created and on the removal of carbon dioxide from the atmosphere itself. And just as all industries will be affected by the green transition, so too all business functions within companies will need to adapt how they work. Strategy, risk, finance, and mergers and acquisitions departments will have to account for different regulatory and cost regimes and employ new types of advanced analytics. Manufacturing processes and materials will need to be redesigned. Supply chain and facility operations should consider resilience as well as the carbon footprint of their operations. R&D and product development must factor in not only new material and energy requirements, but also consumer demand. Talent recruitment needs to consider how to attract candidates with a commitment to social purpose. Stakeholder relations must be reimagined. In sum, every business will have to embed "green" into how it runs.

Finally, and likely the hardest part of all, the green transitions will require us to change our ways of life. Consumer expectations and demands—so powerful in directing and driving capitalist energy—will need to adapt as much as any business's internal operations. For instance, eating habits will need to evolve to help reduce the agriculture sector's carbon emissions. The way people move, work, and live will change in many subtle and perhaps unpredictable ways—but the aim is that all these various transitions will add up to one greater transformation of the way the economy works.

III. WHAT WE SHOULD DO NOW

III.1. Shared understanding and direction

Warming global temperatures threaten not only our shared natural environment, but our economies, societies, and future generations' wellbeing. One of the central pillars of capitalism's Fifth Stage, then, should be addressing climate change. The report proposes:

• *Every person should live and work in a net-zero world by 2050.*

"Net zero" is already a standard objective, endorsed by governments, international organizations, and many businesses. And it bears repeating: If we can achieve that benchmark by 2050, we might be able to limit average global temperature increases to 1.5° and avoid the worst climate scenarios.

While public understanding of the need to act against climate change has increased, "net zero" remains an abstraction to most. All the more so because meeting the goal requires nothing less than restructuring how capitalism works. The changes needed are hard to grasp. It will require investments of trillions of dollars per year. Industrial infrastructure needs to be converted. Transportation will need to phase out the internal combustion engine. Business operations and management need to be redesigned. Tens of millions of new jobs will need to be created; tens of millions of jobs eliminated or transformed. All this will require an unprecedented level of creative collaboration across stakeholders.

Against the massive scale of the challenge, we will have to make the steps along the way as tangible as possible. Leaders across all sectors will need to be relentless in making the case for a green transition even while acknowledging that they may be criticized for doing so.[100] But here, the report's objective may be helpful. It is, after all, a normative commitment to equality of opportunity. Net zero embodies the belief that all lives, wherever and whenever they are, have equal worth.

Further, this goal focuses attention on a true strategic priority. "You manage what you measure," is an old business cliché. In this case, though, it is valuable. This goal not only helps set the agenda, it also provides clarity to evaluate the impact of different investments, track progress, and stress urgency.

The report's net-zero goal also builds momentum across different countries for tangible action. Despite the scale and complexity, achieving net zero will involve solving a series of discrete problems simultaneously. While we work toward better global governance of climate change, nations, businesses, and others can still move us forward.

Finally, this statement of the goal allows us to reframe the net-zero transition as a positive investment in the future—not a cost—in delivering a stronger economy and better planet.[101]

III.2. Investments

- **Establish enduring national strategy forums:** Achieving net zero is the work of generations. Every country and industry will need to formulate its own net-zero strategy. Such strategies should assess risk, develop policy priorities, and formulate implementation plans with defined resources. They cannot be "one and done." Rather, success will require learning and adaptation based on experience and scientific progress. In turn, we need to create or adapt forums for ongoing dialogue among stakeholders.

  Government: Governments should lead in developing the national public policy strategy to achieve net zero. In many cases, these will be hotly contested. Nonetheless, there is no substitute for a broad political consensus on the fundamentals of a national strategy. Establishing predictable policy boundaries or guardrails helps reduce uncertainty for other stakeholders—especially in business as they plan investments.[102]

  Public-private partnerships: Although governments will lead in developing policy, these strategies must be true "whole of society" efforts. Governments should thus also lead in convening a broad array of stakeholders in support of such strategies. In many cases, though, other groups—industry associations, regional leaders, and so on—could also play an important role in establishing forums to engage stakeholders on an ongoing basis. Nonprofits, academic, and other research institutions could provide convening partners and sources of independent analysis of policies, programs, and investments. There are tested principles to build and sustain such strategic alliances;[103] but there is no standard playbook. Instead, each country will need to build its own approach to sustain stakeholder engagement based on its political and economic system, industry composition, level of development, carbon pricing regime, and so on.[104]

- **Embed "green" into businesses' DNA:** Green cannot be an afterthought. Net zero will only be achieved by a thoroughgoing redesign of how businesses operate. The ways we power and operate businesses account for a significant proportion of global greenhouse gases and, therefore, potential mitigation risks. Businesses must become the net-zero engine of this era's capitalism.

Government: Governments should engage with business throughout the transition process to identify potential statutory, regulatory, or other policy changes to accelerate the transition toward green business operations. Governments should also explore how to use their power as a major purchaser of goods and services to incentivize firms to integrate green considerations into their operations, potentially including requirements for transparency on the carbon footprint of their supply chain.

Business: Even from a relatively narrow shareholder value perspective, the case for integrating green goals into business management is compelling. Climate considerations are already reshaping the business landscape. Future competitiveness will depend on how firms anticipate and adjust to regulatory changes. Imagine, for example, making a capital investment in a new manufacturing facility only to have that factory shut down if its carbon impact is later over some allowance.

Different industries will face different transition costs and opportunities,[105] but they should all be clear eyed and plan for what those are, integrating them into their strategy development, risk management, and strategic decision-making. They should prioritize acquiring and building the analytic capabilities needed to guide their operations during the green transition.

Business leaders also have a critical role to play that goes beyond inherited ideas of their business role to adopt a broader stakeholder perspective. They should embrace their unique role of explaining their enterprises to the world, and the world to their employees.

- **Support "offensive" and "defensive" workforce development:** The net-zero transition will have significant implications for workers in many industries. To put it bluntly, there will be winners and losers. As noted above, according to one estimate, the green transition could lead to over 200 million new jobs and the loss of around 190 million jobs by 2050.[106] Workforce development programs will need to be both "offensive" (for example, adapting new standards before they are mandated) as well as "defensive" (managing displaced workers, especially from oil, gas, and coal extraction, during the transition).

Government: Governments have historically invested in workforce development in different ways. Governments should assess, on an ongoing basis, their green workforce requirements as part of their national strategy reviews. The impact of the green transition on workforces will be concentrated in certain sectors—like the extractive industries, the automotive sector, and power generation—and, therefore, geographies. National strategy reviews should not only influence the design, resourcing, and delivery of traditional workforce development programs, but also inform broader educational and credentialling reforms (*See Chapter 4*).

Business: Businesses in the sectors likely to be affected most dramatically by the green transition should begin assessing their own workforce pipeline requirements now. They should develop workforce transition strategies, "offensive" and "defensive." Industry associations and trade unions should also play important roles in these assessments. Throughout the transition, business leaders should engage with government counterparts to help tailor and sequence programs for an orderly transition over years. Businesses should also engage with their local workforce development partners, which vary based on their national system. Typically, workforce development programs' impact is proportional to the level of collaboration between local training centers and their business partners.

- **Invest in green innovation:** We do not yet have all the technologies and other innovations we need to achieve a net-zero economy by 2050. Investment will be needed to close the gap.

Government: Governments should explore options for investing in new innovations as part of their national green strategy processes. They have a range of potential tools—from direct funding of experimental programs run by businesses and research institutes to more indirect subsidies, tax incentives, trade policies, and procurement policies that promote R&D and scaling of innovations.[107]

Governments can also support innovations through funding for universities and other academic centers.

Governments should also assess how regulatory changes can help accelerate green innovation. And they could consider establishing special green R&D or investment agencies to fund early stage high-risk, high-reward research. Public sector early investment can help companies overcome financial barriers to demonstration and early commercialization of their innovations. This approach is sometimes called the "ARPA" model, after the U.S. Department of Defense's Advanced Research Projects Agency, which pioneered the approach with early investment in such technologies as the Internet, GPS, and mRNA vaccines. The U.S. Department of Energy established its own "ARPA-E" in 2009.[108]

Business: Businesses will naturally provide a significant amount of investment in green innovation, guided by their corporate strategies. Many are already leading the way and working within their own carbon pricing forecasts. Businesses should engage with all stakeholders in their innovation "ecosystems"—including academic institutions, national academies, research institutes and national laboratories, venture capital firms, and other investors—to identify and support new technologies.

- **Promote innovation diffusion:** The net-zero transition is a universal challenge. Every country is in the same metaphorical boat. Promoting diffusion of innovations within and across economies will be important for the net-zero transition.

Public-private collaboration: Building upon successes like SINCERE and JPI, described above, governments and international organizations should explore ways to develop and deliver programs to build green skills and help focus investment in high potential areas. Furthermore, restrictive trade and Foreign Direct Investment (FDI) policies, according to the World Bank, "unequivocally discourage" the transfer of these technologies; therefore, countries seeking access to these innovations should explore ways to increase FDI, such as non-tariff barriers like import quotas and advocacy for multilateral trade liberalization.[109]

- **Compensate the most vulnerable:** The green transition will be costly, and its impact felt unevenly. As noted, electricity prices are expected to rise initially during the transition period before declining as more net-zero power generation capacity comes online. Such increased costs disproportionately hit low-income households, which spend more of their income on energy and goods and services with energy embedded in them. Job disruptions as some industries scale back operations could create additional harm. For reasons of equity and political support for the broader net-zero transition effort, these households should receive assistance during the adjustment.

Government: As part of their national strategies, governments should assess the risks posed by the green transition to specific segments of their citizenry. National strategies should then incorporate compensation programs for these specific groups. Such programs could range from community assistance for economic development to reskilling and unemployment support for affected workers to direct assistance to vulnerable households through cash transfers, tax credits, or other subsidies and support. The mix of programs and funding mechanisms should be tailored to the unique needs of these affected individuals, households, and communities.

III.3. "Rules of the road"

- **Accelerate green finance:** Credit has always been the lifeblood of capitalism ever since the Dutch pioneered it in the seventeenth century. So, too, in this era. The financial sector has a unique role to play incentivizing and supporting firms through the green transition.

Government: Central banks should start regular and universal climate stress tests to assess climate risks across financial systems. As described above, the idea of central banks taking an explicit role in promoting green developments is controversial, especially among some central bankers who rightly caution against expanding beyond their traditional stability mandates. Without prejudging the outcome, the significance of the green transition warrants open dialogue among central bankers and with their main stakeholders about whether central bankers' mission should be expanded to reinforce other government actions by gradually and cautiously adopting green monetary policies, while avoiding undermining their market neutrality.

Business: Asset managers and creditors should ask all the companies they invest in (or lend to) to provide information consistent with the framework developed by the Task Force on Climate-related Financial Disclosures (TCFD). That way, the financial sector can prioritize placing resources with companies leading the green transition, while indirectly penalizing laggards. Stock exchanges should also develop common guidance on climate disclosures consistent with the TCFD recommendations. This will improve market transparency.

- **Build voluntary carbon markets:** Many companies seek to purchase carbon credits not for compliance reasons, but to meet their own self-imposed net-zero targets. These credits can, in turn, help fund climate projects. The Taskforce on Scaling Voluntary Carbon Markets, sponsored by the Institute of International Finance, estimates that demand for such credits could increase by a factor of 15 by 2030, with the market worth roughly $50 billion.[110]

Business: Businesses have already started to come together under the auspices of the Taskforce on Scaling Voluntary Carbon Markets, which released its first report in January 2021. The report set out the path to expand such markets and recommended a new independent governance structure. Businesses should continue to collaborate with the Taskforce to identify and resolve any bottlenecks to the smooth functioning of these markets.

- **Integrate climate into corporate governance:** Boards and executives should be incentivized to make progress in managing the net-zero transition. Reliable information on how companies are planning to manage climate risk and opportunities is still "hard to find, inconsistent and fragmented."[111] Many boards have viewed climate change as just another factor potentially affecting financial risk and opportunity. Even many large enterprises have not made significant progress on this front: fewer than half of the FTSE 100 companies set measurable environmental, social, and governance goals and targets, according to PricewaterhouseCoopers.[112]

Business: Following the Greenhouse Gas Protocol Corporate Standard, companies should clarify targets for direct and indirect emissions, including from their global value chains. The lack of transparency so far makes it more difficult for investors to assess and compare risks across potential investments. Investors should push companies to draw up real climate transition plans. Investors should also press rating agencies to encourage firms to adopt accounting standards for green transition factors and for boards to manage climate transition and mitigation risks. Through such transparency, investors would be able to assess their own risk portfolios and direct their resources more effectively. This way improved transparency on green risk factors would help create additional market-incentives for boards to integrate green considerations into their corporate governance, rather than relying upon top-down statutory or regulatory mandates. Climate concerns should be built into boards' regular risk and strategy reviews. Furthermore, boards should link executive compensation to specific green transition targets. Such targets would depend on industry and the enterprise's overall strategy.

- **Promote green labeling:** As awareness of climate change increases, more consumers want to be part of the solution by making "climate friendly" decisions in the market. Green labels that identify a product or service's GHG footprint not only inform consumers, but also help communicate through everyday interactions the importance of broader net-zero commitments.

Government: Most governments have regulatory powers to set consumer information and safety standards for products and services. If similar industry solutions for green labels do not emerge, governments should explore formal regulatory requirements.

Business: Customer-facing businesses should explore approaches to standardize green labeling for their industries. Industry associations could provide the mechanism to establish voluntary standards. Participating firms could then use such labeling as part of their brand building. A variation upon this approach could be for firms or industries to collaborate on creating an independent certification nonprofit organization modeled after Underwriters Laboratory (UL).[113]

III.4. Trilateral recommendation

● *Establish a "Climate Club" among advanced economies*

International agreement on a global carbon pricing regime has remained an aspiration ever since the Kyoto and Paris Accords put their emphasis on voluntary commitments. Progress has been halting, however, as outlined earlier, because the move to carbon pricing involves solving a huge "public goods" issue. This has meant in practice, as William Nordhaus argued in his 2018 Nobel Prize acceptance address, "the present free rides, while the future pays."[114]

While governments should continue to seek a broader global regime, the Trilateral countries should consider accelerating progress on both reducing emissions and incentivizing greater international cooperation through more limited agreements among leading emitters to form so-called "climate clubs."[115]

The basic design, originally proposed by Nordhaus in 2015, involves a group of countries joining together to accept common carbon pricing policies and agreeing to penalize imports from countries without the same policies. This prevents so-called "carbon leakage," whereby industries might migrate from a country with a carbon pricing regime to a free rider without one. The price of admission? Agreement to a carbon price floor to ensure the minimum price is consistent with global carbon targets, while providing leeway to countries that want to go higher.

The major advantages of such an approach are that it is voluntary, can be coordinated more rapidly and less formally among like-minded governments than forging a global consensus, and yet also includes real incentives for compliance and others to join. Countries outside the club, according to the concept, will be incentivized to adopt new carbon policies and make investments in carbon reduction to be more competitive. To help smooth the transition, the club's price floor could increase in a gradual and predictable way. The principle of common but differentiated responsibility would provide the foundation for such an approach. Along the line of the Canadian example, it would allow countries to adopt carbon pricing schemes consistent with local conditions. (*See Box 2.4.*)

A move toward a "club" carries risks that require deliberate mitigation. To help manage the potential impacts of increased prices, the most vulnerable households should receive tax relief or "carbon dividends" from the revenues of this sort of approach. Furthermore, as many developing countries argue, revenues should also help accelerate investments in green technologies in their economies. Standards for carbon accounting will also be critical. Lastly, a club approach should be crafted to preserve its integrity and not become opportunistic protectionism under a green banner. Any club should be consistent with World Trade Organization rules.

Membership in a "climate club" could be adaptable. The Trilateral mainstays such as Australia, the European Union, Japan, South Korea, and the United States are all potential candidates. China and India would make a significant impact as the largest emitters among developing economies if they were willing to join. Given the urgency and limited progress to date on the global track, this sort of experimentation is warranted.

Practically speaking, the European CBAM could provide a starting point for conversations leading to a broader "climate club." The EU could engage through the G7 or G20 fora. Another approach could be for the EU to explore the potential of extending in some way its CBAM through bilateral trade discussions with the United States, Canada, United Kingdom, and Japan. Together these countries would cover 44% of the world's trade.[116] China could also be engaged. Another approach to jumpstart a "climate club" approach could be to focus first on a sector-based approach rather than attempting to secure agreement across entire economies.

In sum, the Trilateral countries should lead in accelerating action on international carbon pricing through a "climate club" approach. Catalyzing agreement among a smaller number of countries in a "climate club" promises to be easier than working just through existing multilateral fora. Although difficult, a success would shift incentives for additional collaboration, leading to broader multilateral agreements.

All these paths involve difficult economic diplomacy. The virtue of the approach remains, however, that these paths could be less difficult than the comprehensive global one.

3

A DIGITAL FUTURE FOR ALL

The digital revolution has delivered amazing innovations and is helping us work together in ways previously unimaginable. Equality of opportunity in the twenty-first century will depend to a significant degree upon digital access—to connectivity, skills, technologies, data, and to the market itself. To develop a more equitable and inclusive growth model, democratic capitalism will need to address the digital divides for individuals and organizations.

I. HOW WE GOT HERE

I.1. An accelerating revolution

The digital revolution epitomizes the immense power and potential of capitalism's engine for innovation and change. New digital tools, techniques, and ways of working have already delivered incredible material benefits, connecting humanity as never before, and helping solve previously unsolvable problems—and they promise more. Our best hope for tackling climate change and other challenges, for example, moves through the digital domain in this Fifth Stage of capitalism.

Yet, at the same time, digital advances generate tensions. Without access to a computer or the Internet, or without the skills to use them, individuals are locked out of the knowledge economy. This can fuel inequality. The digital revolution has created other risks, too, ranging from negative mental health impacts on individuals to the concentration of market power in a few large enterprises across the global economy.

The COVID-19 pandemic highlighted the limits and vulnerabilities in our dependence on the digital. In response to the pandemic, schools around the world shut down. They then tried to transition to remote learning. This approach ran headlong into a harsh reality: an estimated 1.3 billion school-aged children did not have access to the necessary technology in their homes. All told, over 460 million children were entirely shut out. Over the course of a few weeks, education, the bedrock of equality of opportunity (*Chapter 4*), crumbled for many. The projected long-term economic impact is staggering. This generation of students risks losing up to $17 trillion in lifetime earnings, according to a December 2021 report by UNESCO, UNICEF, and the World Bank. That is roughly equivalent to 14 percent of today's global GDP,[1] and the losses will disproportionately come from the future paychecks of those who are already disadvantaged.

To understand how to capture the good of the digital revolution while mitigating the negative, we need to walk through how the revolution started. It really began about 70 years ago in the heyday of Managed Capitalism, when entrepreneurs, businesses, higher education, and the government collaborated to innovate within capitalism. These legacies continue to shape our lives in technologies, centers of innovation, and networks of firms and investors today.

The emergence of California's Silicon Valley as the quintessential innovation "cluster" shows Managed Capitalism's long reach into the present.[2] In the 35 years after the founding of Hewlett-Packard (HP) in 1939, what became Silicon Valley emerged from an amalgam of talent, higher education institutions, established businesses, investors and capital, entrepreneurial experience, and network effects generated by proximity, mobility, and informal collaboration among innovators—all with plenty of government support and guidance.

Remarkably, much of Silicon Valley's success can be traced to one firm, Fairchild Semiconductors, its eight founders, and their network of mutual support. Founded in 1957, Fairchild grew as a government contractor with the Apollo program in the 1960s. Its founders eventually led and invested in a series of start-ups that helped define the Valley. For instance, Intel introduced the first microprocessor in 1974, while the venture capital firm Kleiner-Perkins was founded by a Fairchild founder and a former HP executive. Fairchild's impact cascaded through the decades. A 2014 analysis concluded over 2,000 companies, 92 of them public companies then valued at $2.1 trillion, could be traced back to Fairchild and its founders.[3]

In parallel, other digital innovation hubs eventually emerged as technologies evolved, capital flowed, and markets opened around the world during the neoliberal stage of capitalism. From Tokyo to Tel Aviv, Singapore to Stockholm, Bangalore to Beijing, centers for digital innovation took root in different national contexts.[4]

Or consider the Internet, a defining technology of our era. Its origins are found under the shadow of a potential nuclear war between the Soviet Union and the West, when in 1964 Paul Baran developed the concept of "packet switching" as a potential approach to a new, more resilient communications network. Typical of this era, Baran had recently completed his graduate work at one of the emerging powerhouses of public higher education, the University of California, Los Angeles. He worked at RAND Corporation, a new type of organization designed to harness the best technical minds to serve the government, in this case under contract to the U.S. Air Force. Based off of his research, in 1969, the Department of Defense's Advanced Research Projects Agency then funded the development of a communications network that would become the ARPANET. When the first commercial Internet service provider launched in 1989, it was built in part on these ideas, developed through just one of Managed Capitalism's many public-private collaborations.[5]

At first, progress in communications, information, and digital technologies seemed to outpace their real economic impact. Toward the end of the 1980s, the Nobel laureate Robert Solow famously joked that "you see the computer age everywhere but in the productivity statistics."[6] Some analysts countered that traditional productivity failed to capture the growth in the "intangible economy," but Solow's quip also reflected an important reality: It takes years to build the networks, develop the skills, and innovate how work gets done before capturing the full benefits of digitalization.[7]

That part of the process accelerated in earnest soon after Solow's remark, with the arrival of the World Wide Web, email, chat, and e-commerce, mobile connectivity, Global Positioning Systems (GPS), and Wi-Fi networks. Then came advanced algorithms and analytics as well as smartphones, apps, and social media. Computing power continued its increase. As institutions and individuals adapted to these innovations, the results showed in even traditional productivity measures.[8] The world experienced an explosion of global data flows, increasing 45 times between 2005 and 2016,[9] and as measured by patent applications, digital and computer technology was the most innovative sector—a position it still holds.[10]

By the 2010s, digitalization had touched virtually every person in some way.[11] But the impact remained uneven, across countries and within them. The United States and China emerged as the clear leaders in the race, while much of Europe lagged. Europe's digital frontier firms, for instance, were only about 60% as digitized as comparable American firms. Propelled by the falling cost of smart-phones and high-speed connectivity, India emerged as one of "the world's largest and fastest-growing bases of digital consumers" and was accelerating past many other economies, developing and developed alike.[12] And as a recent report for Brookings pointed out, across Africa "the relentless spread of networks, sensors, arti-ficial intelligence, and automation" boosted the digital revolution in the most dynamic urban areas, widening the gap with underde-veloped rural regions.[13]

Within countries, some sectors made more use of the digital revolution than others. Not surprisingly, information and com-munications technology, media, finance, and services led the way. More fragmented and locally-based sectors like construction, hos-pitality, and agriculture were largely untouched. Government and education sectors were particularly weak in digitalization, too. And even within industries, digital maturity was uneven across firms. In fact, a relatively small number of "superstar" firms were emerg-ing to create a disproportionate share of digital value.[14] Overall, though, the digital revolution still had huge unrealized potential as the 2020s began.

I.2. The Artificial Intelligence wave

In the 2010s, the continued expansion of computing power, explo-sion of data, and refinement of algorithms set the stage for another wave of digital innovation centered around Artificial Intelligence (AI).

AI is a broad concept that, as IBM notes, combines "computer science and robust datasets, to enable problem-solving,"[15] includ-ing tasks such as perception, learning, problem solving, and even creativity. AI is not a single technology, but a set of technologies and approaches that can knit together and accelerate a variety of other innovations. Practically speaking, the use cases for AI range from robotics, voice recognition, natural language learning and translation, visual perception, and autonomous vehicles to algorithmic prediction.[16]

Already, a massive acceleration of research and investment is underway. Journal articles, conference presentations, and patents filed and granted all show explosive growth. In the decade leading to 2021, global patent filings increased over 47% per year from 2,949 to 141,241 (*Exhibit 3.1*). Global corporate investment in AI followed in lockstep, also growing roughly 47% per year between 2013 and 2021.[17] Between 2020 and 2021, the increase was even more substantial; private investment grew over 100% to $93.5 billion over that span.[18]

Exhibit 3.1

Trends in AI patents and investment

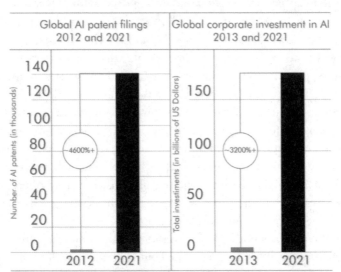

Source: Stanford Institute for Human-Centered Artificial Intelligence Center for Security and Emerging Technologies, Netbase Quid, The Trilateral Commission

With so much attention, it is easy to get carried away about AI's potential; indeed, an innovation's appearance is often followed by a "hype cycle," as the market analysis firm Gartner calls it, whereby its introduction generates over-inflated expectations, followed by disillusionment when those expectations are not met, and then finally the emergence of a more realistic path to adoption.[19] AI and its related technologies appear to be following this cycle too.

It will take time before AI reaches its full potential. But even so, early effects are already visible. We rely on AI applications in our smartphone maps, in our traffic guidance, and in our vehicles' automatic warning detection, breaking, and parking capabilities. AI has transformed customer experience with personally tailored recommendations (think Netflix and other streaming services) and algorithm-driven chatbots answering account questions, 24/7, 365. We now expect easy, accurate translations of many languages with a click.[20]

Over time, narrower improvements like these will build on each other to shape and accelerate the "Second Machine Age" and "the Fourth Industrial Revolution."[21] A particular driver will be greater capture and exploitation of "big data" arising from various sources including the Internet of Things (IoT), commercial activities, public records, social media, and satellite tracking. With power potentially *trillions* of times greater than today's supercomputers, quantum computing promises to redefine what a computer can do. Faster digital connectivity, powered by 5G, will give access to more rapid and stable wireless networking, connect a higher number of devices, and enable, in turn, richer, more varied streams of data. Equally important, so called "trust architecture" through distributed ledgers, such as blockchain, will reduce the cost of complying with security regulations, lowering operating and capital expenditures associated with cybersecurity, and enabling more cost-efficient transactions.[22]

Of course, as with other waves of digitalization, the spread of technology will not be even. The United States and China are the clear frontrunners in the race so far. Universities and institutes in the United States (MIT, Stanford, Michigan, Harvard, and Carnegie Mellon) and China (Academy of Sciences, Tsinghua, Shanghai Jiao

Tong, Zhejiang) dominate AI research publications. Germany's Max Planck Institute is the only non-American or Chinese institution in the global top ten for research publications.[23]

Corporate innovation shows a similar pattern. Ten of the top twenty firms for patent applications are American, and five are Chinese (*See Exhibit 3.4*). So, too, for private investments and new firm start-ups. In 2021, the United States secured over $52.9 billion in private AI investment, China $17.2 billion, and, lagging, the EU countries only $6.4 billion. That year the United States' 299 AI startups were over ten times the number of AI firms launched in Israel (28), France (27), Germany (25), India (23), Canada (22), and South Korea (19). Only China (119) and the United Kingdom (49) came within an order of magnitude of the United States for new firm creation.[24]

Meanwhile, a December 2021 survey indicated that, around the world, an average of 56 percent of organizations had adopted some form of AI in their operations. Asian economies led, with India at 65 percent, developed countries in Asia-Pacific at 64 percent, and developing markets including China at 57 percent. North American firms are around the global average, at 55 percent, and European firms lag at 51 percent.[25] A Stanford assessment of countries' overall AI "vibrancy," based on measures of research and development as well as distribution of AI capabilities, puts the United States, China, and India as the head of the pack (*Exhibit 3.2*).[26]

Following overall patterns of digitalization, the rates of AI adoption not only vary across firms but also among specific business functions within companies. For example, about 45 percent of high-tech and communications firms around the world have adopted AI to improve product and service development, while less than 20 percent of automotive and assembly, professional services, and consumer goods firms have for the same function. And across all firms, AI's potential remains largely untapped in certain critical functions. Strategy and corporate finance remain virtually untouched, for example, with fewer than 15 percent of organizations across all sectors employing some form of AI.[27]

Adding to the unevenness, the governance of AI and related technologies lags the pace of these technological and business changes.

Exhibit 3.2

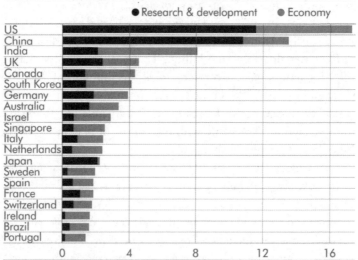

Global AI Vibrancy Ranking, 2021
Weighted index scores in research &
development and economy

Source: Stanford Institute for Human-Centered Artificial Intelligence, The
Trilateral Commission

THE TRILATERAL COMMISSION

Starting with Canada and Finland in 2017, countries have started to
develop their own national AI strategies.[28] In May 2019, the OECD
adopted a set of principles and high-level recommendations to guide
countries' development and adoption of AI.[29] The OECD also
established its AI Policy Observation to collect and share data and
best practices, including a living collection of national strategies and
major policy initiatives.[30] Despite this progress, there is as yet little
true international governance of AI. Regulatory agencies within
countries often have relatively limited capacity compared to major
technology companies. At the level of individual organizations,
there are often gaps between recognition of potential risks arising
from AI and steps to mitigate these risks. In a 2021 survey, for
example, 29 percent of organizations identified equity and fairness

as a potential risk in AI adoption, and only 19 percent were taking steps to address such concerns.[31]

AI's future potential is massive and multifaceted (*Box 3.1*). "Digital technologies are doing to human brainpower what the steam engine and related technologies did to human muscle power during the Industrial Revolution," argues MIT professor Andrew McAfee.[32] Its ultimate impact, though, will depend upon access.

Box 3.1: Role of digital technologies in
reducing greenhouse gas emissions

Digital data collection and analytics create new opportunities to optimize energy use and decrease greenhouse gas emissions.[33]

According to a recent Center for Climate and Energy Solutions (C2ES) report, "digital technologies are already being deployed across power grids, transportation networks, industrial facilities, buildings, and beyond. As their deployment increases, so too does their potential to accelerate decarbonization."[34]

We see AI's impact in other sectors too. "Fourth Industrial Revolution" manufacturing, C2ES notes, "can optimize energy and resource use, improve supply chain management, and allow for differentiation of products based on environmental attributes." Digital agriculture is already improving the use of water, pesticides, and fertilizers, thereby mitigating the environmental impact. Likewise for the transportation sector where data-driven methods have improved planning of transport systems and infrastructure as well as designing engines for greater efficiency and optimizing electric vehicles charging.

AI will play an essential role in the green transition. Part of the shift toward low-carbon energy systems will involve more "distributed power generation, distributed storage, and advanced demand-response capabilities," reports the World Economic Forum, and all of these "need to be coordinated

---

and integrated through more networked, transactional power grids."[35] At the same time, the combination of data with AI will offer more effective and timely monitoring of environmental trends, strengthening predictive capabilities. Thus, AI will help improve not just our technological solutions but also environmental planning, decision making, tracking green impact for policymakers, managers, and investors, and the management and monitoring of environmental policies.

II. WHERE WE ARE TODAY

The digital revolution is accelerating the transition to the Fifth Stage of capitalism. Its reach is already broad and deep, and it will extend further as technologies develop. The exact scale, scope, and distribution of that impact, however, remains uncertain.

A critical question today, therefore, is whether these digital innovations will improve equality of opportunity for all—or only for some. How well we respond will help determine how Fifth Stage capitalism manages a variety of challenges. For instance, navigating the narrow path to a successful green transition necessarily involves every country, every industry, and every individual in some way. We will only be able to succeed in that journey if we take full advantage of all our tools, especially the digital ones (*Chapter 2*).

To ensure that the digital revolution addresses inequality rather than worsening it, we will have to ensure access to these transformative innovations while managing their risks. This involves access for individuals as well as organizations to these innovations, both now and in the future. While there are many potential approaches to survey this digital landscape, this section will examine the digital revolution and how to capture its potential through the lens of access from multiple perspectives. We start with the individual and then move to the firm's viewpoint.

II.1. The perspective of the individual

It is impossible to imagine a new capitalism that prioritizes equality of opportunity for individuals without addressing the digital divide.

First, every person that is left behind represents lost equal opportunity as well as lost economic and social potential. Second, to the extent that access to the digital revolution remains uneven, it risks compounding other inequalities and work to undermine the legitimacy of the system as a whole.

II.1.1 Access to the Internet

The divides in digital access are clear (*Exhibit 3.3*). At the highest level, access is correlated with overall levels of economic development. The United Nations estimates that almost half the world's population—3.7 billion people, the majority of them women, and mostly in developing countries—are still offline.[36] Non-OECD countries have roughly half the number of high-speed mobile Internet subscriptions per person and one-third the number of fixed broadband subscriptions as OECD nations.[37]

Exhibit 3.3

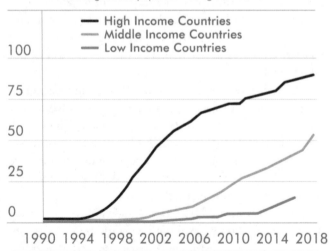

A wide access divide

Percentage of the population using the Internet

Source: World Bank, The Trilateral Commission

THE TRILATERAL COMMISSION

89

Although connectivity is especially weak in developing countries because of their often-underdeveloped infrastructure, significant numbers of people in developed economies remain excluded from digital life as well.[38] This is sometimes a function of the "last mile problem," especially for those living in rural and remote areas where it may not be profitable to extend a network to their home. Across countries, affordability is a recurring challenge as well.[39] Some Internet service providers have effectively abandoned some low-income urban neighborhoods as unprofitable, which critics have described as "digital redlining."[40] In the United States, for example, 21 million people lack Internet access, while in the United Kingdom, 12 percent of surveyed 11- and 18-year-olds reported not having Internet access at home from a computer or tablet.[41]

Even where access is widespread, the available technology may be out of date. Among OECD nations, for example, fiberoptic connections remain a relatively small share of broadband connections in many countries, standing below 5 percent in Austria, Belgium, Germany, Greece, Israel, and the United Kingdom. High-speed Internet is especially sparse in rural areas. (By contrast, fiberoptic connections make up 82 percent of broadband subscriptions in South Korea and 79 percent in Japan.) The most advanced digital tasks require the most advanced connections, and those starting with slower Internet and older devices will struggle to keep up and risk falling further behind as technologies and skills evolve.[42]

Ensuring access to the technologies that are increasingly necessary to learn and work seems an obvious way for governments and businesses to promote equality of opportunity. The COVID-19 pandemic has made the case for childhood Internet access. And from the perspective of lifelong learning, ability to interact with new technologies will be critical for re-skilling and to remaining competitive in the labor market.

Governments can also boost broadband deployment with grants or other financial support, promoting private investment, and setting coverage minimums for rural areas in spectrum auctions.

While governments have a critical role in establishing the essential regulatory and infrastructure foundations for access, private businesses—operating independently or in public-private partnerships depending upon the country—will play a critical role in finding innovative solutions to extend connectivity. Major technology companies such as Amazon, Google, and SpaceX, as well as a variety of startups and local providers, are innovating solutions to extend affordable Internet connectivity to underserved communities across the world. In India, for example, the opening of the telecommunications market led to the rapid spread of cheap handset devices with low-cost data plans. These devices are the most common access point to the Internet in the country. The number of Indians online is projected to increase from 622 million in 2020 to over 900 million in 2025.[43]

II.1.2 Access to skills

After access to digital connectivity, the next question is how to ensure access to the skills needed for an individual to thrive in our increasingly digitalized economies. All the way back to Britain's Luddite uprisings when textile laborers smashed their machines in 1810s, a recurring subtheme in capitalism's history is some workers' fear that technological change will upend established ways and throw them out of work.[44]

The AI-led changes across industries raise similar anxieties today, and with some justification. Capitalism, after all, generates "creative destruction." Entrepreneurs emphasize the "creative" in Schumpeter's phrase, while workers often experience the "destruction" when their jobs change or are eliminated.

The digital transition to "the Second Machine Age," as coined by Eric Brynjolfsson and Andrew McAfee, is accelerating and amplifying these trends.[45] This is an era of "skills-biased technical change," one that "favors people with more education, training, and experience."[46] The flip side is the vulnerability of many workers with lower skills as machines replace people.

Those possessing the highest digital skills and agility—the "knowledge workers," the creatives, the technical experts and engineers, the most skilled problem solvers—can be excited by the prospects of integrating AI into their work. Such technologies expand their opportunities for impact and increase their value in the labor market.

Most other workers, however—those without technical skills, educational credentials, or networks—may contemplate the same trends with fear. They now see outsourcing of jobs to globalization replaced by outsourcing to automation. They feel their jobs are precarious. They fear being left behind. Such anxieties are not just anecdotal. Since the 1980s the labor share of GDP has declined in most countries as firms decided to invest in new technologies rather than labor to drive efficiencies.[47] AI has begun to extend these dynamics from the manufacturing shopfloor into traditional middle-class "white collar" jobs such as accounting, retail, and legal.

From a global perspective, the scope and scale of these changes is significant. According to some likely scenarios, up to 375 million workers will need to adapt, build new skills, and change occupations by 2030. These impacts would not be spread evenly across countries. Due to a function of income level, industry structure, and underlying demographics, some countries would experience very little impact by 2030, while others would have about 30% of work activities displaced.[48] While less than 5 percent of occupations appear to be fully automatable, about 60% of occupations could have at least 30% of their tasks automated.[49]

Automation will continue to focus first on routine, predictable tasks, like bookkeeping and data processing, clerical work, and repetitive physical movement. Such tasks can be easily automated because they follow clear patterns and procedures that can be codified in software and performed by machines. Non-routine tasks that require problem-solving, emotional intelligence, intuition, persuasion, creativity, in-person interaction, situational adaptability—like writing a novel or designing a corporate strategy—are much harder to automate, at least for now.[50]

Based on historical experience, then, technology should lead to the adaptation of work more than the elimination of different occupations. Since 1950, only one job—elevator operator—has been fully automatized and removed from the 270 detailed occupations listed in the 1950 U.S. Census, while scores more have been added.[51] Moreover, even when some tasks have been automated, it has opened time for workers to do more complex labor. Take the example of the Automatic Teller Machine (ATM) that was introduced in 1970. Many expected it would kill off the job of bank teller. However, the number of bank tellers increased because their profession has evolved. The routine cash-handling tasks tellers used to do receded, while they have taken on a broader range of "relationship banking" services.[52]

Both governments and businesses have roles to play in smoothing the transition by equipping workers with the "nonroutine, creative, and higher-level skills that [new] technologies demand," wrote Brookings' Zia Quereshi, while working to "support workers during the adjustment process." Traditional formal education, the byproduct of the First and Second Industrial Revolutions, "must be complemented with new models and options for reskilling and lifelong learning. As the old career path of 'learn-work-retire' gives way to one of continuous learning ... the availability and quality of education must be scaled up." *(See Chapter 4.)*[53]

On this front, the digital revolution will need to help itself. The massive workforce development challenge will demand, as Quereshi explained, "innovations in the content, delivery, and financing of training, including new models of public-private partnership."[54]

Given the speed of transformation in today's labor market, moreover, governments should adopt policies that get people back into the workforce after a disruption through new unemployment programs and retraining services. Meanwhile, notes Quereshi, "well-functioning labor market institutions—collective bargaining, minimum wage laws, labor standards—are important to ensure that workers get a fair share of economic returns, especially at a time of rising market power of dominant firms."[55] (See *Chapter 4.*)

Lastly, this transformation will also impact capitalism as a "cultural system" in how we value work itself. Regardless of the pace of digital revolution, hundreds of millions of workers will continue in critically important occupations that will not be digitalized.[56] Consider all the skilled trades who literally help build and operate the world—from power grids and transportation networks to home healthcare and motorcycle repair.[57] Or large parts of the so-called "gig economy," where software and algorithms provide the platform to sell specific services performed by real workers. In an era of digital transformation, we will need to remember that "low tech" work does not equal low skill or low value.

How we value work for every person will shape the capitalism we build in the twenty-first century.

II.2. The perspective of firms

Capitalism is propelled forward by firms. They operate within the market "rules of the road" established by governments across the varieties of capitalism. It is their strategies, investments, innovations, and ability to perform with operational excellence that largely set the pace and reach of innovation and economic change.

So, too, in today's digital revolution. Understanding firms' abilities to access the capabilities and opportunities generated by the digital revolution is, therefore, another critical question.

Of course, there is no singular "perspective" on this question, but many from different industries, countries of operation, and levels of digital maturity. The interactions among firms, innovations, and the market is inherently complex and defies easy summary.

However, considering three broad categories of firms—defined by how they try to access and participate in the digital revolution— helps us simplify this complexity and analyze the main features of the challenges ahead. First, *creators* are the digital innovators in both content and operation. They typically conduct their own research and development to create new products and services for the market. This category includes many of the so-called frontier firms and spans from the largest global digital firms like Microsoft, Apple, Meta, Alphabet, Amazon, Tencent, and Alibaba to niche startups.

Consumers are the businesses that rely upon others to create digital solutions to improve their own internal operations and processes. Most firms fall into this category. They range from large multi-nationals to local retailers. They purchase digital goods and services from creators. However, especially when they face technical or implementation challenges beyond their experience, the consumers may engage a third category of firms.

This third category, the *constructors*, occupies an intermediary position in the market, providing expertise and services to the consumer firms to help design and then construct their digital capabilities out of the materials produced by the creators. Sometimes the constructors then help consumers implement changes and operate new digital approaches. A variety of technology and professional services firms fall into this final category.

This categorization informs this report's exploration of three general questions of access: access to and adoption of digital technologies, access to the data to run a successful business, and, lastly, access to the marketplace itself. Across these three questions we see different dynamics among the three broad categories of firms, and, significantly, different potential roles for governments to play in accelerating the digital revolution.

II.2.1 Access to technologies

From a macro-level perspective, how well technological innovation diffuses within economies matters greatly for both productivity growth and income distribution. Between 2001 and 2013, labor productivity among cutting-edge firms in advanced economies rose by around 35%; among non-frontier firms (the bottom 95 percent in terms of productivity within each industry), the increase was only 5%.[58] When productivity stagnates, wages in less competitive firms do as well. This can contribute to inequalities (*Chapter 4*).

From the perspective of businesses overall, access to digital technologies, tools, and techniques shapes their competitiveness and profitability. Early innovators and adopters have proven this. As described above, the wave of digital innovation, investments, new startups, and value creation continues to accelerate. While many digital *consumer* firms have begun to adopt new AI-enabled capabilities in some way, the breadth and depth of the digital revolution continues to be uneven across geographies, industries, and business functions within firms.

The digital *creator* firms and their investors continue to see this unevenness as presenting massive market opportunities. Untapped geographies, industries, and business functions are so-called "white space" of unmet consumer need. More simply, profit drives innovation. Consider the explosion in financial technology, or fintech, to improve people's access to finance. In addition to well-publicized innovations in trading platforms and cryptocurrency investing, fintech *creators* are developing new products and services to address the massive populations of the un- and underbanked, who have been excluded from traditional banking and credit markets.[59]

Digital *creator* firms may even offer "free" products and services to *consumer* firms to improve business performance. Such *creator* business models can work because a distinctive feature of the digital revolution is that the marginal costs to scale in the digital domain may effectively be zero; this differs from production of physical products where each additional unit shipped brings additional costs. The business logic is that basic services can be provided free to attract new customers who then end up purchasing services with greater capabilities. During the COVID-19 pandemic, for instance, digital *consumer* businesses and individuals made countless video conference calls because a variety of different *creator* firms offered them free of charge. Likewise, consider the range of free personal productivity services and apps—schedulers and project management tools—as well as free productivity draining online games and other entertainment.

The challenge, therefore, is not access to digital products and services in the marketplace per se, but access to paths to adoption by digital *consumer* firms. Why some firms are slower to take up new technologies often comes down to their management. Adoption requires investments and adaptation in business models, strategies, systems, and skills and capabilities. Digital transformations in *consumer* firms, therefore, often pivot upon the art and science of "change management." Not surprisingly, therefore, the move to digitally transform enterprises, large and small, has led to a steady growth in digital *constructor* firm services as they help other *consumer* firms manage their transitions.

But scale matters too. The scale of *consumer* firms influences how well they can adopt and use new digital capabilities. Larger firms can make upfront investments in advanced computing power, data storage, and advanced AI. They have advantages in recruiting technical and managerial talent to knit everything together. And there are the benefits of data, at scale. The larger the firm, the easier it is to establish a virtuous, self-reinforcing cycle where adopting new approaches provides better analytic insights that leads to better business results that generates more and richer data, that then feeds back to improve the algorithms and analytics. The bigger firms have a higher probability of taking full advantage of potential "network effects."[60]

Not surprisingly, for instance, major "traditional" retailers like Tesco, Walmart, Carrefour, and Seven-Eleven have often led the way in investing in digital capabilities; they could improve their operations based upon their data, ranging from customer transactions to supply chain deliveries. Analogous dynamics are at work in manufacturing and other sectors. These scale effects then cut both ways. Small and medium-sized businesses, which are typically engines of employment and growth, have a harder time adopting the new digital approaches and competing against larger scale enterprises.[61]

In sum, while many of the challenges related to adopting digital capabilities should be addressed by firms' management, there are structural factors related to scale that can slow adoption among small and medium-sized digital *consumers*.

It is this gap, therefore, where businesses, governments, and public-private collaborations can best focus their efforts to improve small and medium-sized *consumers'* access to these technologies. Industry associations can build and mobilize networks to adapt world-class techniques to learning best practices to adopt and use digital capabilities from exemplar firms and one another. For instance, firms can visit exemplar organizations to learn by walking the shopfloor or office to put into practice principles like the Toyota Production System's *Genchi Genbutsu* ("actual place, actual thing").

Businesses, government, and higher education institutions should also collaborate to develop new lifetime learning and workforce development programs to support these digital transitions (*Chapter 4*). They can also collaborate and invest in technology and innovation centers to help small and medium-sized firms build the capabilities they need to compete. In the United States, ManufacturingUSA provides one model for these sorts of collaborations.[62] The German Fraunhofer institutes offer another example (*Box 3.2*).

Box 3.2: Spreading innovation among small and medium-sized enterprises

The Fraunhofer-Gesellschaft, founded in 1949, has become not only Germany's leading applied research organization, but a global leader as well, with eight international affiliates. By early 2022, it had over 30,000 employees—mostly technical experts—in 76 institutes across Germany.[63]

The Fraunhofer's current organizational model was introduced in 1973 to strike multiple balances—between public and private sector, between local and national, and between autonomous and coordinated—to deliver consistent results.

Its public-private funding model provides roughly one third of its funding from the federal and state governments, and the rest through contract work with businesses and public sector organizations. This reliance on contract work incentivizes entrepreneurship and focused, practical applied research for businesses.

Each institute develops its own research agenda and engages in contracted work tailored to its local community. At the same time, the institutes remain legally part of the overall governance structure.

While researchers define their own programs, a flexible approach of cross-institute groups, initiatives, and clusters of excellence also creates national virtual research collaborations.

The institutes' close ties to industry are ultimately the foundations for its impact. The institutes specialize in bridging the gap between innovative research and the work of small and medium-sized enterprises. These linkages accelerate not

---

only the development of innovations but their commercialization from climate and AI to digital healthcare and hydrogen.

Its Fraunhofer Academy, established in 2006, serves as a hub for continuing education training that transfer knowledge from the institutes' research to businesses.[64]

The institutes are also a critical part of Germany's overall workforce development system, and help accelerate innovations through the industrial sector.

II.2.2 Access to data

In 2017, *The Economist* dubbed data as the "new oil" for this era of capitalism.[65] If fossil fuels were essential to propelling earlier industrial revolutions, then the digital revolution runs on data. Access to data, as described above, is the lifeblood of new AI-enabled business operations. All this is made possible by the continued development of advanced analytic techniques and the decline in costs for storing and using data.[66] These dynamics reward and reinforce scale, which, in turn, can erect barriers to entry from competition.[67]

The upshot of these trends, as the OECD has reported, is that data ownership that is becoming more concentrated as data volumes explode. This raises potential risks to privacy and market competition.[68] Therefore, the competition over data—and the policies defining how data can be used—are fundamental to the future of the digital revolution in capitalism's Fifth Stage.

Where some see potential antitrust issues tied to such data concentration (*discussed in Section II.2.3 below*), other digital *creator* firms see market opportunities. Here, three examples of market-driven innovation in not just technologies but also in branding and business models show how even the largest digital incumbents can be challenged in the market, at least in market segments.

All involve control over data or privacy. First, Google's position in the lucrative internet search business—with nearly 90% of global market share—appears dominant.[69] A variety of smaller *creators* are attempting to turn the Google model of free search with sharing of personal data on its head with a paid subscription search model, with no advertising, designed around protecting user data and privacy.[70]

Second, in a clash among "big tech" competitors, Apple has tried to position its brand as a protector of an individual's privacy. In 2021, Apple innovated by requiring online companies to ask permission to track users' activity as it rolled out a new version of its iOS mobile operating system. Given this option, around two thirds of customers said no, dealing a revenue blow to firms that rely upon digital advertising revenue like Facebook.[71]

Third, the Canadian e-commerce platform firm Shopify's model challenges Amazon's marketplace by ensuring that its retail partners, who are Shopify's *consumer* firms, retain exclusive control over their own data. This differentiates Shopify's value proposition: some retailers will pay a fee to retain control over their own data rather than entrusting Amazon with their transaction data from its marketplace.[72]

These types of market-based solutions are partial, addressing aspects of the data challenge, market segment by market segment. They also follow a certain, potentially unsettling pattern. They suggest the customer digital market may be evolving toward two fundamentally different models based upon consumers' willingness and ability to pay for privacy and data protections. As Professor Scott Galloway of New York University argues, the digital world appears to be bifurcating into what he calls the iOS World and the Android World, named after the dominant mobile smartphone operating systems.[73] In the iOS World, customers are willing to pay a premium for "more privacy, [and] a more elegant solution." The Android World, on the other hand, is where customers appear to get products for free—such as search, email, social media, access to marketplaces, etc.—but they effectively trade for these products their personal data, which the Android World *creator* firms then monetize in different ways such as targeted advertising, product development, and reselling data. This trend raises, in turn, ethical issues about commodification of personal data.[74]

Striking the right balance between the use and protection of data is essential to defining the type of digital world we will live in.

Public opinion polling suggests a good share of the public around the world is concerned about these issues. A landmark study in July 2020 showed, for instance, that 7 out of 10 people worldwide are "concerned about sharing personal information," while two-thirds of the global population does "not like the current privacy practices of most data collectors."[75] When given the option in practice, however, the majority of customers opt for the "free" "Android World" product and thereby effectively surrender control of their data.

This dilemma helps reframe the access question: Who should be able to grant access to data?

Different varieties of capitalism tend to answer this question differently. To simplify, democratic types of capitalism tend to grant the ownership of data either primarily to firms (liberal democratic capitalism) or citizens (social democratic capitalism), whereas authoritarian capitalisms view data as, ultimately, an asset of the state.

Furthermore, countries differ in how far they have advanced in formal statutory and regulatory policy changes related to data and privacy protections. Exemplifying contrasting approaches among advanced democracies, the United States has not enacted such regulations, while the EU has deliberately moved early to set standards. Adopted in 2016 and entering into force in 2018, the European Union's General Data Protection Regulation, known as GDPR, sets the global standard for access to data. GDPR's focus on data protection and personalized control, according to the European Parliament, "creates a regulatory model that puts the user and the generator of data in control, and possibly limits the power of enterprises."[76]

In this context, cooperation on data policies have proved challenging among the advanced democracies, but some recent progress provides grounds for modest optimism. Coordination between the European Union and the United States, for instance, has been limited due to the considerable differences in domestic laws regulating privacy, surveillance, and national security.

To attempt to address these challenges and others, in June 2021, the European Union and the United States announced the establishment of a Transatlantic Trade and Technology Council (TTC). It convened for the first time in September 2021. As announced in its inaugural joint statement, the TTC's foundational purpose is to "coordinate approaches to key global technology, economic, and trade issues; and to deepen transatlantic trade and economic relations, basing policies on shared democratic values." The TTC dialogues are "without prejudice to the regulatory autonomy of the European Union and the United States and should respect the different legal systems in both jurisdictions." TTC established a working group dedicated to Data Governance and Technology Platforms to "exchange information" and, among other topics, "engage in a discussion on effective measures to appropriately address the power of online platforms and ensure effective competition and contestable markets."[77]

In March 2022, the United States and EU announced a new Trans-Atlantic Data Privacy Framework whereby the United States committed to reforms to strengthen the privacy and civil liberties protections related to signals intelligence. This move was designed to address concerns raised by the Court of Justice of the European Union and also help open the door to greater collaboration in the TTC.[78]

Meanwhile, although the tensions between democratic countries about privacy policy reflect differences of degree, the clash between them and more authoritarian approaches represents a stark difference of kind. China's data strategy, for instance, risks abusive data collection on foreign nationals and companies. Furthermore, its data governance framework offers a form of "data protectionism," where China holds data as a state asset and does not share with others.[79] This and related measures to restrict data flows from outside means the Chinese digital environment is increasingly separated from the rest of the world.

Looking more broadly, debates over data and overall digital policy are increasingly comingled with geopolitical contests among states. China, Russia, and other autocracies are coordinating on an alternative digital vision from democratic countries to shape technology standards through groups like the Shanghai Cooperation Organization, write Richard Fontaine and Jared Cohen in *Foreign Affairs*, "whose members have agreed to collaborate on information security, robotics, and e-commerce, among other areas. They also work through global forums such as the International Tele-communication Union, where some of the same countries have supported international standards that would facilitate unaccount-able surveillance."[80] Growing alignment among authoritarian regimes in the digital domain risks the spread of technologies for digital autocracy, eroding liberal norms, and accelerating the move toward "splinternets"—that is a fragmenting of the internet along political or social lines. The impact of expansive digital sanctions against Russia for its invasion of Ukraine may be a harbinger of such an increasingly fragmented and contested digital world that pits democratic versus authoritarian governments.

Against this backdrop, we should expect the competition between different variants of capitalism in the digital domain to be not just about digital standards and rules of the road, but also how data and these technologies fit into geopolitical competition (*Box 3.3*).

Box 3.3: Great power rivalry in digital technology

Access to digital technologies will not only affect internal dynamics within capitalist economies but will also influence the economic competition and the geopolitical race between its democratic and authoritarian variants. Digital technolo-gies already play a critical role in the effectiveness of tradi-tional military "hard" power and their supporting networks, and their importance is only expected to increase in the coming decades.[81]

Such technologies will also open more opportunities for social control. While in the 1990s, explained Ian Bremmer in *Foreign Affairs*, many expected the computer age to foster the freer flow of information, challenging the grip on power of authoritarian regimes, digital technologies are now revers-ing things, blurring the boundaries between the digital and physical realm, the civilian and the military world. "Tech companies are increasingly shaping the global environment in which governments operate," noted Bremmer, determining how they "project economic and military power."[82]

The day when China can challenge the advanced democracies on the technology front may not be too far off. China, for example, is already a peer of the United States in AI.[83] As Bremmer writes, "President Xi Jinping named Alibaba and Tencent, along with the search engine Baidu and the voice recognition iFlytek, to China's 'national AI team',," which gave them a major role in shaping Beijing's AI future.[84] In many areas, such as 5G, facial recognition, and quantum computing, China is already ahead.[85] China pursues building these industries as a strategic priority, and deploy the power of the state behind them. China focuses a significant amount of these efforts on internal security and social control.

Russia's model of digital authoritarianism is not as sophisticated as China's, but it could still inspire other autocrats. In the past decade Russia has used the Internet for disinformation campaigns, digital manipulation, and cybersecurity operations. Russia deployed these tools during the initial invasion of Ukraine but their public impact was largely countered by the effective counter-information operations by Ukraine.[86]

II.2.3 Access to the market

From the perspective of firms, the final question of access is whether or not they can access a fair and competitive market. Of course, the central importance of competition to ensure a vibrant capitalist system and its concomitant benefits has a long lineage at least to Adam Smith and his allies in the eighteenth century.

This question becomes more pointed in the context of the digital revolution precisely because, as outlined above, the nature of AI-led innovation tends to advantage larger scale digital *creator* firms as well as those other large enterprises that possess enough resources and proprietary data at scale to build their own digital capabilities to compete in their markets. The top companies in the world for AI patent applications reflect these trends (see *Exhibit 3.4*).

The risk to competitive markets arises from the potential that a dominant *creator* firm's scale could reach a tipping point where the market itself is jeopardized. Dominant firms could act to limit or eliminate competition through a variety of monopolistic tactics like unfair pricing, product development, preemptive acquisitions to stymie budding competition, and the like. Such actions could impact their digital *consumer* firms directly, through pricing or competition in specific goods or services categories, or indirectly, by slowing the pace of innovation in the market. If firms with such concentration of power exert influence in the market and government to "lock in" their market position, that would distort the capitalist market over the long run with a cascade of negative consequences for the economy and innovation.

Exhibit 3.4

AI patent applications

Top 20 companies, 2010-2019

1	IBM		11	Alibaba	
2	Microsoft		12	Toyota	
3	Google		13	Huawei	
4	Ping An		14	Meta	
5	Baidu		15	Qualcomm	
6	Samsung		16	Amazon	
7	Tencent		17	Philips	
8	Intel		18	GE Global Research	
9	Siemens		19	Adobe	
10	NEC corp.		20	General Electric	

Source: Center for Security and Emerging Technologies, PARAT dataset, The Trilateral Commission

THE TRILATERAL COMMISSION

While antitrust regulatory action is designed to monitor and act to prevent such distortions of capitalist markets from taking place, we should not discount market competition itself as a countervailing force to these sorts of risks. As outlined above, innovators are challenging some global digital *creator* firms with alternative value propositions, for instance, centered around protecting privacy. Furthermore, firms like TikTok have demonstrated that market incumbents can be disrupted by innovative products even in the largest digital markets.

Realistically, however, market competition alone may prove insufficient or too slow a check on excess market concentration. Even in those segments of the digital market where competition is intensifying, monopolies may turn into oligopolies rather than truly competitive markets.[87] "Big tech firms," *The Economist* recently explained, "are diversifying as their core products mature, new technological opportunities emerge, and regulatory threats mount." Microsoft and Alphabet are competing with Amazon in the cloud. Amazon is increasingly more active in digital advertising. Giants of the old economy, such as Disney and Walmart, are now gaining market share in, respectively, streaming services and online sales. "Firms," continued *The Economist*, "think in terms of subscribers who could be persuaded to buy a fluid range of services, rather than protecting a static monopoly at all costs." But to succeed in this world requires a disproportionate amount of human and financial capital that only a few actors have access to.

The major digital *creator* platforms and firms thus pose a fundamental "paradox" to antitrust authorities in Fifth Stage Capitalism.[88] Regulators could intervene, in an effort to open the field to competitors, but, in the process, they would reduce economies of scale and possibly undermine the very services that consumers seek—and services consumers receive "free." They could alternatively let the market dictate outcomes, in which case key companies might enjoy semi-monopolistic positions until new entrants disrupt them, if ever.

The antitrust question is complicated further by the potential intersection of geopolitics with these questions related to scale and digital market concentration. Representatives of "big tech" firms in the United States, in particular, have argued against antitrust action on the grounds that it would strengthen Chinese competitor firms and weaken U.S. international competitiveness.[89]

The potential negative impacts from digital market concentration are roughly equivalent for all capitalist systems. That said, antitrust and other approaches to manage such challenges vary substantially across the capitalism spectrum. This is partly because the regulatory incentives might differ significantly depending on whether a government is regulating a foreign or domestic digital company; but it is also partly because the pace of change has been so fast and the potential downstream implications of certain antitrust actions remains uncertain.

Rather than attempt a comprehensive survey of these efforts, instead, here we offer snapshots of recent regulatory actions from across major economies and the capitalist spectrum. When assembled these snapshots convey movements of legislators and regulators trying to catch up to the digital market. While there is a near consensus of concern regarding the burgeoning power of "big tech" among regulators around the world, these snapshots show they are far from unified in their viewpoints.

Starting with the liberal capitalist end of the spectrum, recent antitrust in the United States has generally accepted market leadership earned by competition in the market as long as it does not negatively impact consumers directly through monopoly pricing.[90] In 2020, the U.S. House of Representatives concluded a multiyear investigation reporting on possible abuses of market concentration including using a "gatekeeper position" to maintain their dominant positions by leading tech firms.[91] Skepticism of the major digital *creators* is rife in both the Republican and Democratic Parties, especially after dramatic evidence revealed by a Facebook whistleblower in 2021, and a number of regulatory statutes have been proposed.[92] State attorneys general have collaborated to sue "big tech" too. In early 2022, the Biden Administration advocated for significant budget increases to build its antitrust capabilities in the Department of Justice and Federal Trade Commission.[93]

The United Kingdom established a new Digital Markets Unit to oversee a new pro-competition policy in the digital space, including powers, for instance, to ensure interoperability across platforms and to pursue a variety of antitrust actions against the major tech firms such as ordering Facebook to divest Giphy.[94]

In the Asia Pacific region, Australia challenged Facebook and Google with a law requiring platforms to pay publishers for news content,[95] and its Australia Competition and Consumer Commission (ACC) established a new Digital Platforms Branch to scrutinize digital platforms.[96] The Japanese Act on Improving Transparency and Fairness of Digital Platforms to ensure platforms disclosed essential terms and conditions to consumers went into effect in February 2021.[97] The Japan Fair Trade Commission also investigated the Apple's App Store in 2021 on a relatively focused issue involving developer account management and came to an agreement.[98] The Korea Fair Trade Commission has sanctioned Google and the local browser company Naver for anti-competitive conduct,[99] and issued in early 2022 new *Guidelines on Anticompetitive Conduct in the Platform Sector.*[100]

In contrast to the American approach, Europe has tended to protect competitors against powerful market leaders.[101] In response to challenges posed by Big Tech companies, meanwhile, the European Commission has proposed the Digital Services Act, the Digital Markets Act, and the AI Act.[102] They all outline responsibilities and liabilities for tech companies around concept moderation, the power of gatekeepers, and the need to mitigate harm from high-risk AI applications. In many respects, these EU reforms hold the potential to establish more international norms as digital firms adapt to comply with EU regulations, as they did with GDPR, which *de facto* sets a global norm.[103]

On the judicial track, following Facebook's acquisition of WhatsApp, courts have argued that the existing merger controls regime should be updated to include proposed acquisitions of less established companies by those that may contain significant quantities of personal data.

At the non-democratic end of the spectrum, China's approach to managing potential market concentration stands out. In the past few years, China's regulation of its own digital *creator* firms—like Alibaba—has been forceful and rapid. The disappearance from the public eye of some major technology leaders is disconcerting and implies harsh intimidation tactics. The state's overturning of the private tutoring industry virtually overnight effectively destroyed a multi-billion-dollar industry without warning or pretense of protecting property rights or investments. Like other countries, the Chinese government has many potentially legitimate reasons to want to rein in its tech giants, but its tactics to silence opposition may eventually weaken Beijing's ability to achieve technological self-reliance in this decade.[104]

In considering this range of regulatory steps to try to ensure competitive markets in the digital domain, it is easy to conclude that when faced with a new digital disruption, regulators tend to respond relatively late, and thereby reinforce the status quo and slow the pace of innovation. There is some truth to this point.[105]

But it is also true that regulators can move too soon—before they have all the information and insights they need—and thereby distort the market dynamics negatively as well. Living with these risks of negative consequences from action tends to make regulators cautious and more accepting of the risks of their inaction.[106]

One potential path forward for regulators to help ensure access to markets is the idea of "regulatory sandboxes." In essence, a "sandbox" is a way for firms to test out new products and services with real customers for a limited duration without complying with all current regulations. A predefined data-collection and assessment plan means that at the end of the "sandbox" phase, potential regulatory arrangements can be assessed in a fact-based way. This is a more data-driven, even experimental approach to assessing potential market impacts from innovative products and services.

Launched by the United Kingdom's Financial Conduct Authority in 2016, "sandboxes" have been used successfully to test Fintech products. Regulators in Singapore, Australia, Denmark, Canada, and other countries and some U.S. states have also adopted the approach.[107] While not a replacement for traditional antitrust enforcement measures, adapting "sandbox" approaches in other digital domains could help move toward a more collaborative, experimental, data-driven, and proactive approach to regulation.

III. WHAT WE SHOULD DO NOW

III.1. Shared direction

Harnessing the full potential of the digital revolution is central to the new spirit of capitalism. Without it, a more sustainable and equitable economic system will remain out of reach. This report therefore proposes:

- *Every person should have access to full benefits of the digital revolution*

Like the other goals for climate change and inequality, this goal emphasizes equality of opportunity. A world divided permanently between digital haves and have nots is inequitable. Access to digital infrastructure is akin to indoor plumbing, electricity, and telephones. But access alone is insufficient. It must be combined with digital literacy along with data and privacy protections. To make the most of the digital revolution, meanwhile, innovation must be sustained and shared, not constrained by monopolies.

This goal also embodies a commitment to smart growth. Our economies need to be able to manage the potential downside risks arising from the digital revolution. If we cannot, disruptions will threaten the functioning of capitalism. Success here requires a modernized state to be an effective partner with other stakeholders.

Although bold, the goal is realistic. First, it is not partisan. People across the political spectrum appreciate the necessity of the basic infrastructure and skills for success in the digital age. Second, it is potentially affordable. Many digital innovations will dramatically lower the costs of education or organization. And private sector businesses will have tangible market incentives to continue to extend access to as broad a population as possible.

III.2. Investments

- **Establish inclusive national digital strategies:** Achieving access for all will require clear national strategies. These should not champion net growth, but rather smart or "good" growth that delivers long-term impact across stakeholders. Limited public resources must be directed in the most efficient and effective fashion.

Government: While national digital strategies will share many common features, each country should tailor its own to its level of development, existing infrastructure, industry composition, and the balance between state and market in delivering public goods. But first and foremost, such strategies should explicitly promote inclusive access across all of society, as well as innovation and economic growth.

Public-private collaboration: For each strategy, the mix will vary, but all such efforts will engage the public, private, and nonprofit sectors. Business models and financing will vary across capitalist systems. Some strategies will rely more heavily on direct state investment in building out digital infrastructure, for instance, whereas others may rely more on regulatory and tax incentives to encourage private sector investment. Such national strategies should also clearly communicate the digital revolution's central role in enabling other transformations, most notably in life-long education and training.

- **Close the connectivity gap:** Connectivity is a prerequisite for equality of opportunity in this era. Billions of people still do not have easy or affordable access to essential digital services. In the coming decades, that must be fixed.

Government: In addition to helping design, and sometimes fund, programs to close the connectivity gaps, governments should consider leveraging their regulatory powers to require providers to offer access to all citizens as a public good. Some governments may also invest directly in acquiring and managing free, open internet networks. Lithuania, Croatia, and Estonia lead the world with the fastest public Wi-Fi speeds as a result of their own long-term investments.[108]

Public-private collaboration: The barriers to access vary by country. Some countries lack the basic communications network infrastructure. Closing the connectivity gaps in these countries, or regions within countries, involves expansion of communications networks. Multiple technologies are in the mix, including fiberoptic, broadband, 5G, and innovative alternative approaches such as satellite-based systems.

Each country's approach and level of investment to close the connectivity gap will be unique. They will involve varying degrees of public-private collaboration depending on the country's ownership structure for communications. Funding and delivery models will likewise vary from direct funding to consumers to incentives to providers to state grants to local communities to bridge remaining "last mile" gaps.

- **Promote universal digital literacy:** Establishing basic digital literacy today is analogous in importance to the mass education reforms of the nineteenth century, which drove a step change in literacy and numeracy in many countries, in turn helping accelerate economic growth across a range of industries. Universal digital literacy is essential for success in today's global economy.

  Government: Our approaches to education should be transformed to enable true life-long learning for all (*Chapter 4*). Digital technologies are foundational to the design and delivery of such reforms at scale. They can reach unlimited populations, effectively sidestepping the physical constraints of traditional education (e.g., physical schools, transportation, etc.). Governments should ensure universal digital literacy is a core to any curriculum, alongside literacy and numeracy.

  Public-private collaboration: Governments, businesses, higher education institutions, and non-profits should explore the potential to develop together ubiquitous, free basic digital literacy training in all languages and formats accessible to all audiences. Such programs could be designed for local delivery, or, in coordination with other national efforts, as programs to help accelerate development in other countries.

- **Empower employees with digital tools:** Similar to education for younger people, life-long learning and skill building in the digital domain should be accessible to all workers. This will help them succeed in their current roles and be more agile as industries change.

Government: The digital revolution is already reshaping work and skill requirements across economies, but government policy can shape the future timing and scale of demand for worker training arising from these transitions. For example, it can guide the pace of rollout of autonomous vehicles to make sure that workers in the trucking industry are not hit all at once. Governments should include in their national strategy reviews analysis of the potential for digital disruption across industries. Such analyses should inform policy goals and also the targeting of additional training resources.

Business: As with the broader education and training reform agenda, businesses should play an important role in the design and delivery of digital training for their workforces. Management philosophy and approach matter. Business leaders should emphasize the opportunity that the digital transformation creates for workers to upgrade their skills and be better positioned to succeed in the future. Engaging workers in the process is critical, including asking them to think about how their own strengths could be better used.[109] Special attention should be paid to "portable" certifications with recognized standards for basic digital skills.[110]

- **Establish hubs to disperse digital innovation:** Firms will have to harness digital capabilities to transform their business models and operations, but not all are equally positioned to do so. Leading innovative firms can help others reimagine their business operations through cooperative hubs or centers to share experience and expertise.

Government: Governments should support the creation of such hubs and the dispersal of industrial best practices through research, data sharing, convening, and financial support ranging from grants to tax incentives. The ManufacturingUSA and the Fraunhofer-Gesellschaft networks are examples.

Business: In addition to collaborating with governments to establish hubs, business, trade, and industry associations should combine financial and technical resources to build physical or virtual technology centers to help companies understand new digital best practices for business operations and worker upskilling.

Public-private collaboration: Different organizations can take the lead in convening and structuring collaborations to identify and share best practices within and across industries. Their orientation can range from more research and development to skill-building and application. An alternative approach is for non-profits to serve as neutral conveners and thought leaders to bring together diverse stakeholders and business interests. The World Economic Forum's Global Lighthouse Network, for instance, is a model for showcasing examples of success to inform and inspire others (*see Chapter 2, Box 2.1*).[111]

- **Transform government operations:** With the notable exceptions of countries like Estonia, the public sector remains one of the least digitalized in most countries. Improving state capacity is critical for the success of capitalism. It involves both internal operations and also the quality of citizen experience. The state should be a competent counterpart to the private sector. And a more capable democratic state provides more effective and efficient services, ranging from policy design and regulation to business licensing and taxation to social services and education. Digital transformation should provide the backbone for such efforts.

Government: Governments should prioritize the modernization of their service delivery. This will require multiyear investment strategies, which in turn will require sustained engagement with legislators and other stakeholders. Like other sectors, much of the daily work of government will be affected by the introduction of new approaches to management and operations. AI-based approaches can already automate many basic customer service interactions, thereby enabling workers to shift to more complex and valuable customer interactions and problem solving.

In many countries, the transition will require proactive dialogues with public sector unions. Most public sector organizations do not have the digital talent in-house to design and implement such transformations. Governments, therefore, should develop and expand innovative models to bring private sector expertise to bear. As one example, the Government Digital Service (GDS) in the UK launched in 2011 helped transform digital services for citizens. Its success then inspired other efforts like the United States Digital Service, the Canadian Digital Service, and the DigitalService4Germany.[112]

III.3. "Rules of the road"

- **Adapt antitrust for the digital age:** The scale, scope, and market concentration of some digital enterprises poses risks. Some digital firms have even acknowledged exploiting their market position to reduce competition through preemptive acquisitions and mergers. Inherited approaches to antitrust do not always work in an industry where customers often receive "free" products and services in exchange for access to their data.

Government: To support their traditional pro-competition regulatory agencies, governments should invest in the institutional capacities of these agencies; such investments should ensure the agencies possess the analytic capabilities to evaluate complex digital market dynamics and implications of potential courses of action. Some countries may conclude statutory updates their legal codes would help match the unique features of digital technologies. Regulatory agencies should explore the potential for "sandboxes" or "test beds" to allow businesses to try out new services or products in a different regulatory environment to assess potential options in a more data-driven manner. Other potential regulatory moves to consider could include: requirements for social media platforms to share more information about their algorithms and their impact with the government and independent researchers; customer data ownership rights covering privacy, portability, and interoperability across platforms; and separation of platforms operating in adjacent lines of business.

- **Develop a plurilateral World Trade Organization framework on digital trade:** Digital trade is rapidly growing. The WTO is the quintessential twentieth century organization struggling to remain effective and relevant in the twenty-first. Despite its challenges, the WTO plays a unique role in sustaining an equal playing field in trade.

International: In December 2017, a group of WTO member countries began discussions for international rules to govern e-commerce. Progress has been slow and halting. Meanwhile, bilateral and regional digital agreements have proliferated among

WTO member states. This proliferation creates uncertainty in international trade. Governments should commit to work with the WTO to find a shared path forward.

- **Secure the cyber-infrastructure through new standards:** The world is increasingly vulnerable to cyberattacks.[113] Mitigating systemic hazards to the cyber-infrastructure is key to preserve essential digital services. This requires sharing the burden of cyber-security, with private companies building a resilient digital ecosystem and governments providing more timely and comprehensive threat information.

Government: In order to tap the digital revolution's full potential, the hardware and software that deliver its benefits must remain trustworthy, resilient, and operational. Governments should invest in digital infrastructure, ensure fair competition, and protect the most vulnerable from digital disruptions, while contributing human and financial resources toward institutions designed to prevent, counter, and recover from cyber-incidents. As Marietje Schaake urged in a recent *Foreign Affairs* piece, "democratic countries must extend norms and rules to ensure safety in the digital world," establishing agreements to fend off threats in cyberspace. The starting point, she wrote, is to identify "which digitized systems are vital for the public interest, public safety, and the functioning of society," and then institute standards and regulations to ensure their security that both private and public actors need to comply with. Moreover, explained an IMF report, "enhanced consistency in regulatory and supervisory approaches would reduce costs of compliance and build a platform for stronger cross-border cooperation and information sharing."[114]

Public-private partnerships: Writing for the World Economic Forum, Paul See and Chaitra Chandrasekhar explained that "business and government expose each other to significant cyber-risks because they are interconnected and rely on the same network of software vendors." For this reason, a strong collaboration between the two actors is needed. Moreover, they should collaborate to train the next generation of cybersecurity professionals—whose shortage is currently estimated to be close to three million worldwide. Finally, firms should invest in upgrades to embed security into devices to reduce cyber vulnerabilities due to human errors from the start. In a recent set of principles on the topic that was sketched out by Australia's eSafety Commissioner, it is established that "safety should never be the sole responsibility of the consumer, and that companies mitigate risk factors for all users before releasing services to the public."[115]

III.4 Trilateral recommendation

• *Establish an alliance of "techno-democracies"*

If there is one observation that underpins all the other recommendations, it is this: most of our international institutions are inherited from the twentieth century and have not been adapted to the digital age. In the Fifth Stage of capitalism, we need to do better. Extending access to—and capturing the full potential of—the digital revolution requires it.

At the same time, no advanced democratic capitalist country has been sheltered from the downside risks and digital threats of this era, which range from state-sponsored disinformation campaigns to cybercrimes. The war in Ukraine and the resulting exit from the Russian market of most Western technology and social media firms marks a new chapter in the digital world—one more fragmented and perhaps even more dangerous.

Today, the Trilateral countries lack a natural home for collaboration across the range of cross-cutting digital issues spanning from scientific and technical to economic and commercial to security, military, and law enforcement.

Likeminded democracies and technological leaders should, therefore, establish a forum or alliance to fill this gap. Such an alliance could help ensure a digital order that preserves and promotes open societies, combats the illiberal use of emerging digital technologies, and maximizes the economic potential of these innovations.

The Financial Stability Board (FSB) provides a potential analogue of the type of organization or network to consider on the digital front. The world's major economies established the FSB in 2009 in response to the 2007–08 global financial crisis. It built upon the successes of its predecessor, the Financial Stability Forum. The FSB was designed to fix vulnerabilities in global finance while promoting more coherent policymaking. Under the auspices of the G20, the FSB matured until it evolved into an independent nonprofit organization based in Switzerland.[116] A similar forum should be established for the digital economy.[117]

While there are a range of potential organizational models for such an alliance of "techno-democracies," the most productive path likely starts with a more informal, bureaucratically "light" group and then evolves through practice and results, as the FSB has.[118] A less-structured approach would afford flexibility to support dialogue, coordination, and working groups including government, business, academic, and nonprofit organizations. Through time, a more formal, robust organization could evolve through this sort of organic approach.

Such an informal alliance could start by bringing together experts and officials to set common standards regarding digital technologies and definitions of cybercrime, discuss common approaches to antitrust rules, and develop a framework to address its most pressing ethical issues, while working together to harmonize their policies concerning privacy, or data ownership. Interoperability and common rules about data portability and transfer are critical to achieving economies of scale and enabling connectivity and stability. Eventually, this forum could evolve to address more sensitive digital topics such as exchanging information about online propaganda, disinformation, and cyber threats to counter the misuse of digital technologies by autocratic regimes. It could also help coordinate investments and share intelligence among the leading democratic digital countries.

The G7 governments' recent progress on digital coordination could provide a seed for this effort.[119] Notably, the G7 countries include not only the United States but also six more of the top 16 most advanced AI countries in the world.[120] Building upon this momentum, the G7 should launch an initiative to develop this new alliance among techno-democracies.

Starting with the G7 members, the membership could move to engage other like-minded democratic countries that possess disproportionate influence in the digital space. Logical candidates include Australia and South Korea from the Asia Pacific region, Finland and Sweden from Europe, and Israel from the Mediterranean region. Including India, another global leader in AI, in the alliance would strengthen its developing "rules of the road" aligned with democratic capitalist values and interests.[121] The membership could be open to all like-minded countries as the alliance takes form and establishes momentum. Establishing this group within the next 12–24 months should be a priority.

4

TOWARD A MORE EQUITABLE FUTURE

Inequalities emerge from the workings of capitalism. The challenge is when such inequalities become locked in and persistent. Children's postal codes should not determine their destiny. Addressing these inequalities is fundamental to defining capitalism in the twenty-first century.

I. HOW WE GOT HERE

I.1. Another peak in inequality

Inequality within and between societies long predates capitalism. They have been a constant across cultures and throughout history. From pharaonic Egypt and czarist Russia to Victorian England, the Ottoman Empire, and China under the Qing Dynasty, the pattern has been the same: wealth concentrates in the hands of a privileged elite.[1] Most of the great temples, royal palaces, pyramids, and castles are the enduring legacies of inequality. At the apogee of the Roman Empire, the richest aristocrat in Rome possessed a fortune that was 1.5 million times the average per capita income of that era. That is about the same as the wealth gap between Microsoft founder Bill Gates and the average American household.[2]

In the last 1,000 years, the world has reached two major peaks of inequality: in late medieval Europe, on the eve of the Black Death, and in modern times, on the eve of World War I.[3] Both were followed by cataclysmic events that restored some balance. The Black Death killed 30–50 percent of all Europeans and destroyed much of the continent's workforce, boosting the value of labor relative to landed wealth. Similarly, the combined World Wars of the twentieth century not only devastated many of the physical, financial, and human assets of the wealthy but also accelerated the embrace of Managed Capitalism that contributed to compressing inequality (*Chapter 1*). While specifics varied across countries, this form of capitalism saw the emergence of the modern welfare state, rapid expansion of higher education, and improvements in health and well-being.

Now, we approach a third peak. The Neoliberal Capitalism era witnessed concerning levels of inequality. In 2010, 388 billionaires owned as much private wealth as the poorer half of the global population; by 2016, a mere eight people did.[4] The overall global trends are even more telling. According to the World Inequality Database, among G7 countries, the top 1 percent of individuals by wealth held about 20 percent of total national wealth and 9 percent of total national income in 1980; about 25 years later, the top 1 percent held 27 percent of total wealth and 13 percent of total income.[5]

What separates this most recent peak in equality from previous ones is that even though inequality is rising within countries, there is less inequality between countries than there was 40 years ago (*Exhibit 4.1*). Over the last 30 years, Asia's stellar economic performance has allowed once low-income countries to close the gap with advanced economies. According to data from the World Bank, higher-income countries' share of global wealth has fallen,

Exhibit 4.1

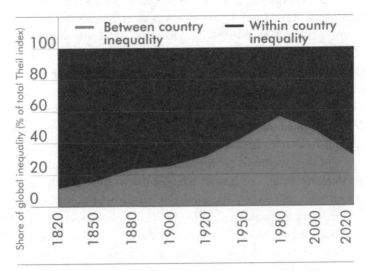

Rising domestic inequality

Global income inequality, 1820-2020: Theil index

Source: Chancel and Piketty (2021), The Trilateral Commission

THE TRILATERAL COMMISSION

from 80 percent in 2000 to 71 percent in 2014. Middle-income countries' share rose from 14 to 22 percent.[6] Although the gap between nations is still substantial—the average income of some-one living in North America, for example, is 16 times higher than that of a person in sub-Saharan Africa—only one third of global inequality today is due to differences between countries.[7] Two-thirds is due to inequality within them.[8]

Domestic inequality is a challenge for capitalist systems every-where. The origins are found in capitalism itself. Capitalism's genius is that it relies on entrepreneurs and firms to take risks and innovate in the relentless pursuit of profit. Some bet big and lose, others win. And the winners initially reap outsized rewards for their risk taking. Thus, capitalism begets inequality of outcomes. But these advantages—in truly competitive markets—do not become entrenched. Eventually, other firms adopt the new innova-tions, their performance improves, and inequality starts declining. At an individual level, talent, skills, drive, tolerance for risk—all these factors are not evenly distributed in society. They eventually work through the market system to yield different rewards. From this perspective, inequality is just another term for rewarding tal-ent, hard work, creativity, and entrepreneurship. That is an old idea, but it is an especially compelling one today because of the way labor and capital are structured.[9] In this telling, inequalities should be temporary, not enduring.

But the world is messy. Inequality has accelerated at different rates in different places. A complex interplay of a country's level of development and industry structure, its prevailing model of capitalism, and other local, sometimes unique contextual factors all can affect inequalities in practice. Inequality tends to increase at lower levels of development because enterprises have access to a larger pool of lower-wage workers, and then declines through time as the competition for talent becomes more intense. Similarly, industries vary in the economic value they create and thus different wages they command—for example, mining differs from manufac-turing. A country's mix of industries, therefore, influences its position relative to others and also affects the dynamics of inequal-ity among is citizens.

The different varieties of capitalism also exhibit broad patterns or tendencies in their relative inequality (*Exhibit 4.2*). In general, authoritarian capitalist systems tend to be more unequal than their democratic counterparts, as measured by Gini coefficients. And liberal democratic capitalist countries, which tend to emphasize the market more, tend to be more unequal than social democratic ones (*Box 4.1*).

Within these categories, policy preferences help shape variation across countries. Within the social democratic category, for instance, Japan has lower inequality than Italy and France, but more than Norway or Sweden. Japan's position is partly due to a high inheritance tax rate, currently at 55 percent, that can erode the wealth of a single family over three generations.[10]

Exhibit 4.2

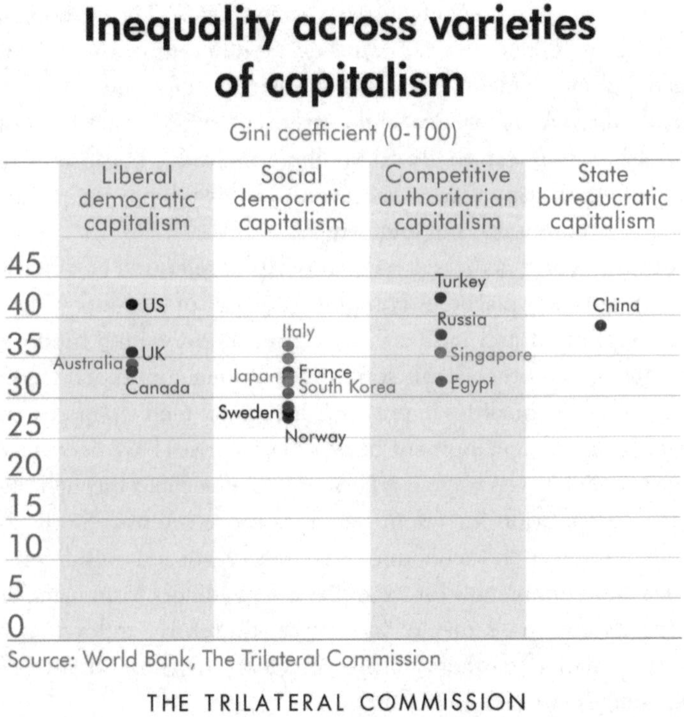

Inequality across varieties of capitalism

Gini coefficient (0-100)

	Liberal democratic capitalism	Social democratic capitalism	Competitive authoritarian capitalism	State bureaucratic capitalism
45				
40	● US		Turkey ●	China
35	Australia ● ● UK	Italy ●	Russia ● ● Singapore	●
30	Canada	Japan ● France ● South Korea	● Egypt	
25		Sweden ●		
20		Norway		
15				
10				
5				
0				

Source: World Bank, The Trilateral Commission

THE TRILATERAL COMMISSION

Among the Trilateral countries, the United States stands out because of its high inequality. Between 1980 and 2017, the income for the bottom 90 percent of the population barely increased. Most of the aggregate income growth was appropriated by the country's top 10 percent—in particular, by the top 1 percent.[11]

In Western Europe, income for the bottom 90 percent was likewise relatively stagnant. Meanwhile, although income for the wealthiest did rise, most affluent Europeans are still considerably less well off than their American counterparts (*Exhibit 4.3*). Consider the share of pre-tax income that accrues to the richest 1 percent in both places. In Europe, it rose from 8 percent to 11 percent between 1980 and 2017, while in the United States, it jumped from 11 percent to 21.[12] Europe is not just less unequal than the United States, it is the least unequal region in the world.[13]

Exhibit 4.3

Sharp decoupling between Europe and the US

Growth incidence curve (1980-2017)

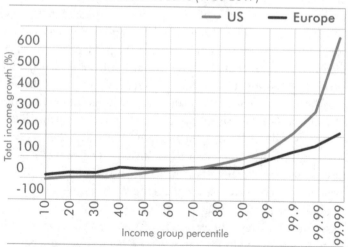

Source: Blanchet et al. (2019), The Trilateral Commission

THE TRILATERAL COMMISSION

Developing Asia experienced a broad and dramatic reduction of poverty in the last fifty years, but progress in improving income distribution proved uneven.[14] During the 1960s–1980s, inequality in most developing Asian economies remained stable even as economies grew, noted the Asian Development Bank in a 2020 report. Since the 1990s, however, rapid growth and poverty reduction have come with rising income inequality, as technological progress and globalization have led to rising wage gaps between skilled and less-skilled workers among other factors.

Looking at one specific country, India, its economic success story of recent years has come at the cost of an explosion in income inequality.[15] Under British colonial rule (1858–1947), inequality in India was very high, with the top 10 percent's income share around 50 percent. After independence, due to socialist-inspired development plans, this share dropped to around 35 percent. And it is now up to 57 percent. Similar figures characterize South America and Sub-Saharan Africa as well.[16]

In addition to these regional and national patterns, several trends contribute to the recent wave of inequality. They include the declining negotiating power of trade unions, slowing labor productivity growth, skills-biased technological progress, accelerating globalization, and less progressive tax systems.[17] These factors trace back to the priorities of the Neoliberal Capitalist stage which emphasized market liberalization and deregulation (*Chapter 1.*).

Technological progress tends to boost the productivity of higher skilled workers, particularly those working at frontier firms, while contributing less for those at the bottom of the skills distribution. Meanwhile, the advent of information and communication technologies has increased the demand for educated workers, further hiking their wages, while allowing for the outsourcing of other work—domestically, internationally, or to automation (*Chapter 3*).[18] Globalization further accelerated these processes by enabling the division of production across complex global value chains, often designed in pursuit of the lowest cost labor possible.

In some countries, the evolution of their tax systems contributed to inequality with tax rates for the highest income earners having trended down for decades. Consider the United States. Although the U.S. federal income tax rate technically goes from

0 percent for those who earn the least to 37 percent for those who earn the most, in 2018, the effective tax rate paid by the richest 400 households was just 23 percent. That was five percentage points lower than the average rate for the population as a whole.[19] This was not the case until the 1970s, when the threat of capital flight and global tax competition changed Americans' attitudes toward progressivity. Similar patterns, in less extreme forms, are found across most developed economies because they faced the same underlying global forces. Average tax rates for the bottom 90 percent have remained roughly the same since the seventies, whereas they have flattened sharply for the top 10 percent.[20]

Beyond these structural trends, recent contingencies have exacerbated the inequality dynamics in many countries. The risks and costs related to climate change fall disproportionately on the most vulnerable in a variety of ways—from vulnerability to natural disasters to potential higher energy prices (*Chapter 2*).[21] The COVID-19 pandemic increased inequality within countries.[22] Lower income households suffered relatively more poor health outcomes. Also, lower income workers suffered proportionately more unemployment during the early attempts to flatten the epidemiological curve. At the same time, higher income and more skilled workers had a higher probability of working remotely, while the wealth of the most affluent increased in lockstep with stock-market valuations. Looking forward, the return of high inflation—which is fueled by global supply chain disruptions due to COVID-19 and rising commodity prices due to the Russia-Ukraine conflict—risks eroding the purchasing power of the middle class.

These explanations help explain parts of the recent acceleration in inequality. Yet they tend to elide some fundamental questions—namely, why are some people and places being left behind while others prosper? If capitalism is so dynamic, why are inequalities passed down across generations, thereby defying notions of equality of opportunity? Every society, no matter how prosperous, has such people and places that are left behind. And in every country, we see inequalities entrench and persist. Too often a child's fate—regardless of her talent—is decided by the postal code where she lives.

Tackling this challenge is critical to capitalism's success in the twenty-first century.

Box 4.1: Inequality in authoritarian and democratic capitalisms

The type of political regime and state capacity influence the balance of power within countries. Different regimes affect the level of inequality. A study of 47 democracies and 61 autocracies revealed authoritarian regimes tend to have higher degrees of inequality, as measured through Gini coefficients, than democratic ones (*See Exhibit 4.4*).[23]

Exhibit 4.4

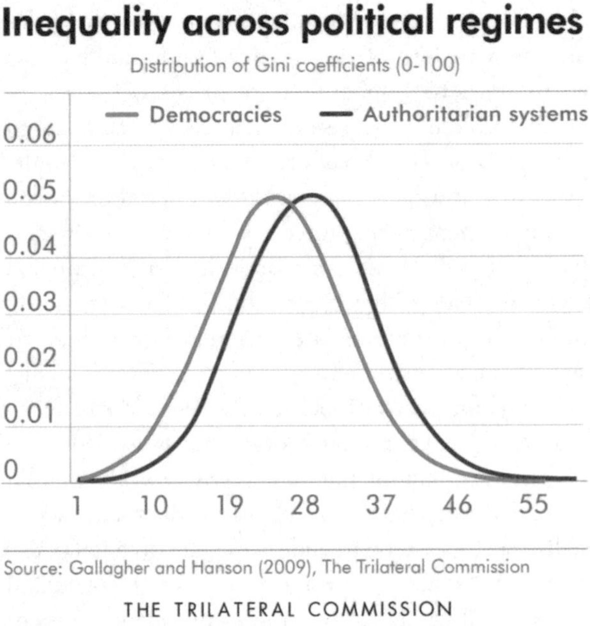

Inequality across political regimes

Distribution of Gini coefficients (0-100)

Source: Gallagher and Hanson (2009), The Trilateral Commission

THE TRILATERAL COMMISSION

This distribution also shows the level of inequality varies substantially from country to country of the same basic regime type. Autocrats may be threatened by rivals within their political party or elite (horizontal pressures) as well as by popular unrest (vertical pressures). Authoritarian rulers employ a mixture of repression and redistribution to keep both kinds of challenger at bay.[24] Redistributive policies to counter or reduce pressures created by horizontal accountability tend to produce greater inequality, while policies aimed at vertical pressures tend toward lower inequality.

For example, autocrats may gain the loyalty of the political elite by allowing rents, offering state resources, appointing them to important posts in the party or government, defending their wealth from redistributive claims, and so on. China's inequality, for example, is partly due to decision-makers' control over access to business opportunities.[25] Bank loans go disproportionately to politically connected firms. This encourages their unconnected competitors to borrow from shadow banks at high rates. The side effect is rising inequality, with corrupt officials and entrepreneurs both taking advantage of the system to increase their wealth.

Russia provides another example of deep inequality in an oligarchic and kleptocratic society.[26] After the fall of Communism, Moscow privatized public assets in a short time span, offering large blocks of stocks on generous terms to selected and well-connected individuals, especially in the energy sector. Recent studies show that the top decile's share of total income, which was just over 25 percent in 1990, rose to 45–50 percent 20 years ago and has remained there ever since. The top 1 percent now controls 25 percent of national income, up from 5 percent in 1990.[27]

Alternatively, authoritarian rulers may win the acquiescence of the masses by distributing resources through subsidies or the provision of other public goods. Saudi Arabia, for example, has traditionally used its oil revenues to fund generous welfare programs to preserve domestic consensus and political stability. Despite such efforts, Saudi Arabia is still one of the most unequal societies in the world.

Exhibit 4.4 shows similar variations in the distribution of the Gini coefficients across democracies too. From a purely theoretical point of view, it is somewhat puzzling to find high levels of inequality within democracies, because democratic institutions are expected to better empower those who stand to benefit more from redistribution.[28] However, a large literature, including work by scholar Jonathan Hanson, has shown that "electoral systems, governmental forms, and different geographical distributions of the poor all affect the extent of redistributive spending. Proportional representation systems deliver higher levels of social spending compared with majoritarian systems" because smaller interest groups manage to be represented within the parliament.[29] Likewise, parliamentary systems are linked to greater social spending than presidential systems, where the executive does not derive its democratic legitimacy from the legislature and so it feels less the pressure coming from smaller interest groups.

II. WHERE WE ARE TODAY

We follow in this section the path of a life journey from birth and home to formal education and then the labor market and workplace to understand better how inequality of opportunity plays out in practice. Along the way, this journey highlights the types of barriers to equality of opportunity that slow or impede an individual's success. While we can accept real "merit-based" inequality, we should resist "status-based" inequalities that are inherited, not earned.[30] These barriers include place or location, as well as such factors as family, class, ethnicity and race, and gender. They distort the operation of market-based systems to the ultimate detriment of all.

This sketch is not comprehensive. Nonetheless, it is meant to help illustrate the types of obstacles that governments, businesses, and nonprofit organizations should focus on removing to help capitalism deliver more effectively and equitably. Each country has its own challenges, its own places and people left behind. Each will need to tailor its solutions.

A guiding idea here is that markets and their operation should be designed to create fairer outcomes from the start. Such predistribution stresses the greater effectiveness of interventions designed to promote equal opportunity from the beginning than of those trying to rectify things later through redistribution. (This said, in many cases redistributive programs through taxation and disbursements will need to continue.)[31] Success in life and position in the income distribution is partly the result of luck, partly the result of innate talent, and partly—and more importantly—reflects the skills, experiences, and certifications a person accumulates during their life. Pre-distribution focuses on steps to improve how workers can succeed in the market. It switches attention from the sphere of distribution into the sphere of production. Shaping markets by offering equal opportunities to all is a more effective approach than fixing unequal market outcomes after the fact. The need for redistribution through taxation and subsidies is reduced when the distribution of economic power is made fairer and more equitable in the first place.

II.1.1 From family to school

The English philosopher Bertrand Russell once joked "choose your parents wisely." He captured an intuition about inequality: some people are born ahead. Children from different family backgrounds face "diverging destinies."[32]

The bluntest mechanism for perpetuation of inequality remains inherited wealth. At the same time, across OECD countries, new laws and regulations have diminished inheritance taxes. On average across these countries, 0.5 percent of total tax revenues today come from inheritance tax, and a majority of inheritance goes untaxed in many places.[33]

Before birth, a child's odds of success are also influenced by their parents because so-called assortative mating—when people of similar education status and income level marry—is a major driver of intergenerational inequality. In 1970, only 13 percent of young American men in the top ten percent of male earners married similarly high-earning young women. By 2017, that figure had risen to almost 29 percent—thanks also to the higher incidence of educated women in the population. According to Branko Milanović, "about one-third of the inequality increase in the

United States between 1967 and 2007 can be explained by assortative mating."[34] This phenomenon is not limited to the United States; inequality induced this way is especially high in Nordic countries.[35]

After that, health, stability, and household dynamics in the first few years of life matter. Access to basic services and infrastructure is much lower among children born into disadvantaged circumstances. And all of those factors both influence later development, and are hard to make up for in later life through policy interventions. Under-nutrition, for example, has widespread lasting effects on children's physical and cognitive development.[36]

Disadvantaged children have a higher probability of doing poorly in school, often abandoning it early on, and subsequently have lower incomes to provide for their own children, and so the cycle of poverty continues.[37] Adverse childhood experiences correlate with poor adult outcomes.[38] Compared to the environments of intact families, for example, single-parent homes are much less favorable for children's outcomes.[39]

Social norms also constrain households' investment decisions about the education of their children. Where women face disadvantages in the labor market, or where investments in girls' education are not seen as worthwhile, since they will leave the household upon marriage, families will under-invest for the education of their daughters. Gender disparity in education is a prevalent issue in many countries where it is linked to pervasive socio-cultural gender biases.[40] That said, female educational attainment now eclipses males in countries as diverse as Bangladesh and the United States.[41]

The problem goes beyond schooling. Gender inequality is often associated with financial exclusion. Across many societies, as the International Labor Organization (ILO) notes, women do not have "equal access to the full range of needs-based financial services—savings, credit, insurance, payments—and the accompanying financial education" that are necessary for social and economic empowerment. "Even before the pandemic," the ILO continues, "56 percent of all those without a bank account were women." In other words, nearly a billion women are unbanked.[42]

And then there are race, ethnicity, and immigration status. The United States' particularly sticky class divide has a clear racial element. Black Americans start off with significant material disadvantages, with the typical family possessing only an eight of the wealth possessed of the average white family.[43] When it comes to schooling, white students score an average of 1.5 to 2 grade levels higher than black students in the average district.[44] In other countries, immigration status, more than ethnicity or race, can affect school performance and educational attainments.[45] For example, in the European Union, according to RAND research from 2016, migrant children do less well at school on average than their native counterparts.[46] Or, in India, castes still play a fundamental role in defining individual success. The Scheduled Castes or Scheduled Tribes have substantially lower wealth than others.[47]

These different birth-related dimensions of inequality (family backgrounds, race, and gender) are further exacerbated by clustering effects related to the tendencies of people with similar professional and socio-economic backgrounds to concentrate in the same geographic areas. Just look at Paris and London, or New York and Tokyo.

On the flip side, there is solid empirical evidence showing that poor children do better when they grow up in some cities rather than in others.[48] In the United States, the places where poor children fare the worst include Atlanta, the Bronx, Chicago, Los Angeles, Milwaukee, Orlando, West Palm Beach, Tampa, and the lowest-income parts of Manhattan. As reported in the *New York Times*, "all else equal, low-income boys who grow up in such areas earn about 35 percent less on average than otherwise similar low-income children who grow up in the best areas for mobility."[49] In Europe, London and Madrid have some of the highest levels of inequality and economic segregation, whereas Budapest and Oslo boast some of the lowest, with Amsterdam and Vienna sitting in between.[50] In Asia, cities like Tokyo or Seoul have put in place intra-metropolitan equalization schemes to address the negative spillovers of urban sprawl through redistributive grants and tax-base sharing.[51]

The sources of inequality that shape one's youth cast a long shadow into adulthood. Take innovators, for example.[52] "Children's chances of becoming inventors vary sharply with characteristics at birth, such as their race, gender, and parents' socioeconomic class," wrote researchers for NBER in 2019. "For example, children from high-income (top 1%) families are ten times as likely to become inventors as those from below-median income families." Such gaps show up even when children have similar math test scores in early childhood.[53]

What is at stake is not only fairness but the health of capitalist systems over the long term. As lack of equality of opportunity hardens group and class divides, those excluded begin to experience life profoundly differently than the "haves" at the top.[54] Inequality is not the same as poverty; it often makes people feel poor, even when they are not. In fact, "more telling than one's position on the income scale is the subjective process by which one establishes one's own social status." Those who feel poorer than someone in their orbit are "more likely to suffer from depression, anxiety disorders, cardiovascular disease, obesity, and diabetes—regardless of their true socioeconomic situation."[55]

II.1.2 From college to the first steps into the workforce

Education may be one of the greatest methods for reducing inequality; data from various countries shows that government spending on education can reduce the importance of family background in future success.[56] According to the International Monetary Fund, for people born in the 1960s cohort, "an increase of 2¾ years in education is associated with an improvement from the third quartile to nearly the median of the distribution of intergenerational mobility in education"[57] largely through access to better jobs. Indeed, in the United States, individuals with a college degree earn, on average, almost twice as much as people with only a high school degree.[58] While there's a great deal of variation across capitalist economies, the college degree premium tends to be sizeable everywhere.

While primary and secondary education are supposed, at least on paper, to provide the basic skills to allow a person to pursue his career aspirations by removing early-life barriers, tertiary education is very much supposed to exalt the talent or the hard work of an individual. But meritocracy might turn out to be more apparent than real, hiding sharp inequalities of opportunity. This is because capitalism is also a cultural system that interacts with the society— and all its ideas about class, race, gender, and more—around it. (*Chapter 1*). Capitalism can reinforce existing disparities; wealthy people, who might belong to the dominant ethnic or socio-economic group, hand down wealth and advantages to their children, ensuring intergenerational privilege. And capitalism can create new ones; admission into elite colleges in the United States and Great Britain depends a lot (but not exclusively) on whether one's parents also attended them, creating a new upper class.[59]

Some studies show, for example, that applicants to Oxford or Cambridge University are more likely to be admitted if a distant relative attended these schools two centuries earlier.[60] Equally, both universities recruit more students from eight private schools than from 3,000 state schools put together.[61] Or take the United States.[62] Even in the absence of noble titles, origins still contribute to determining one's chances for success in life. Being admitted to an Ivy League university depends a lot (but not exclusively) on family background. Well-educated parents have the means to raise ideal college applicants, and to afford rising tuition costs. Since top employers seek recruits from top universities, class privilege risks being perpetuated from generation to generation. The most glamorous American universities have more students from the 1 percent of the income distribution than from the entire bottom half.[63]

Similarly, even in a highly meritocratic society like Singapore, where pupils are continuously tested and assessed to be then assigned to one school or another, there is a risk that family backgrounds more than talent end up affecting school performance.[64] The competitive "streaming" of students by exam results at an early age risks stigmatizing the least privileged, limiting educational attainment and reducing intergenerational mobility.

Examples like these weaken the idea that anyone today is able to improve and realize their potential in a free capitalist system. In the United States, over the last 50 years, a child's chances of out-earning his or her parents have fallen from almost 90 percent to

50 percent.[65] In fact, the American Dream is more alive in Denmark (*Exhibit 4.5*). Part of the explanation, but not all of it, is that in Denmark the government, and not the market, provides several basic public goods like health care or education that shape the future career opportunities of an individual.[66] This goes back to our discussion about the varieties of capitalism and the extent of the role played by the state in each individual system.

There is no easy way to guarantee access to high quality higher education. In countries like the United States or the United Kingdom, high tuition fees might represent an insurmountable obstacle for talented kids who have managed to overcome some birth-related obstacles. Only a handful of U.S. colleges and universities offer need-blind admission *and* full-need financial aid grants to all students. In the United Kingdom, both Cambridge and Oxford are increasing admissions from public schools (known as "state schools" in the UK) to the detriment of elite private schools in order to reduce the per-

Exhibit 4.5

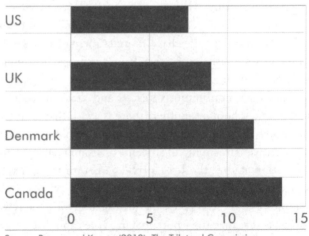

Stalled social mobility

Probability of a child moving from bottom to top income quintile (%)

Source: Reeves and Krause (2018), The Trilateral Commission

THE TRILATERAL COMMISSION

petuation of undeserved privileges.[67] In countries like Denmark, college is free and students are even guaranteed a stipend while in school. Looking at a more extreme example, in China, a recent crackdown on private tutoring, which was meant to avoid letting privileged children get easier access to the best schools, was joined with additional funding for public schools and childcare services.[68]

Then, there is a gender dimension to the problem. Even among OECD countries, young women are under-represented in higher education in mathematics, physical science, and computing programs.[69] In OECD countries, women make up 20 percent of entrants in tertiary-level computer science programs and only around 18 in engineering.[70] This is not only a loss for women themselves, but for society at large. By facilitating the entry of more women and girls into the STEM sector, the European Union could increase its GDP per capita to 3 percent in 2050.[71] People without an appropriate education, and not necessarily from an elite university, lose access not only to better salaries but also to jobs for which they are perfectly qualified. It is common for employers to use academic degrees as screening mechanisms, even if those degrees are not really needed for a specific job. As a result, people with the right skills and experience are screened out of the selection process, missing opportunities that would be mutually beneficial for employer and employee.

This so-called degree gap may be worsening.[72] For example, in 2015, 67 percent of production supervisor job postings asked for a college degree in the United Kingdom, according to reporting in the *Nation*, while only 16 percent of employed production supervisors had one. In other words, the people currently doing the work do not have the degrees required of those who will replace them. In such a system, everyone is worse off. Companies pay higher salaries for having unnecessarily qualified workers. Employees, who feel overqualified for the tasks that are assigned to them, tend to be under-productive. And those willing to do the job, who usually belong to already marginalized groups, are left out.

Perhaps realizing as much, there are already examples of both governments and firms removing university degree requirements from their job posts in order to maximize hiring opportunities for those with the right skills (*Box 4.2*).[73] Apprenticeships, which combine class time with job experience, are widespread in Europe as an alternative to four-year degrees.

Beyond degrees and certifications, though, there is also the problem of education not being appropriate, at least for those who do not belong to the professional elite, for the jobs that actually exist. Today's model is a legacy of the First Industrial Revolution. The so-called factory model of education was meant to train students as future factory workers. Workers now need to be agile learners who can adjust their skillsets as the nature of work changes (*Chapter 3*).

They also need to learn over their whole lifetimes so that they can seize opportunities in new sectors and handle shocks in declining industries. But for private firms, retraining a workforce often looks less appealing than things like automation or finding cheaper workers abroad. Not surprisingly, in its 2015 Economic Report of the President, the U.S. Council of Economic Advisers reported that the share of American workers receiving re-training fell steadily from 1996 to 2008. Equally, according to Eurostat, as of 2017, only about 10 percent of the eurozone's labor force tended to undertake some type of formal or informal training, and the share declines sharply with age.

Box 4.2: Skilled Through Alternative Routes

Employers often hire workers based on their academic and other credentials more than on their skills. According to the nonprofit Opportunity@Work, 71 million American workers are what it calls "STARS" or "Skilled Though Alternative Routes." Opportunity@Work defines STARs as individuals at least 25 years old, currently active in the workforce, with a high school diploma, but not a bachelor's degree.

STARs have developed valuable skills on the job, through military service, in community college, or through other methods. They are found in every field and occupation across the labor market, from travel and hospitality to retail, health care, information technology, and manufacturing. They also represent the full racial, ethnic, and cultural diversity of the country. According to the nonprofit's research, millions of STARs have demonstrated skills for roles with salaries at least 50 percent higher than their current job.[74]

STARs are not only an American phenomenon. Every economy has some. Around the world, their untapped potential means economies are squandering significant human capital. Typically, STARs are in roles not adequate for their competencies, while even more qualified workers are stuck in jobs where a STAR would fit well. Consequently, a better approach to assessment—one that considers more than formal educational experience—and allocation of talent could significantly increase an economy's productive capacity and also reduce the need for governmental redistributive interventions.

Maximizing the potential of STARs requires moving beyond the inherited standard HR practices that use degree requirements to screen out candidates. Instead, new assessment approaches would consider a candidate's holistic experience and value non-linear career trajectories. After careful evaluation of their real capabilities, STARs are then ideal candidates for additional training to refine existing skills, acquire new ones, and increase their competitiveness in the labor market.

II.1.3 In the labor market

The sources of inequality that shape one's youth and education tend also to shape one's working adulthood. Indeed, where you started tends to determine where you end up.

Looking at regular employees, the situation is not much different. Gender represents a persistent barrier to thriving in the labor market. According to the International Labor Organization, the current global labor force participation rate for women is just under 47 percent, as opposed to 72 percent for men.[75] Meanwhile, women often receive lower starting salaries than their male counterparts because across many cultures they tend to be less aggressive in negotiating salaries. A minor difference of $1,000 per year in starting salary can compound over a career to a cumulative loss of $500,000 in earnings.[76] This implies enormous human capital losses for a global economy that operates below its potential.

Especially in the United States, race remains a great obstacle in employment. As Brookings notes, "Black men have the highest unemployment rates of any race/gender group, and the lowest labor force participation and employment rates among men." This is due to a combination of low education, poor health, and social discrimination.[77] In Asia, immigrant workers are often employed in insecure and poorly paid jobs, and face substantial discrimination. In a recent survey conducted by the International Labor Organization, when asked if migrant workers are a "drain on the economy," 30 percent in Singapore, 32 percent in Japan, and 40 percent in Thailand answered in the affirmative.[78]

Overlaid on these dynamics are policy or cultural factors that compound existing inequality. Even when workers possess the right academic credentials and can get good jobs, salary differentials might not always reflect genuine differences in responsibility or talent. One striking factor of the last four decades is the steep increase in executive compensation that has been combined with the wage stagnation of average workers in most advanced economies.[79] Looking at the apex of the corporate hierarchy, from 1978 to 2016, the average compensation of the typical CEO of a large American corporation has risen by more than 800 percent, as typical workers' salaries have gone up by 11.2 percent.[80] In 1978, CEO earnings in the United States were roughly 30 times larger than the average worker's salary, but more than 300 times larger by 2014.

CEO-to-worker compensation ratios, which should be seen as a proxy about the earning gap between those at the top of a corporate hierarchy and those in the middle, vary quite sharply across countries (*Exhibit 4.6*), with Austria the lowest and the United States the highest, probably reflecting the underlying ideological features of each capitalist type.[81] Even where the ratio is lower, though, wages for workers have stagnated, pointing to a feature of

Neoliberal Capitalism, particularly the decline in workers' power due to globalization and the fall in union membership.[82]

Beyond pay differences throughout a company's hierarchy, an individual will also face differences in pay for the same job between companies and industries.[83] In fact, only one third of the increase in income inequality in the United States in the last several years is due to differences in earnings within the same firms—that is pay gaps between top executives and staff. The remaining two-thirds is due to differences between firms.[84] The best-performing firms pull away from the rest, recording high productivity growth that allows them to pay generous salaries to their workers. High-wage employees tend to cluster in high-wage firms. As the *Harvard Business Review* has noted, fast-growing companies attract more top

Exhibit 4.6

The CEO-to-worker gap

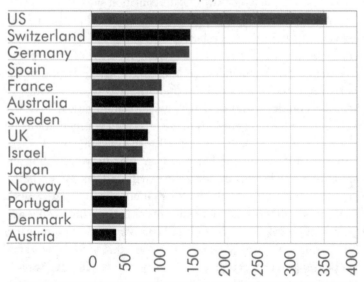

CEO-to-worker pay ratio

Source: Kiatpongsan and Norton (2014), The Trilateral Commission

THE TRILATERAL COMMISSION

talent by offering generous payouts, benefits, and perks, further fueling their own momentum, while employees in less-successful companies continue to be poorly paid, with their companies falling further behind over time.[85]

In a way, this seems logical. An industry in decline cannot pay as well as an industry on the ascent, and the rise and fall of new companies is part of capitalism. However, pay differentials in the real world are not always related to growth potential. Rather, low competition and poor regulation of new industries often play a role, and governments tend to address these issues with considerable delays, when monopolistic or oligopolistic positions have already crystallized.

When a new technology disrupts an existing industry or creates an entirely new one, regulators can be caught by surprise, and it takes some time for them to react (*Chapter 3*). New firms are able to take advantage of that fact, perhaps through monopolistic behavior that leads to higher profits, dividends, and salaries compared to saturated and regulated sectors. Old sectors, too, with powerful interest groups, may have the upper hand. In the United States, for example, finance has enjoyed a long wave of deregulation since the 1990s.[86]

Sometimes, firm-level inequality is the result of poor wage setting rules. If the salary gap between the top executives and the average employee is too wide, there might be issues of corporate governance that lawmakers can address. When firms operate in poorly regulated sectors and respond primarily to the instances of their shareholders, and deal with weak trade unions, they will likely end up paying generous dividends, high compensations for their top executives, and low wages for their average workers.

By contrast, when the bargaining power between labor and capital is more balanced, companies will end up paying better wages, reducing internal levels of inequality. For example, Germany's codetermination creates more balance between shareholders and workers on corporate boards and other committees (*Box 4.3*). In general, labor-market reforms that increase workers' negotiating power through legal protections are effective ways to flatten inequalities without harming growth. Examples include rules about minimum wages, and employment protections, trade unions, and wage coordination.[87]

Box 4.3: Germany's codetermination: culture and institutions matter[88]

In Germany's corporate governance, as *Harvard Business Review* describes it, workers have a say in company decision-making and contribute to shaping the business strategy. They elect a large share of the board and form groups of employees that consult with management about decisions. There is evidence suggesting the codetermination model leads to a more equitable distribution of company profits.

As discussed in Chapter 1, each variety of capitalism has its own distinctive elements that are often rooted in a country's particular context and culture. Collaborative structures like Germany's work councils are deeply embedded in German corporate history and practice. They work because of the level of trust between employers and employees.

In other countries, such trust cannot simply be assumed, especially where there is a history of tensions between labor and management. Nor should one expect the replication of the German approach on paper would necessarily lead to similar results.

Codetermination, moreover, is the byproduct of specific institutions. German work councils are effective because of the country's centralized wage-setting structure. In economies like the United States, as *HBR* notes, where firms have the primary responsibility for determining wages, worker involvement in corporate governance would be very different, and perhaps more contentious, than in a German context.

Finally, the state itself might inadvertently reinforce many sources of inequality by "imposing administrative burdens that loom larger for citizens with lower levels of human capital," explain the authors of an article for the *Public Administration Review*.[89] And then there are the psychological costs that "arise in the form of stigma from participating in unpopular programs, the experience of disempowerment, feelings of subservience and loss of autonomy, and related stress." The authors note that "means-tested programs will, because of their inherent need to verify eligibility, be more burdensome and alienating than a universal program designed to be accessible to nearly everyone."

III. WHAT WE SHOULD DO NOW

III.1. Shared direction

The preceding analysis affirms the new spirit of capitalism should have a bold goal to guide efforts to make capitalism more equitable. The report proposes:

- *Every person should have equal opportunity to achieve their potential*.

These ten words explicitly focus on equality of opportunity. To be clear, this goal embraces the varieties of human experience. It does not imply one concept of the "good life," nor the desirability of identical outcomes. Some people will focus on individual achievement while others on their community's. Some will emphasize innovation while others will preserve traditions. Judgment will be needed to apply this principle in our different countries. But the bedrock principle is solid. And a corollary is that we remove barriers within capitalism to opportunity where we can. Above all, we should fight permanent inequalities—or the "locking in" of privilege.

This goal is intuitively attractive from a normative perspective, but it also leads to sound policy. Capitalism succeeds in proportion to the talent and creativity it taps. We all suffer when geniuses cannot flourish, or when a talented child cannot contribute. And focusing on the beginning of opportunity—with policies emphasizing pre-distributive investments and removing legacy barriers—is more efficient and effective than redistribution after inequality is already baked in. Being born rich or poor, man or woman, black or white, should not determine success in life. This approach also changes the perspective on how we assess achievements. Instead of praising someone for his accomplishments, and so the endpoint, it is more important to look at the starting point.

This goal is also pragmatic. It is aligned with the effective functioning of markets and capitalism. Investments in our people, better functioning labor markets, and the breaking down of barriers erected to protect special interests all make capitalism stronger. By tackling inequality within our countries—alongside successes in curbing climate change and harnessing the digital revolution—we will also help address inequality more broadly. Lastly, a commitment to foundational equality gives all people a stake in the system and less reason to upend it.

Pre-distribution is powerful because it can be applied within any capitalist context, regardless of its institutional and cultural features. China's common prosperity strategy, for example, is aimed at reinvigorating the middle class and pushing companies to be more "empathetic."[90] According to the rhetoric of the Chinese Communist Party, the goal is to eliminate the "unfair" sources of inequality, while letting talent be rewarded in a meritocratic fashion—even if, in an authoritarian system, the government has a high degree of discretion about what merit is.

A bolder approach to income disparities in the West is important for democratic capitalism to build fairer societies and win the competition with its authoritarian counterparts. Social democracies are better positioned in this sense than liberal democracies. In Europe and parts of Asia, interventions in the form of educational investments, labor market regulation, wage settings and so on are more widespread than in the United States or the United Kingdom and, by their very nature, they are relatively more favorable to low and middle-income groups.

III.2. Investments

- **Ensure a fair start:** Equality of opportunity begins in childhood. Early investment in a child's life is therefore critical to promoting greater equity in their life.

  Government: Governments should play the leading role in supporting equality of opportunity from the start. They should con-

147

tinue and reinforce family-friendly policies and programs to ensure that every child has what is needed to ensure healthy development. Specific approaches range from prenatal education and healthcare programs, to basic nutritional support, to initiatives for early childhood intellectual development. More social-democratic countries have already proven the benefits of state-supported early childcare programs, expansive family-leave policies, and direct cash payments to qualified families. More liberal market countries, like the United States, have demonstrated the impact of indirect financial support through tax policies, especially Earned Income Tax Credits. These programs, which often win support from across the political spectrum, can boost school attendance and future earnings.[91]

Business: Businesses should also contribute to a "fair start" through generous paid leave policies and other assistance, such as on-site daycare.

Public-private partnerships: Other approaches can involve governments working with non-profits to design and deliver "fair start" programs backed in part by state funding. For example, "Parents as Teachers" in the United States and elsewhere is an evidence-based model, where parents agree to have home visits from qualified aids who give guidance on how to best accelerate their children's development.[92]

International: Today governments can learn from one another's policy interventions through the sharing of best practices, as they have in the past.[93] Systematic, comparative analyses of the advantages and disadvantages of Universal Basic Income experiments is one potential area for collaboration.

- **Improve infrastructure for families:** Among their other positive economic impacts, investments in better transportation, housing, communications, and digital connectivity disproportionately benefit the lower and middle classes.

Government: In planning infrastructure, governments should prioritize investments in affordable mixed-use housing, mass transit, parks and recreation areas, and digital access. Such investments help families have a fair start by lowering the costs of living and also freeing time for parents to spend with their children. (*See Chapter 3 for more details on digital investments.*)

- **Transform education for lifetime learning:** Our educational systems require transformation to meet the challenges of the twenty-first century. Success will take boldness and creativity similar to that which drove the mass education reforms of the nineteenth century and the dramatic expansion of higher education in the twentieth century. Every person should have affordable access to high-quality lifetime learning.

Government: Through policies and direct investment in institutions of higher education, governments need to incentivize and support true educational reform at all levels. Too often, we have inherited educational systems with calendars shaped by the rhythm of agriculture, and approaches designed as mass assembly lines for human capital. But the labor market is changing fast. Many in-demand occupations—especially in the high-tech sector—did not exist a decade ago. More dramatic, 65 percent of children entering primary school today may end up in jobs that do not yet exist.[94] Experience and research affirm, therefore, the necessity of ongoing lifetime learning. As described in Chapter 3, we should harness the digital revolution's full potential to extend and deliver education as never before, on a scale previously thought unimaginable. Exemplifying the sort of revolution in education needed, for example, Arizona State University has launched a program to reach 100 *million* more students in the coming decade (*See Box 4.4*).[95]

Box 4.4: Transforming education: Arizona State University's 100 Million Learners

Arizona State University (ASU) has become one of the most innovative higher education institutions in the world under the leadership of President Michael Crow.[96] ASU has consistently innovated to expand its access and impact, and experiment with new models.

In 2022, ASU challenged the art of the possible when it launched one of the most ambitious innovations in higher education—the Francis and Dionne Najafi 100 Million Learners Global Initiative.[97]

In collaboration with the Thunderbird School of Global Management, the initiative will offer five management online courses, each of which awards a micro-certification badge upon completion. Upon completing all five courses, a student is awarded 15 credit hours which can count toward a degree at Thunderbird, ASU, or other universities. The program is designed for lifetime learners of all types with three tracks: for learners without a high school diploma, at the undergraduate level, and at the graduate level. The courses will be accessible online through computers or smartphones.

The initiative plans to reach 100 million students worldwide by 2030.

The program is free and open to all. ASU hopes 70% of the participants will eventually be women. Behind this model is a collaboration between a public higher education institution—ASU—and private philanthropy.

The initiative can achieve its unique combination of reach and affordability because it relies upon an innovative mix of ASU professors teaching, reinforced by AI and machine learning capabilities to help teach and grade the courses. Furthermore, working with Google, the program will use a purpose-built translation engine to deliver the courses in 40 languages, from Arabic to Zulu, within four years.

The program began in 2022 with a 54-hour "Global entrepreneurship and Innovation Bootcamp" with no prerequisite certificates or credentials.[98]

The 100 Million Learners initiative presages the power of the digital revolution to transform education for true lifelong learning, affordably and on a global scale.

Business: Businesses also have a critical role to play. A significant part of lifetime learning will not occur inside traditional academic institutions. Rather, learning will be more "real time" and tailored to specific work or career requirements. And it will happen on the job. Before the COVID pandemic, the global workplace training industry was estimated to be worth over $370 billion.[99] Looking forward, such investment will be even more important. The challenge is not just quantity, but quality. Businesses will need to stay on the cutting edge of content development and delivery of such training either through their own tailored programs or support by specialized firms.

- **Attack legacy barriers to opportunity:** Despite much progress, a range of legacy barriers continue to slow or stop individuals from achieving their potential. These barriers vary by country, level of economic development, and sometimes culture. Overcoming them will require focused effort. Support for equal opportunity among women provides an illustrative example of how such interventions improve performance within capitalism. But similar arguments could be applied to race or other traits that hold back specific minority groups.

  Government: Decades of research validates the effectiveness of public programs targeting women's literacy and health. The impact of such programs disproportionately affects not only the women's lives but also broader economic development in their communities.[100] Financial education is especially important for helping women achieve better business results, better equality, and more empowerment.

  Business: There is a strong business case for improving the diversity of leadership in the private sector. Diversity improves business performance.[101] Women, however, are still underrepresented in senior leadership roles, including on Boards of Directors. A root cause is that fewer women are promoted to manager. That means the first rung in the career ladder is broken, which has far-reaching consequences.[102] Addressing these challenges requires businesses to invest time, resources, and visible senior leadership commitment to recruiting and mentorship of women.

- **Modernize credentialing:** Access to a good job is critical to equality of opportunity. Too often, people with the skills and potential are excluded from opportunities because of inflated credential requirements. Labor markets, therefore, can be hugely inefficient. Capitalism works best for the individual and as a system when the labor market has real insight into a person's real skills, experience, and potential, and not just a formal credential.

Government: As an important part of the broader educational transformation, governments should promote alternative career paths, the adoption of micro-certifications, and different learning models. While preserving essential continuing education requirements for professions such as physicians, engineers, and other high risk or technical fields, they should also explore professional certification and licensing reforms to help improve workforce mobility (e.g., enable a licensed practitioner in one jurisdiction to practice in another) and reduce artificial barriers to entry in some careers (e.g., five U.S. states still require a professional license and 1,500+ hours of training to braid hair).[103] As major employers themselves, governments should also re-evaluate their hiring criteria and, where appropriate, move job requirements toward skills and away from educational credentials. Some already are. For example, in March 2022, the State of Maryland, in partnership with the non-profit Opportunity@Work, became the first state government in the United States to eliminate the 4-year degree requirement for thousands of state jobs (*Box 4.2*).[104]

Business: Businesses have a central role in shaping labor markets. Across industries, there are plenty of opportunities to accelerate reforms to credentialing and hiring. This is ultimately in businesses' own self-interest, since it expands the pool of potential candidates. But they will need to develop new approaches to assess candidates' full range of skills and capabilities. Businesses should also commit to reviewing job requirements for all positions to ensure that they do not include unnecessary exclusionary requirements. High-tech and digital firms have been a vanguard in jettisoning college degree requirements and accepting alternative forms of certification. Under the pressures of the tightened COVID-19 labor market, others have followed.[105] But more can and should be done.

- **Tackle stagnating wages:** Well-paying jobs are important to address challenges of inequality. In the past 30 years, however, corporate valuations and profitability have increased in tandem with a declining share of income for labor, slow wage growth for most workers, and, therefore, increasing income inequality. Declining worker power is an important factor behind these trends.[106] Between 1960 and 2019, unionization rates among OECD countries fell from 38% to about 16%.[107]

Government: Governments should support true minimum living wage requirements, which will, in turn, affect labor rates across the market. While it is unrealistic to seek a rapid re-unionization in many economies, governments can reaffirm trade unions' role as an effective partner with management.

Business: In many more social-democratic systems, management-union relationships have remained relatively cooperative through informal norms as well as formal corporate governance mechanisms. Germany, for instance, has perhaps the strongest tradition of "co-determination" in Europe, including labor representation on corporate boards. While individual business leaders have embraced more "people-focused" management, many more need to make the transition to embracing labor and unions as critical stakeholders for their enterprises' success.[108] Unions, too, need to modernize to attract new members, for instance by offering new skill building and job services to their members or by helping provide cooperative insurance and benefits to "gig" workers.

- **Enhance role of data and analytics:** How services are delivered is often as important to a program's effectiveness as the policy intent itself. The success of other investments to counter inequality depends in part upon public sector institutions with twenty-first century capabilities for data-driven design and delivery.

Government: Programs are still too often launched or continued without critical assessment. Governments need to invest in building foundational state capacity for twenty-first-century management. This involves tapping not only into the full potential of the digital revolution (*see Chapter 3*), but also using advances in behavioral economics and experimental economics, and data on customer experience and design thinking. To date, for example, behavioral economics expertise in the U.S. and British governments has informed some "nudges" to move citizens toward better choices and design more effective regulations.[109]

Governments should accelerate "open data" initiatives to enable both public staff and private researchers to analyze budget and program effectiveness.[110] Governments also need to redouble efforts to make it as easy as possible for citizens to be informed about and receive benefits. The COVID-19 pandemic forced many governments to adapt to digital life rather than requiring citizens to come into physical offices. Such changes can have a disproportionately positive impact on lower-income citizens, who cannot afford time away from work or childcare.

III.3. "Rules of the road"

- **Address market concentration:** Concentration of market power is always a potential threat to capitalism and democratic governance. Concentrated power seeks to entrench its position by economic and political means. That, in turn, can "lock in" inequalities, including those shaping labor markets and constraining wage growth. (*See also Chapter 3.*)

  Government: Governments should resource their agencies sufficiently to monitor market concentration across industries and then take regulatory action. Data shows that market concentration has increased in many sectors of the American economy. These sectors range from agribusiness to pharmaceuticals to the high-tech sector, which was traditionally perceived as highly competitive.[111]

  Business: Adding to the strength of "superstar firms" are non-compete agreements for employees, especially among highly skilled workers, that prevent them from working for other businesses in the sector. But such agreements may limit entrepreneurship by preventing individuals with good ideas from establishing their own start-ups.[112]

- **Enhance workforce pay and demographics transparency:** Inequalities can arise from pay differences and lack of diversity in businesses. Considering how these dynamics impact women provides an illustrative example of how "rules of the road" should be adapted to help market mechanisms function better to address inequalities.

Government: Governments should consider whether formal legal requirements for pay and demographic data transparency are needed. A number of U.S. states and cities, including New York City, have recently passed pay transparency laws, but there is no data yet on their impact.[113] Such laws are in a similar spirit to laws prohibiting a future employer from asking about past compensation history, another common behavior that tends to perpetuate lower salaries for women.

Business: Firms and industry associations should establish consistent reporting standards for basic workforce pay and demographic information. This will help establish industry benchmarks and help firms prioritize efforts to address imbalances. The transparency will also help investors and other stakeholders assess any given firm's commitments to equality. Data on compensation ranges for positions, promotion rates, and the diversity of leaders could be captured in standard human resource systems. At the same time, other factors, such as executive-to-worker pay ratios, could be reported. Together transparency about such data would increase workers' bargaining power and thereby help reduce pay differentials. It would also help identify those businesses that are distinctive in their equitable personnel policies as examples to follow.

- **Provide an equity stake to workers.** Extending equity ownership to workers would increase the fairness and the efficiency of the system. Even if history shows that capital income tends to grow faster than labor earnings, the goal of such a proposal is not to boost workers' financial returns because the odds of single stocks to even outperform Treasury Bills are low. The rationale is more to increase their degree of engagement in their daily jobs and thus their productivity, while contributing to lengthen the strategic horizon of their companies.[114]

Public-private partnership: There is no ideal way to design worker ownership plans. Workers can own stocks in their companies through profit-sharing or pension plans, or through schemes to share ownership. Also, the underlying nature of the capitalist system will likely play a role. In some cases, the government will take the lead; in other cases, firms will be in the driver's seat. In 2019, for example, France passed a law for mandatory profit-sharing schemes for employees in firms with more than 50 workers. In the United States, the *Wall Street Journal* reports, a coalition of more than 60 groups, including banks, pension funds, and private equity firms, has backed a new nonprofit, Ownership Work, that promotes broad-based stock ownership, setting standards for designing ownership programs and advocating for more widespread adoption of them. Or in China, telecommunications firm Huawei has its labor union hold 98.6 percent of shares on behalf of shareholding employees, with the remaining 1.4 percent owned by its founder, Ren Zhengfei.[115]

- **Tax consistently:** Regardless of the absolute value of taxes at stake, consistent application of tax policies matters to the confidence in the fairness of the system. Faith erodes when the wealthy can "play by their own rules" by venue shopping.*

Government: In most jurisdictions, on top of more favorable tax rates than for labor income, there are normative provisions that allow for special tax treatments of capital income—which is usually the primary source of income for the wealthy. For example, if a person in the United States holds onto assets without selling them and bequeaths them to heirs, the increase in the assets' value is not subject to income tax. Closing loopholes in the tax system would not necessarily require taxing richer people more, but simply asking them to pay their share of taxes. But better structured capital income taxes likely will not be enough to address the deepest sources of inequality without being complemented by some form of wealth taxation.[116] According to a 2018 OECD paper, "wealth inequality is far greater than income inequality, and there is some evidence suggesting that wealth inequality has increased in recent decades. In addition, wealth accumulation operates in a self-reinforcing way and is likely to increase in the absence of taxation."[117] Finally, increasing taxation on large inheritances might not significantly boost tax revenues, but might send a signal of a broader

---

* Not all Task Force co-chairs agreed on this recommendation.

social commitment to equality of opportunity. Some countries might go a step further, and target revenues from such a tax toward helping lower-income families invest in their children and, thereby, help increase intergenerational economic mobility.

Cross-government cooperation: Governments should intensify their international tax coordination, including standard setting, information sharing, and enforcement. In a globalized financial system, one country's public policies may be undermined by tax competition with another country. Most simply, if billionaires fear their home country's tax policies, they might move their fortunes to a more favorable tax jurisdiction. According to a recent study in the *American Economic Review*, in Scandinavia, "the probability of hiding assets offshore rises sharply and significantly with wealth, including within the very top groups of the wealth distribution.... As a result, the wealth in tax havens turns out to be extremely concentrated: the top 0.01 percent of the wealth distribution owns about 50 percent of it." The report continues that "tax evasion is possible for the very rich because there is an industry that helps them conceal wealth abroad, and most of their income derives from wealth."[118] Recent progress in international efforts to introduce a 15 percent minimum global corporate tax signals both the difficulties and potential of greater cross-border tax coordination.

- **Address large inheritances:** Regulating inheritance necessarily involves balancing individual freedoms with social good. How states manage the issue sends a strong message on the value they place on equality of opportunity.

Government: Large inheritances are more a matter of symbolism than a significant route toward increasing total tax revenues. Policies to reduce inheritances may signal a broader social commitment to equality of opportunity. Some countries might go a step further, and target revenues from such a tax toward helping lower-income families invest in their children and, thereby, help increase intergenerational economic mobility. The costs and benefits of such reforms, however, should be evaluated, weighing the potential to preempt potential unintended negative consequences.

- **Eliminate administrative burden:** Administrative burden is a tax on the poor. Whether to validate eligibility for public benefits or register a business, cumbersome bureaucratic requirements can slow or prevent citizens from receiving the services they deserve as well as create barriers that favor incumbent businesses or special interests. Such burdens also offer opportunities for petty public corruption.[119]

Government: Governments should commit themselves to continuous improvement in eliminating administrative burden. They should undertake regular reviews of how they engage with citizens—from regulation to taxation to provision of social services—to identify extraneous administrative burdens. They should seek any required regulatory and/or statutory change to enable streamlining processes. Increased government capacity for data-driven analysis, program design, and implementation will contribute to these efforts.

III.4. Trilateral recommendation

- *Ensure quality life-long learning accessible to every person by end of the decade*

Previous stages of capitalism both fueled and were fueled by transformations in education. Recall, for instance, the introduction of compulsory primary education in many countries in the nineteenth century. Entering the Fifth Stage of capitalism, we again face the opportunity and the necessity of reimagining education so that it can contribute to both equality of opportunity and economic vibrancy.

Today, the Trilateral countries have the opportunity to launch a "moonshot" initiative to remake education on the scale of the reforms of the nineteenth and twentieth centuries, namely by ensuring every person can access high-quality life-long learning by the end of this decade. Such training will be designed to fit an individual's personalized needs by role, experience and age, sector and industry, and geography.

To design education with this granularity, the public and private sectors alike will have to rely on AI to mine insights from vast data sets available through social media, employment firms, and public sources. The programs will be delivered through multiple digital channels in an individual's language, relying again on AI enabled multi-language translation and graded and interactive exercises. We already see this potential in initiatives like Arizona State University's plans to reach 100 million more students this decade through the innovative use of AI technologies (*Box 4.4*). While this recommendation would not include access to physical "hands on" training for all, it will offer virtual reality opportunities to help bridge the gap for developing specific physical skills. All this can only be achieved through developing and applying at scale a series of digital innovations.

Like the Apollo program announced by U.S. President John F. Kennedy sixty years ago, in announcing such a bold goal, the Trilateral countries would not yet have in hand all the design and technical capabilities to achieve their goal.[120] As in the 1960s, though, most of the required infrastructure and digital capabilities already exist or will soon exist. And as in the Apollo era, the bold goal will help focus a set of potentially divergent efforts and innovations toward a singular historic objective.

Unlike the moonshot of the 1960s, however, such an effort will not involve a single engineering project led and funded by one government. Rather, it will be more like an "initiative of initiatives," one that knits together a number of recommendations from across this report. A single public sector organization—like the National Aeronautics and Space Administration (NASA) with the Apollo program—will not program manage the effort as during the era of Managed Capitalism. Instead, success will emerge from diverse networks involving private enterprises, educational institutions, governments, nonprofits, individual entrepreneurs and thought leaders.

A purpose-built, international non-profit enterprise could provide coherence to such an effort. Its core functions would include: *catalyzing* research and program priorities across networks; *convening* leaders, experts, innovators, and other stakeholders to learn, motivate, and mobilize; *coordinating* informally across networks and institutions to help the division of labor to address major gaps in access; and *communicating* and serving as a *clearinghouse* of best practices, programs, innovations, and lessons learned. Ideally, such an enterprise would combine public and private resources with an independent international management team.

This concluding Trilateral recommendation integrates the profound potential of the digital revolution (*Chapter 3*) with the imperative of advancing equality of opportunity. Importantly, such a transformation in education for all people is a prerequisite to achieve all the other goals and transition to a more sustainable and equitable capitalism in the twenty-first century.

5

TOWARD A NEW SPIRIT OF CAPITALISM

We live in a world shaped by capitalism. Its impact is far-reaching, extending over centuries. This long history was never a straight line, but it brought unprecedented prosperity and helped extend countless lives and their quality to levels unimaginable just two centuries ago.

Yet, today, many people around the world feel frustrated. The capitalist system and institutions we inherited from the twentieth century no longer work as they once did. For many families, prosperity and security are harder to find. For them, the future does not appear as promising.[1]

Before the outbreak of the COVID-19 pandemic, global surveys highlighted that most people felt their countries were already on the "wrong track."[2] There are a host of factors behind such feelings, and many of them are not linked to capitalism directly. That said, efforts to respond to climate change proved inconsistent. Digital technologies changed people's daily lives, the industry landscape, and our politics—and not always in positive ways. And inequality grew within countries while it declined across them. As China and other emerging Asian economies' growth rebalanced the global economy toward Asia, many families in advanced economies faced income stagnation while unmatched wealth accrued for the few. In turn, trust in established institutions continued to erode. Political instability followed in many countries. As the COVID-19 pandemic entered its third year, uncertainties about the future lingered only to be heightened by Russia's invasion of Ukraine and further disruptions to the global economy with the signs of rising inflation.

Such feelings are understandable, especially when viewed against the backdrop of history. We are now moving through a historic transition from one form of capitalism to another. This is the transition to the Fifth Stage of capitalism. This process touches nearly every life on every continent. Success is not certain.

Whether or not we act to shape the future of capitalism is thus a defining question of our time.

The Trilateral Commission Task Force on Global Capitalism in Transition was unified in this conviction: We must act. Capitalism remains the most powerful engine of prosperity and well-being. Yet capitalism will not inevitably settle onto a favorable path. If we do not act, the current trajectory will continue. We can already see outlines of a future defined by inaction. A hotter planet as climate change creates a cascade of economic, social, humanitarian, and political consequences. Lost opportunities for digital transformation. A withering of the innovation and dynamism that propel capitalism. A more unequal world, one defined as much by people and places "left behind" as by opportunity and upward mobility. However, if we do face these challenges and act, we will then have opportunities not only to increase our collective material wealth, but also to raise the overall well-being of billions around the world.

How we decide to act therefore matters a great deal. History reminds us to be humble. Capitalism is a complex cultural system. It shapes and is shaped by billions of independent, decentralized decisions every day. These range from the mundane choice of what to buy for dinner to strategic decisions such as whether to build a new multibillion dollar semiconductor facility.

This complexity defies reducing change to one dimension. Instead, a complex interplay of factors has shaped—and will continue to shape—capitalism's development. What technologies we develop and spread matter. Where we invest matters. How we educate matters. How we work together matters. Where we place factories and supply chains matter. Whether we cooperate or compete to define "rules of the road" matters.

And which ideas and values move us matter too. This was a core insight of the great sociologist Max Weber more than a century ago as he contemplated the rise of capitalism.[3] We cannot understand capitalism, he concluded, without understanding its foundations. And these foundations are found in the mind and heart more than material and machines. These foundations include our values and aspirations for the future. They remain powerful, if often unseen forces. They inform all the individual decisions and actions that ultimately make capitalism work. These ideas together become the animating "spirit" of an era's capitalism.

This report to the Trilateral Commission Task Force, therefore, calls for a new "Social Compact with the Next Generations." We need to commit ourselves to ensuring a better future for our children, grandchildren, and great-grandchildren. The quality of their lives matters as much as ours today. Such a compact will influence the direction of capitalism's evolution. It embodies equality of opportunity. Self-interest and the simple profit motive are not sufficient; they never have been. We should deliver high-quality growth for a broad common good, not just high-volume growth. We then view today's decisions through the lens of decades, not quarters. We can adapt and expand market incentives. Our perspective by necessity also broadens to consider impact across different stakeholders. In doing so, we recognize our diversity while seeking to work together whenever possible.

The Social Compact can become real through the test of addressing the three defining challenges of our era—namely, how to fight climate change, manage the digital revolution, and reduce inequality. Without exaggeration, if we do not get these right, all else is at risk. But we cannot lose sight that the reverse is also true: if we do successfully tackle these challenges the benefits will be mutually reinforcing whereby green innovations and harnessing the digital revolution's potential can lead to better lives and reduced inequalities. The preceding chapters, therefore, argue for three goals to serve as the main pillars supporting the new Social Compact:

- Every person should live and work in a net-zero world by 2050.
- Every person should have access to full benefits of the digital revolution.
- Every person should have equal opportunity to achieve their potential.

These three goals are not necessarily comprehensive. Together they provide a starting point for engagement—discussion, debate, decision. Others may be added. But these are essential. And they share some fundamental characteristics.

- All three are *right* because they accord with moral intuitions across belief systems. Birth should not be destiny. Capitalism's Fifth Stage must aim to help every person. Everyone deserves opportunities, and we need an aspirational compass bearing to guide us.
- All three are *wise* because they improve how capitalism works. Our prosperity depends upon expanding opportunities, investing in all our people, making our institutions work, countering risks, and removing barriers to innovation and competition.
- All three are *smart* because they balance ambition with pragmaticism. The basic ideas have momentum. They can appeal to aspirations of diverse peoples and across the political spectrum. Different countries can translate them into policies, programs, and actions tailored to the variety of capitalisms. We should not be naïve: these changes will involve a hard journey over decades, just as in past transitions in capitalism's history.

This report offers initial recommendations to deliver on the promise of each of these goals. These recommendations are not comprehensive, of course. But they are deliberately framed to point in a common direction. They are also flexible: they can be adapted to different models of capitalism. Practically, we must accept different rates of progress and different approaches in different countries. This shared direction of action, though, matters greatly.

This report also recognizes the unique power of collaboration among the advanced democracies of the world that help comprise the Trilateral Commission. Collaboration among them to advance common interests and values could never be more impactful—

especially in this time of transition uncertainty marked by rising geopolitical tensions, fragmenting global supply chains and data flows, and the return of inflation to levels not experienced in decades. The three recommendations for collaboration among advanced democracies stand out:

- For the Green Transition: Establish a "Climate Club" among advanced economies.
- For the Digital Revolution: Establish an alliance of "techno-democracies."
- For reducing Inequality: Ensure quality life-long learning accessible to every person by end of the decade.

Considering the three chapters' recommendations together highlights some cross-cutting ideas. Together, these can help guide the exploration of additional recommendations to translate the new spirit of the age into action.

- *We should act early but always with a long view:* We need urgency. Effects compound through time. Better to address the root cause of an issue today than attempt to redistribute resources later. Attacking problems early usually delivers the greatest, most efficient impact—whether through pre-distribution interventions to expand children's opportunities or the introduction of green technologies. But such actions should always be defined starting with a view of their long-term impact. This requires leaders, investors, voters, and consumers to look beyond the quarterly earnings call or the next election to enduring impact.
- *People provide the most important source of capitalism's power.* Their creativity, dedication, innovation, entrepreneurship, and management provide the fuel for capitalism's engine. Therefore, the most important investments are in their opportunities and skills. Today we need to match the scale and scope of the nineteenth and twentieth centuries' educational reforms to extend life-long learning to the world. Our fellow citizens are the architects and builders of our shared future.
- *Business enterprises remain the main vehicle of capitalism.* If people provide the energy, how they design and run business enterprises will create the vehicles that move capitalism forward.

165

How businesses operate—from research to the design of products to the management of the shop floor to corporate governance—are critically important. Within the limits of antitrust, we need to find ways for businesses to learn from one another to solve this era's challenges. None of these challenges can be addressed without thoughtful business leaders. And it will be the best among these leaders who set a new standard for this era of capitalism. They will broaden their own and their team's perspectives, first, to embrace the guiding purpose of advancing broader positive change, and then to translate it into specific high impact and profitable products and services.

- *Balance among stakeholders improves capitalism.* We have seen how an overly restrictive view of shareholder value risks eroding capitalism's legitimacy over time. When workers and consumers are more empowered, the results tend to be more equitable and, ultimately, more sustainable. By adopting a broader perspective on their potential impact, business leaders can then play the fulcrum in finding a constructive balance.

- *Healthy competition leads to healthy capitalism.* Over 250 years ago, Adam Smith spoke against the distorting influence of monopolies. The risks endure today. Market concentration matters. Too much of it, and capitalism can ossify and lose its dynamism. Then we all lose eventually. Targeted reforms and incentives can improve competition and keep capitalism's innovation flywheel spinning. Often, realigned incentives will provide the key to unlock many solutions.

- *The state remains an important partner.* Across the different varieties of capitalism, the state will play a critical role in realizing the new Social Compact. In democracies, strengthening essential state capacity—improving government's basic competence in policy design and delivery—ultimately serves all stakeholders. Sometimes, this era's challenges will demand the state take the lead whether alone or catalyzing new public-private partnerships. Even the limited state should be a highly competent one.

- *Hang together or we will hang separately.* Many of the challenges and opportunities of this age require international cooperation. Finding common ground amid the diversity of interests and histories is, as an understatement, difficult. Nonetheless, political and business leaders alike must remain engaged and search for creative solutions. Some solutions will be forged among allies, some with rivals, and some with both. That said, the world's democracies should work together to ensure this era's rules, standards, and norms reinforce not just their shared interests, but also common values. This is an age for statesmen and stateswomen.

* * *

From its outset, this Trilateral Commission Task Force report aims to contribute to a positive change in global capitalism in four ways: by building understanding and shared direction of where capitalism should evolve in its Fifth Stage; suggesting ways of working to achieve those goals; identifying the necessary investments in skills and capabilities; and, lastly, sharing select examples that show change of the sort described is possible.

Above all, this report hopes to explain and help set the agenda to guide us during the transition to the Fifth Stage of capitalism. By understanding capitalism and its evolution, we can see better how to bend the curve of its development. Especially in times of such uncertainty, thinking with the long view in mind can provide a compass bearing for the future. The Social Compact for the Next Generations sketches the spirit for this new age of capitalism. Its goals and recommendations provide a starting point.

Most important, the idea of the Social Compact helps us focus on fundamentals. It is easy to get lost in complexities or overwhelmed by the scale of the challenges ahead. In many ways, we may now feel more divided than only a few years ago.[4] The power of this Social Compact lies in its ability to cut through this complexity with a simple question: Is the decision I am about to make right for the next generations?

That is a question everyone—regardless of country, regardless of industry, regardless of position—can ask themselves. And if we do, we will all be on a path to a more equitable and sustainable capitalism.

APPENDICES

MEMBERS OF THE TASK FORCE ON GLOBAL CAPITALISM IN TRANSITION

- **Bruce Andrews**, Corporate Vice President and Chief Government Affairs Officer at Intel Corporation; former U.S. Deputy Secretary of Commerce.

- **Ajay Banga**, Vice Chairman, General Atlantic; former President and CEO, Mastercard.

- **Carl Bildt** (co-chair), WHO Special Envoy for the Access to COVID-19 Tools Accelerator; former Prime Minister of Sweden.

- **Hon. Julie Bishop**, former Minister of Foreign Affairs, Australia.

- **Nicola Brewer**, Non-Executive Board member, Iberdrola; former Vice Provost UCL and former British High Commissioner to South Africa.

- **John Bruton**, former Taoiseach of Ireland.

- **Edoardo Campanella**, Research Director, Task Force on Global Capitalism in Transition, Trilateral Commission; Senior Fellow at the Mossavar-Rahmani Center for Government and Business, Harvard Kennedy School.

- **Mark Carney**, Vice-Chairman, Brookfield Asset Management; former Governor of the Bank of England, former Governor of the Bank of Canada.

- **Vladimir Dlouhy**, President of the Czech Chamber of Commerce.

- **Makiko Eda**, Chief Representative Officer, World Economic Forum Japan; Member of Executive Committee, World Economic Forum.

- **Andrew Erdmann**, former Chief Operating Officer, State of Missouri.

- **Naushad Forbes**, Co-Chairman of Forbes Marshall, India.

- **Sigmar Gabriel**, Chairman, Atlantik-Brücke; former Foreign Minister of Germany.

- **Armando Garza Sada**, Chairman of Alfa.

- **Kelly Grier** (co-chair), U.S. Chair and Managing Partner and Americas Managing Partner, Ernst & Young.

- **Luigi Gubitosi**, former Chief Executive Officer, Telecom Italia.

- **Marillyn Hewson**, former Chairman, President, and CEO, Lockheed Martin.

- **Mellody Hobson**, current Chairman of Starbucks, current CEO and Chair of Ariel Investments.

- **Akinari Horii**, Special Advisor, Member of the Board of Directors, Canon Institute for Global Studies.

- **Bhairavi Jani**, Executive Director, SCA Group & Chairperson, IEF.

- **Bilahari Kausikan**, former Permanent Secretary of the Singapore Ministry of Foreign Affairs.

- **Lawrence Lau**, Ralph and Claire Landau Professor of Economics, The Chinese University of Hong Kong.

- **Bo Lidegaard**, Managing Director (Europe), Macro Advisory Partners.

- **Doris Magsaysay Ho**, President and CEO, Magsaysay Group.

- **Cecilia Malmström**, Non-resident Senior Fellow, Peterson Institute for International Economics; former European Commissioner for Trade.

- **James Manyika**, Senior Vice President of Technology and Society at Google; Chairman Emeritus, McKinsey Global Institute, and Senior Partner Emeritus, McKinsey & Company.

- **Takehiko Nakao**, Former President, Asian Development Bank; Chairman, Mizuho Research & Technologies.

- **Takeshi Niinami** (co-chair), Chief Executive Officer, Suntory Holdings.

- **Meghan O'Sullivan**, Chair of the Trilateral Commission, North America Chapter; Jeane Kirkpatrick Professor of the Practice of International Affairs and the Director of the Geopolitics of Energy Project at the Harvard Kennedy School.

- **Susan Schwab**, Professor Emeritus University of Maryland; Board Member of FedEx, Marriott, and Caterpillar; former U.S. Trade Representative.

- **Lawrence H. Summers**, Charles W. Eliot University Professor and President Emeritus, Harvard University; former U.S. Secretary of the Treasury.

- **Bark Taeho**, President of Lee & Ko Global Commerce Institute; Professor Emeritus, Seoul National University; former Minister of Trade for Korea.

- **Akihiko Tanaka**, Chair Trilateral Commission, Asia Chapter; President of the National Graduate Institute for Policy Studies.

- **Helle Thorning-Schmidt**, Co-chair Oversight Board; former Prime Minister of Denmark.

- **Jean-Claude Trichet**, former Chair Trilateral Commission, Europe Chapter; former President of the European Central Bank.

- **Axel A. Weber**, Chair of the Trilateral Commission, Europe Chapter; Chairman of UBS.

- **Hans Wijers**, Chairman, ING Group; former Dutch Minister for Economic Affairs.

- 25 May 2021, "Setting the agenda," with Branko Milanović, Senior Scholar at the Stone Center on Socio-economic Inequality, author of *Capitalism, Alone.*

- 10 June 2021, "Getting to Net Zero," with Henry M. Paulson, Jr., current Executive Chairman of TPG Climate Rise Fund, former U.S. Secretary of the Treasury, former Chair and CEO of Goldman Sachs.

- 14 July 2021, "Levelling the Digital Playing Field," with Eric Schmidt, co-founder, Schmidt Futures, former CEO and Executive Chairman, Google/Alphabet, and Marietje Schaake, International Policy Director, Stanford Cyber Policy Center, former Member of the European Parliament from the Netherlands; columnist, *Financial Times.*

- 20 October 2021, "Sharing the Pie More Fairly," with Keyu Jin, Associate Professor of Economics, London School of Economics.

- 3–5 November 2021: Virtual Global Meeting on Capitalism in Transition [with entire Trilateral Commission].

  - 3 November 2021, "Is Capitalism in Crisis?" with Jacob Wallenberg, Chairman, Investor AB; and Raghuram Rajan, the Katherine Dusak Miller Distinguished Service Professor of Finance at the University of Chicago's Booth School.

  - 3 November 2021, "Toward Net Zero," with Arunabha Ghosh, Founder-CEO, Council on Energy, Environment, and Water, Joseph Stiglitz, University Professor, Columbia University; and Laurence Tubiana, CEO, European Climate Foundation.

  - 4 November 2021, "Sharing the Pie More Fairly," with Ngozi Okonjo-Iweala, Director General, World Trade Organization; Keyu Jin, Associate Professor of Economics, London School of Economics; and Yasuyuki Sawada, Professor, Faculty of Economics, University of Tokyo, former Chief Economist, Asian Development Bank.

- 5 November 2021, "Levelling the Digital Playing Field," with Eric Schmidt, co-founder, Schmidt Futures, former CEO and Executive Chairman, Google/Alphabet; Maria Chiara Carrozza, President of the National Research Council, Italy; Mike Froman, Deputy Chairman, MasterCard; and Rohini Srivathsa, National Technology Officer, Microsoft India.

- 29 November 2021, "The State vs the Market," with Luigi Zingales, Robert C. McCormack Distinguished Service Professor of Entrepreneurship and Finance and George G. Rinder Faculty Fellow, University of Chicago; and Susan Thornton, Senior Fellow and Visiting Lecturer, Yale Law School; former acting Assistant Secretary of State for East Asian and Pacific Affairs.

- 14 December 2021, "The Role of Corporations in Driving Sustainable Growth," with Rebecca Henderson, John and Natty McArthur University Professor, Harvard University; author of *Reimagining Capitalism in a World on Fire*; and Dambisa Moyo, Economist and best-selling author of *How Boards Work*.

- 12 January 2022, "A New International Architecture," with Mariana Mazzucato, Professor in the Economics of Innovation and Public Value at University College London and author of *Mission Economy*; and Anne-Marie Slaughter, CEO of New America and Bert G. Kerstetter '66 University Professor Emerita of Politics and International Affairs at Princeton University.

- 4 April 2022, "Discussion of Draft Report."

NOTES

FOREWORD AND PREFACE

1. Crozier, Michel, Samuel P. Huntington and Joji Watanuki. *The Crisis of Democracy: Report on the Governability of Democracies to the Trilateral Commission*. New York University Press, 1975.
2. The most important titles include: Bastani, Aaron. *Fully Automated Luxury Communism*. Verso, 2019; Collier, Paul. *The Future of Capitalism: Facing the New Anxieties*. Harper, 2018; Henderson, Rebecca. *Reimagining Capitalism in a World on Fire*. PublicAffairs, 2021; Mazzucato, Mariana. *Mission Economy: A Moonshot Guide to Changing Capitalism*. Harper Business, 2021; Rajan, Raghuram. *The Third Pillar: How Markets and the State Leave the Community Behind*. Penguin Press, 2019.
3. For more on capitalism as a cultural system see: Appleby, Joyce. *The Relentless Revolution: A History of Capitalism (Norton Paperback)*. Reprint, W. W. Norton and Company, 2011.
4. Weber, Max. *The Protestant Ethic and the Spirit of Capitalism (Norton Critical Editions)*. First, W. W. Norton and Company, 2008.

1. CAPITALISM'S FIFTH STAGE

1. Zitelmann, Rainer. *The Power of Capitalism: A Journey Through Recent History Across Five Continents*. LID Publishing, 2019.
2. McCraw, Thomas, ed. *Creating Modern Capitalism: How Entrepreneurs, Companies, and Countries Triumphed in Three Industrial Revolutions*. First Edition (U.S.) First Printing, Harvard University Press, 1998.
3. "GNI per Capita, Atlas Method (Current US$)—China." *World Bank*, data.world-bank.org/indicator/NY.GNP.PCAP.CD?locations=CN. Accessed 15 Apr. 2022.
4. Frieden, Jeffry. *Global Capitalism*. Reissue, W. W. Norton and Company, 2020.
5. See, for example: Henderson, Rebecca. *Reimagining Capitalism in a World on Fire*. PublicAffairs, 2021.

6. McCann, Duncan and Christine Berry. "Shareholder Capitalism." *New Economics Foundation*, 2017. https://neweconomics.org/uploads/files/NEF_SHARE-HOLDER-CAPITALISM_E_latest.pdf

7. Griffin, Paul. "Carbon Majors Report 2017." Climate Accountability Institute, 2017. https://climateaccountability.org/pdf/CarbonMajorsRpt2017%20Jul17.pdf

8. Marc Zuckerberg, the CEO of Meta (formerly Facebook), coined the motto "move fast and break things." For a critique of this mindset, see: "The Era of 'Move Fast and Break Things' Is Over." *Harvard Business Review*, 23 Jan. 2019, hbr.org/2019/01/the-era-of-move-fast-and-break-things-is-over.

9. "World's Billionaires Have More Wealth than 4.6 Billion People." *Oxfam International*, 20 Jan. 2020, www.oxfam.org/en/press-releases/worlds-billion-aires-have-more-wealth-46-billion-people.

10. Fine, David, et al. "Inequality: A Persisting Challenge and Its Implications." *McKinsey & Company*, 23 June 2021, www.mckinsey.com/industries/public-and-social-sector/our-insights/inequality-a-persisting-challenge-and-its-impli-cations.

11. In the United States, a child's chance of out-earning his or her parents have fallen from almost 90% in the 1970s to 50% now. See: Chetty, Raj, et al. "The Fading American Dream: Trends in Absolute Income Mobility since 1940." *Science*, vol. 356, no. 6336, 2017, pp. 398–406. *Crossref*, https://doi.org/10.1126/science.aal4617.

12. See: "Axios | Momentive Poll: Capitalism and Socialism." *SurveyMonkey*, www.surveymonkey.com/curiosity/axios-capitalism-update. Accessed 14 Apr. 2022.
    In March 2021, a Fortune/Survey Monkey poll found that almost 40% of Americans aged 25–34 preferred socialism over capitalism, as opposed to 15% of people older than 65. See: "Fortune | SurveyMonkey Poll: Streaming and Capitalism." *SurveyMonkey*, www.surveymonkey.com/curiosity/fortune-poll-march-2021. Accessed 14 Apr. 2022.
    Similarly, in a 2020 survey, 38% of 18–38 year olds expressed in 2020 a favor-able view of socialism versus 20% for older "Baby Boomers" (55–73 year olds).
    It is worth noting, 50% of the 18 to 58 years old cohort viewed "socialism" unfavorably. See: "Poll: Sanders Rises, But Socialism Isn't Popular With Most Americans." *NPR*, 19 Feb. 2020, www.npr.org/2020/02/19/807047941/poll-sanders-rises-but-socialism-isnt-popular-with-most-americans.

13. Niemietz, Kristian Peter. "Left Turn Ahead: Surveying Attitudes of Young People Towards Capitalism and Socialism." *SSRN Electronic Journal*, 2021. *Crossref*, https://doi.org/10.2139/ssrn.3893595.
    This analysis of British younger generations' opinions also finds a relatively thin foundation of understanding. For instance: "Just under half correctly pick the definition of socialism, but one in three mistake the definition of capitalism for the definition of socialism" (p. 41). Further, "the fact remains that large num-bers of people—often around a quarter of respondents—simultaneously agree with an anti-capitalist and a pro-capitalist statement on the same issue" (p. 67).

14. Jones, Jeffrey. "Socialism, Capitalism Ratings in U.S. Unchanged." *Gallup.Com*, 13 Dec. 2021, news.gallup.com/poll/357755/socialism-capitalism-ratings-unchanged.aspx.

   See also: Newport, Frank. "Deconstructing Americans' Views of Socialism, Capitalism." *Gallup.Com*, 17 Dec. 2021, news.gallup.com/opinion/polling-matters/358178/deconstructing-americans-views-socialism-capitalism.aspx.

   Newport notes that approximately one in five Americans view both socialism and capitalism favorably.

15. Participatory socialism implies the abolition of the old capitalist model via a highly progressive income tax and a tax on inherited wealth, which are used to finance both a basic income and a "capital endowment" for every citizen. See: Piketty, Thomas. *Capital and Ideology*. Unabridged, Harvard University Press and Blackstone Publishing, 2020.

16. "How Japan Is Ushering in a New Form of Capitalism." *World Economic Forum*, 8 Feb. 2022, www.weforum.org/agenda/2022/01/japan-new-form-of-capitalism-revive-economy.

17. "China Vows Further Curbs on 'Disorderly Expansion' by Tech Firms—BNN Bloomberg." *BNN*, 27 Sept. 2021, www.bnnbloomberg.ca/china-vows-further-curbs-on-disorderly-expansion-by-tech-firms-1.1657802#:%7E:text=Since%20its%20first%20public%20use%20by%20the%20Politburo,actions%20against%20technology%20moguls%2C%20celebrities%20and%20private%20tutors.

18. For the original chart and analysis, see: Lakner, Christoph, and Branko Milanović. "Global Income Distribution: From the Fall of the Berlin Wall to the Great Recession." *The World Bank Economic Review*, vol. 30, no. 2, 2015, pp. 203–32. *Crossref*, https://doi.org/10.1093/wber/lhv039.

   For updates to and refinements of the original "Elephant Chart" argument, see: Corlett, Adam. "Examining an elephant." *Resolution Foundation Report*, September 2016. https://www.resolutionfoundation.org/app/uploads/2016/09/Examining-an-elephant.pdf; Kharas, Homi and Brina Seidel. "What's Happening to the World Income Distribution? The Elephant Chart Revisited." *Brookings*, 9 Mar. 2022, www.brookings.edu/research/whats-happening-to-the-world-income-distribution-the-elephant-chart-revisited.

19. On the origins of this adage, known as "Miles' Law" after its creator, see: Miles, Rufus E. "The Origin and Meaning of Miles' Law." *Public Administration Review*, vol. 38, no. 5, 1978, p. 399. *Crossref*, https://doi.org/10.2307/975497.

20. Schumpeter, Joseph Alois. *Business Cycles*. Martino Pub., 2006 reprint.

21. Milanović, Branko. *Capitalism, Alone: The Future of the System That Rules the World*. Reprint, Belknap Press: An Imprint of Harvard University Press, 2021.

   Private firms produce about two-thirds of China's output. Between 1978 and 2011, the growth of the private sector accounted for virtually all of the growth in urban employment. Moreover, more than 90% of workers are either hired or self-employed (mostly as farmers in the countryside) and employment in state-owned or state-controlled companies has declined significantly since the late 1990s. In his 2019 Government Work Report before the National People's Congress, Premier Li Keqiang stated the principle that all firms—whether private sector or state-owned and controlled—should be treated equally.

See Tianlei Huang and Nicholas Lardy, "Bias against private sector slows China's recovery from COVID-19", Peterson Institute for International Economics, 20 April 2020, https://www.piie.com/blogs/china-economic-watch/bias-against-private-sector-slows-chinas-recovery-covid-19; and Nicholas Lardy, "The Changing Role of the Private Sector in China", Royal Bank of Australia, Conference Volume 2020

22. Lardy, Nicholas. *The State Strikes Back: The End of Economic Reform in China?* Peterson Institute for International Economics, 2019.

23. Schumpeter, 2006.

24. This definition synthesizes the perspectives in Appleby, Joyce. *The Relentless Revolution: A History of Capitalism* (Norton Paperback). Reprint, W. W. Norton and Company, 2011. Chandler, Alfred, Jr. *Scale and Scope: The Dynamics of Industrial Capitalism*. Harvard University Press, 1991; Kocka, Jürgen and Marcel Van Der Linden. *Capitalism: The Reemergence of a Historical Concept*. Reprint, Bloomsbury Academic, 2018; McCraw, Thomas. ed. *Creating Modern Capitalism: How Entrepreneurs, Companies, and Countries Triumphed in Three Industrial Revolutions*. First Edition (US) First Printing, Harvard University Press, 1998.

25. McCraw, Thomas. *Creating Modern Capitalism: How Entrepreneurs, Companies, and Countries Triumphed in Three Industrial Revolutions*. First Edition (U.S.) First Printing, Harvard University Press, 1998.

26. On this point, see: Appleby, 2011.

27. Hall, Peter, and David Soskice. *Varieties of Capitalism*. Oxford University Press, 2001.

There are several other ways to classify the different capitalist models. See, for instance: Esping-Andersen , Gøsta. *The Three Worlds of Welfare Capitalism*. Princeton University Press, 1990.

See also; Albert, Michel. *Capitalisme Contre Capitalisme*. SEUIL, 1991.

28. Schmidt, Vivien A. "Putting the Political Back into Political Economy by Bringing the State Back in Yet Again." *World Politics*, vol. 61, no. 3, 2009, pp. 516–46. *Crossref*, https://doi.org/10.1017/s0043887109000173.

29. Buzan, Barry and George Lawson. "Capitalism and the Emergent World Order." *International Affairs*, vol. 90, no. 1, 2014, pp. 71–91. *Crossref*, https://doi.org/10.1111/1468-2346.12096.

30. Philippon, Thomas. *The Great Reversal*. Harvard University Press, 2019.

31. Goodin, Robert E, Bruce Headley, Ruud Muffels, and Henk-Jan Dirven *The Real Worlds of Welfare Capitalism*. Cambridge University Press, 2009.

32. Levitsky, Steven, and Lucan Way. "The Rise of Competitive Authoritarianism." *Journal of Democracy*, vol. 13, no. 2, 2002, pp. 51–65. *Crossref*, https://doi.org/10.1353/jod.2002.0026.

33. Iversen, Torbin. "Democracy and Capitalism". In: Wittman D, Weingast B Oxford Handbook of Political Economy. Oxford; New York: Oxford University Press; 2006. pp. 601–623.

34. According to the Polity IV database, the number of democracies jumped from around 40 in 1990 to slightly more than 80 now. "Democracies" are countries that receive a score of 7 or higher in the Polity's democracy indicator (which takes values between 0 and 10), while "non-democracies" are countries with a score below 7. See, "INSCR Data Page." *Center for Systemic Peace*, www.system-icpeace.org/inscrdata.html. Accessed 14 Apr. 2022.

    For more details, see: Mukand, Sharun W., and Dani Rodrik. "The Political Economy of Liberal Democracy." *The Economic Journal*, vol. 130, no. 627, 2020, pp. 765–92. *Crossref*, https://doi.org/10.1093/ej/ueaa004.

    For the concept of illiberal democracy, see: Zakaria, Fareed. "The Rise of Illiberal Democracy." *Foreign Affairs*, 01 Nov. 1997, www.foreignaffairs.com/articles/1997–11–01/rise-illiberal-democracy.

35. This historical synthesis draws upon Acemoglu, Daron, and James Robinson. *Why Nations Fail: The Origins of Power, Prosperity, and Poverty*. Macmillan Publishers, 2012.

    Allen, Robert C. *The Industrial Revolution: A Very Short Introduction (Very Short Introductions)*. 1st ed., Oxford University Press, 2017.

    Allen, Robert C. *Global Economic History: A Very Short Introduction*. Oxford University Press, 2011.

    Appleby, 2011.

    Beckert, Sven. *Empire of Cotton: A New History of Global Capitalism*. 1 ed., Penguin, 2015.

    Chandler, Alfred, Jr. *Scale and Scope: The Dynamics of Industrial Capitalism*. Harvard University Press, 1991.

    Frieden, Jeffry. *Global Capitalism*. Reissue, W. W. Norton and Company, 2020.

    Gordon, Robert. *The Rise and Fall of American Growth*. Princeton University Press, 2016.

    Greenspan, Alan and Adrian Wooldrige. Capitalism in America: A History. Penguin Press, 2018.

    Kocka, Jürgen. *Capitalism: A Short History*. Princeton University Press, 2016.

    Kocka, Jürgen, and Marcel Van Der Linden. *Capitalism: The Reemergence of a Historical Concept*. Reprint, Bloomsbury Academic, 2018.

    Levy, Jonathan. *Ages of American Capitalism: A History of the United States*. Random House, 2021.

    McCraw, Thomas, ed. *Creating Modern Capitalism: How Entrepreneurs, Companies, and Countries Triumphed in Three Industrial Revolutions*. First Edition (US) First Printing, Harvard University Press, 1998.

36. Appleby, Joyce, 2011.

37. Charles Tilly, "Reflections on the History of European State Making," in Charles

Tilly, ed., *The Formation of National States in Western Europe*, Princeton: Princeton University Press, 1975, p. 42.

38. Cipolla, Carlo. *Guns, Sails and Empires: Technological Innovation and European Expansion 1400–1700*. Barnes Noble Books, 1996.

39. Schama, Simon. *The Embarrassment of Riches: An Interpretation of Dutch Culture in the Golden Age*. Vintage, 1997.

40. Fraser, Nancy, and Rahel Jaeggi. *Capitalism*. Wiley, 2018.

41. The use of "Industrial Revolutions" plural is deliberate. There have been three major industrial revolutions and we are entering the fourth now. The First Industrial Revolution ran from the 1760s to the 1840s; the Second Industrial Revolution from the 1840s to the 1950s; and the Third Industrial Revolution from the 1950s to the 2000s. McCraw, ed. *Creating Modern Capitalism*. For a slightly different delineation of these revolutions, see Schwab, Klaus. *The Fourth Industrial Revolution*. Penguin, 2013.

42. Rosenthal, Caitlin. "Big Data in the Age of the Telegraph." *McKinsey & Company*, 1 Mar. 2021, www.mckinsey.com/business-functions/people-and-organizational-performance/our-insights/big-data-in-the-age-of-the-telegraph.

43. Samuel Bowles and Wendy Carlin. "Rethinking Economics—IMF F&D." *Finance and Development*, Mar. 2021, www.imf.org/external/pubs/ft/fandd/2021/03/rethinking-economics-by-samuel-bowles-and-wendy-carlin.htm.

44. For a sense of the management transformations of this era, see Alfred P. Sloan, Jr. *My Years with General Motors*. Currency, reissue edition, 1990.

45. Friedman, Milton. "A Friedman Doctrine—The Social Responsibility Of Business Is to Increase Its Profits." *The New York Times*, 13 Sept. 1970, www.nytimes.com/1970/09/13/archives/a-friedman-doctrine-the-social-responsibility-of-business-is-to.html.

46. Jensen, Michael C., and William H. Meckling. "Theory of the Firm: Managerial Behavior, Agency Costs and Ownership Structure." *Journal of Financial Economics*, vol. 3, no. 4, 1976, pp. 305–60. *Crossref*, https://doi.org/10.1016/0304-405x(76)90026-x.

47. Martin, Roger L. "The Age of Customer Capitalism." *Harvard Business Review*, Jan-Feb 2010, hbr.org/2010/01/the-age-of-customer-capitalism.

48. Ibid.

49. Fraser, Nancy, and Rahel Jaeggi. *Capitalism*. Wiley, 2018.

50. Business Round Table, "Business Roundtable Redefines the Purpose of a Corporation to Promote 'An Economy That Serves All Americans'", Press release, 19 August 2019, https://www.businessroundtable.org/business-roundtable-redefines-the-purpose-of-a-corporation-to-promote-an-economy-that-serves-all-americans; World Economic Forum, "Measuring Stakeholder Capitalism Towards Common Metrics and Consistent Reporting of Sustainable Value Creation", White Paper, September 2020

51. Schumpeter, 2006.

52. Thompson, E. P. "Time, Work-Discipline, And Industrial Capitalism." *Past and*

Present, vol. 38, no. 1, 1967, pp. 56–97. *Crossref*, https://doi.org/10.1093/past/38.1.56.

53. Weber, Max. *The Protestant Ethic and the Spirit of Capitalism (Norton Critical Editions)*. First, W. W. Norton and Company, 2008.

54. Keynes' full quote from the conclusion of his *General Theory of Employment, Interest, and Money* (1936): "The ideas of economists and political philosophers, both when they are right and when they are wrong are more powerful than is commonly understood. Indeed, the world is ruled by little else. Practical men, who believe themselves to be quite exempt from any intellectual influences, are usually slaves of some defunct economist. Madmen in authority, who hear voices in the air, are distilling their frenzy from some academic scribbler of a few years back."

55. This is the fundamental point of the comparative approach by Chandler and McCraw that emerged from Harvard Business School historians.

56. Kocka, 2016.

57. "How Will You Measure Your Life? Clay Christensen at TEDxBoston." *YouTube*, uploaded by Clay Christensen, 17 July 2012, www.youtube.com/watch?v=tvos4nORf_Y.

58. The literature on organizational change is vast. This perspective draws upon Keller, Scott, and Bill Schaninger. *Beyond Performance 2.0: A Proven Approach to Leading Large-Scale Change*. 2nd ed., Wiley, 2019. Heath, Chip, and Dan Heath. *Made to Stick: Why Some Ideas Survive and Others Die*. 1st ed., Random House, 2007. Heat, Chip, and Dan Heath. *Switch: How to Change Things When Change Is Hard*. 1st ed., Crown Business, 2010. Kotter, John. *Leading Change, With a New Preface by the Author*. 1R ed., Harvard Business Review Press, 2012.

2. GETTING TO NET ZERO

1. "Climate Change and Health." *World Health Organization*, 30 Oct. 2021, www.who.int/news-room/fact-sheets/detail/climate-change-and-health.

2. "Climate Change Indicators: Greenhouse Gases." *US EPA*, www.epa.gov/climate-indicators/greenhouse-gases. Accessed 16 Apr. 2022.

3. "Causes of Climate Change." *European Commission Climate Action*, ec.europa.eu/clima/climate-change/causes-climate-change_en. Accessed 16 Apr. 2022.

4. Evans, Simon. "Analysis: Which Countries Are Historically Responsible for Climate Change?" *Carbon Brief*, 05 Oct. 2021, www.carbonbrief.org/analysis-which-countries-are-historically-responsible-for-climate-change.

5. Ibid.

6. Ibid.

7. Delmotte, V., et al. "IPCC, 2018: Summary for Policymakers." In: *Global Warming of 1.5°C. An IPCC Special Report on the impacts of global warming of 1.5°C above pre-industrial levels and related global greenhouse gas emission pathways, in the context of strengthening the global response to the threat of climate change, sustainable development, and efforts to eradicate poverty*. World Meteorological Organization, 2018.

8. "Consistent Multidecadal Variability in Global Temperature Reconstructions and Simulations over the Common Era." *Nature Geoscience*, vol. 12, no. 8, 2019, pp. 643–49. *Crossref*, https://doi.org/10.1038/s41561-019-0400-0.

9. Ibid.

10. Gibbens, Sarah. "2021's Weather Disasters Brought Home the Reality of Climate Change." *Environment*, 6 Dec. 2021, www.nationalgeographic.com/environment/article/this-year-extreme-weather-brought-home-reality-of-climate-change.

11. "Climate Change 2022: Impacts, Adaptation and Vulnerability." *IPCC*, www.ipcc.ch/report/ar6/wg2. Accessed 16 Apr. 2022.

12. Ibid.

13. International Federation of Red Cross and Red Crescent Societies, *Global Report on Internal Displacement 2021*, Geneva, p. 78.

14. Brunetti, Celso, et al. "Climate Change and Financial Stability." *FEDS Notes*, vol. 2021, no. 2877, 2021. *Crossref*, https://doi.org/10.17016/2380–7172.2893.

15. McKinsey Global Institute, *Climate risk and response: Physical hazards and socioeconomic impacts.*, January 2020, p. viii. https://www.mckinsey.com/business-functions/sustainability/our-insights/climate-risk-and-response-physical-hazards-and-socioeconomic-impacts.

16. IPCC (2022).

17. Ibid.

18. "Citizen Support for Climate Action." *Climate Action*, ec.europa.eu/clima/citizens/citizen-support-climate-action_en.

19. "2019–2020 EIB Climate Survey (1/3)." *EIB.Org*, www.eib.org/en/surveys/2nd-climate-survey/climate-change-impact.htm.

20. Funk, Cary, and Brian Kennedy. "How Americans See Climate Change and the Environment in 7 Charts." *Pew Research Center*, 21 Apr. 2020, www.pewresearch.org/fact-tank/2020/04/21/how-americans-see-climate-change-and-the-environment-in-7-charts.

   Paulson, Henry, Jr, and Erskine Bowles. "Biden Should Embrace a Carbon Tax." *Washington Post*, 10 May 2021, www.washingtonpost.com/opinions/paulson-bowles-biden-carbon-tax/2021/05/10/2230cda4-af62–11eb-b476-c3b287e52a01_story.html.

21. For a detailed account, see: Moosmann, L., et al. "The COP26 Climate Change Conference, Status of climate negotiations and issues at stake." Study for the committee on the Environment, Public Health and Food Safety, Policy Department for Economic, Scientific and Quality of Life Policies, European Parliament, 2021.

22. Primary energy is a measure that includes electricity and other types of energy used in industry, transportation, farming, and so on. See *Statistical Review of World Energy*. BP, 2021.

23. Strasburg, Jenny, and Phred Dvorak. "Ukraine War Drives Countries to Embrace Renewable Energy—but Not Yet." *WSJ*, 4 Apr. 2022, www.wsj.com/

articles/oil-gas-russia-renewable-energy-solar-wind-power-europe-11649086062.

24. Grist. "Oil's Biggest Lobbying Group Killed Carbon Prices. Now It Supports Them?" *Grist*, 05 Mar. 2021, grist.org/energy/oils-biggest-lobbying-group-killed-carbon-pricing-now-it-supports-them.

25. Grippa, Pierpaolo, and Dimitri Demekas. "Financial Regulation, Climate Change, and the Transition to a Low-Carbon Economy: A Survey of the Issues." *IMF Working Papers*, vol. 2021, no. 296, 2021, p. 1. *Crossref*, https://doi.org/10.5089/9781616356521.001.

26. Our World In Data, "Why Did Renewable Become So Cheap So Fast?," retrieved 13 April, 2022. https://ourworldindata.org/cheap-renewables-growth

27. Fehrenbacher, Katie. "BMW, Ford, Other Automakers Rev up Carbon Commitments | Greenbiz." *GreenBiz*, 29 July 2022, www.greenbiz.com/article/bmw-ford-other-automakers-rev-carbon-commitments.

28. "Technology and Innovation for the Future of Production." *World Economic Forum*, www.weforum.org/projects/global_lighthouse_network. Accessed 16 Apr. 2022.

29. Schwab, Klaus. *The Fourth Industrial Revolution*. Penguin, 2013.

30. Updates on the GLN and the program's periodic white papers can be found at "Technology and Innovation for the Future of Production." *World Economic Forum*, www.weforum.org/projects/global_lighthouse_network. Accessed 16 Apr. 2022.

31. World Economic Forum, *The Global Network Playbook for Responsible Industry Transformation*. White Paper, March 2022. https://www3.weforum.org/docs/WEF_The_Global_Lighthouse_Network_Playbook_for_Responsible_Industry_Transformation_2022.pdf

32. Ibid.

33. Ibid for details about the Western Digital Penang facility.

34. "Glasgow's 2030 credibility gap: net zero's lip service to climate action Wave of net zero emission goals not matched by action on the ground." Climate Action Tracker, 9 Nov. 2021, https://climateactiontracker.org/documents/997/CAT_2021-11-09_Briefing_Global-Update_Glasgow2030CredibilityGap.pdf.

35. "Net Zero by 2050." *IEA*, May 2021, www.iea.org/reports/net-zero-by-2050.

36. Ibid.

37. Bloomberg estimates that, to accommodate the energy transition, investments in infrastructure will need to rise to between $3.1 trillion and $5.8 trillion annually on average until 2050, up from about $1.7 trillion in 2020. The final bill could be about eight times U.S. GDP in 2019. See: Mathis, Will. "Greening Energy to Fight Climate Threat May Cost $92 Trillion." *Bloomberg*, 22 Feb. 2021, www.bloomberg.com/news/articles/2021-07-21/greening-energy-to-fight-climate-threat-may-cost-92-trillion.

38. McKinsey estimates global annual investments for the green transition in the tune of $9.2 trillion until 2050. See McKinsey Global Institute, *The Net-Zero Transition: What It Would Cost, What It Could Bring*, 22 May 2022, www.mckin-

sey.com/business-functions/sustainability/our-insights/the-net-zero-transition-what-it-would-cost-what-it-could-bring.

39. Stern, David I. "The Rise and Fall of the Environmental Kuznets Curve." *World Development*, vol. 32, no. 8, 2004, pp. 1419–39. *Crossref*, https://doi.org/10.1016/j.worlddev.2004.03.004.

40. Schmidt, John R. "Why Europe Leads on Climate Change." *Survival*, vol. 50, no. 4, 2008, pp. 83–96. *Crossref*, https://doi.org/10.1080/00396330802328990.

41. PTI. "China Defends Joining with India on Coal 'phase down' Instead of 'Phase out' at COP26." *The Economic Times*, 15 Nov. 2021, economictimes.indiatimes.com/news/international/world-news/china-defends-joining-with-india-on-coal-phase-down-instead-of-phase-out-at-%20%20%20cop26/articleshow/87717616.cms?utm_source=contentofinterest&utm_medium=ext&utm_campaign=cppst.

42. McKinsey Global Institute (2022).

43. Ibid.

44. "The Inequalities-Environment Nexus." *OECD Green Growth Papers*, 2021. *Crossref*, https://doi.org/10.1787/ca9d8479-en.

45. Krishnan, Mekala, et al. "The Economic Transformation: What Would Change in the Net-Zero Transition." *McKinsey & Company*, 25 Jan. 2022, www.mckinsey.com/business-functions/sustainability/our-insights/the-economic-transformation-what-would-change-in-the-net-zero-transition.

46. Stern, Nicholas. "The Economics of Climate Change." *American Economic Review*, vol. 98, no. 2, 2008, pp. 1–37. *Crossref*, https://doi.org/10.1257/aer.98.2.1.

47. "Breaking the Tragedy of the Horizon—Climate Change and Financial Stability—Speech by Mark Carney." *Bank of England*, 29 Sept. 2015, www.bankofengland.co.uk/speech/2015/breaking-the-tragedy-of-the-horizon-climate-change-and-financial-stability.

48. "The Knowledge Project with Shane Parrish." Podcast episode 132, 08 Mar. 2022, https://www.listennotes.com/podcasts/the-knowledge/132-ret-gen-stanley-FesMNKdWQEf/.

49. Stern, Nicholas, and Joseph Stiglitz. "The Economics of Immense Risk, Urgent Action and Radical Change: Towards New Approaches to the Economics of Climate Change." *NBER Working Paper*, 2021. *Crossref*, https://doi.org/10.3386/w28472.

50. Market failures do not necessarily imply a failure of the market system, no matter how pervasive they are. Even when the role of the government is minimal, markets are designed through a set of formal and informal rules that define the incentives of economic agents and determine their conduct. When market failures arise, the problem is not the market per se but how its regulatory and normative frame is constructed. It is wrong to believe that the profit motive drives the private sector to spew carbon into the air with reckless abandon. If a negative externality like pollution is perfectly internalized through an appropriate pricing mechanism, then there would no longer be any failure in the form of

excessive pollution. Equally, if the research activities to invent environmentally friendly technologies are properly subsidized by the government to maximize all the possible knowledge spillovers that could spring out of it, then there would not be any failure in the form of underinvestment. In other words, when the market fully aligns the incentives of its participants in the most efficient way, it can achieve the same result of a central planner who cares about the quality of the environment—but without the kind of coercion that would be necessary to achieve that result.

51. Gillingham, Kenneth, and James H. Stock. "The Cost of Reducing Greenhouse Gas Emissions." *Journal of Economic Perspectives*, vol. 32, no. 4, 2018, pp. 53–72. *Crossref*, https://doi.org/10.1257/jep. 32.4.53.

   See also: Jaffe, Adam B., et al. "A Tale of Two Market Failures: Technology and Environmental Policy." *Ecological Economics*, vol. 54, no. 2–3, 2005, pp. 164–74. *Crossref*, https://doi.org/10.1016/j.ecolecon.2004.12.027.

52. This might be due to informational market failures that stem primarily from the absence of a clear, consistent, and transparent globally agreed taxonomy accompanied by disclosure requirements. Several companies across the globe may misrepresent their green credentials to deceive investors and consumers for economic gain or public favor. "When Markets Fail—the Need for Collective Action in Tackling Climate Change." *Speech by Isabel Schnabel, Member of the Executive Board of the ECB, at the European Sustainable Finance Summit, Frankfurt Am Main*, 28 Sept. 2020, www.ecb.europa.eu/press/key/date/2020/html/ecb. sp200928_1%7E268b0b672f.en.html.

53. Steele, Paul. "Why Adaptation Is the Greatest Market Failure and What This Means For." *World Resources Institute*, www.wri.org/our-work/project/world-resources-report/why-adaptation-greatest-market-failure-and-what-means-state. Accessed 16 Apr. 2022.

54. Lovins, Hunter, and Boyd Cohen. *Climate Capitalism: Capitalism in the Age of Climate Change*. First Edition, Hill and Wang, 2011.

55. Climate Leadership Council. "Economists' Statement." *Climate Leadership Council*, clcouncil.org/economists-statement. Accessed 16 Apr. 2022.

56. *Report of the High-Level Commission on Carbon Prices*. Carbon Pricing Leadership Coalition, 2017.

57. *A Path to Zero*, Christopher Bertram, Ottomar Edenhofer, and Gunnar Lederer, IMF, September 2021 https://www.imf.org/Publications/fandd/issues/2021/09/how-to-reach-net-zero-emissions-bertram

58. See Figures 4 and 8 in OECD (2021), *Carbon Pricing in Times of COVID-19: What Has Changed in G20 Economies?*, OECD, Paris, https://www.oecd.org/tax/tax-policy/carbon-pricing-in-times-ofcovid-19-what-has-changed-in-g20-economies.htm. See also Preana Bhat, "Carbon needs to cost at least $100/tonne now to reach net zero by 2050", Reuters, October 25, 2021. https://www.reuters.com/business/cop/carbon-needs-cost-least-100tonne-now-reach-net-zero-by-2050-2021-10-25/#:~:text=The%20International%20Monetary%20Fund%20has,the%20world%20polled%20from%20Sept

59. Boffo, R., and R. Patalano. "ESG Investing: Practices, Progress and Challenges," OECD, 2020.

60. Porter, Michael E., and Claas Van Der Linde. "Toward a New Conception of the Environment-Competitiveness Relationship." *Journal of Economic Perspectives*, vol. 9, no. 4, 1995, pp. 97–118. *Crossref*, https://doi.org/10.1257/jep. 9.4.97.

61. Whelan, Tensie, and Carly Fink. "The Comprehensive Business Case for Sustainability." *Harvard Business Review*, 21 Oct. 2016, hbr.org/2016/10/the-comprehensive-business-case-for-sustainability.

62. McGuire, Martin C. "Regulation, Factor Rewards, and International Trade." *Journal of Public Economics*, vol. 17, no. 3, 1982, pp. 335–54. *Crossref*, https://doi.org/10.1016/0047–2727(82)90069-x.

    See also: Dechezleprêtre, Antoine, and Misato Sato. *Green policies and firms' competitiveness*, OECD Issue Paper, 2018.

63. See, for example, the range of Asia Pacific expert perspectives of the CBAM ranging from "protectionist" to of limited impact, in: "Perception of the Planned EU Carbon Border Adjustment Mechanism in Asia Pacific." *Regional Programme Energy Security and Climate Change in Asia and the Pacific*, 10 Mar. 2021, www.kas.de/en/web/recap/single-title/-/content/perception-of-the-planned-eu-carbon-border-adjustment-mechanism-in-asia-pacific-an-expert-survey.

64. Bordoff, Jason, and Meghan O'Sullivan. "Green Upheaval: The New Geopolitics of Energy." *Foreign Affairs*, 30 Nov. 2021, www.foreignaffairs.com/articles/world/2021–11–30/geopolitics-energy-green-upheaval.

65. Ibid.

66. Jedediah Purdy, "The Politics of Nature: Climate Change, Environmental Law, and Democracy." *Yale Law Journal*, vol. 119, no. 6, 2010, pp. 1122–361, www.yalelawjournal.org/article/the-politics-of-nature-climate-change-environmental-law-and-democracy.

67. Gilley, Bruce. "Authoritarian Environmentalism and China's Response to Climate Change." *Environmental Politics*, vol. 21, no. 2, 2012, pp. 287–307. *Crossref*, https://doi.org/10.1080/09644016.2012.651904.

68. Li, Yifei, and Judith Shapiro. *China Goes Green: Coercive Environmentalism for a Troubled Planet*. 1st ed., Polity, 2020.

69. Malcomson, Scott. "How China Became the World's Leader in Green Energy: And What Decoupling Could Cost the Environment." *Foreign Affairs*, 28 Feb. 2020, www.foreignaffairs.com/articles/china/2020–02–28/how-china-became-worlds-leader-green-energy.

70. Barbara A. Finamore, "China's Quest for Global Clean Energy Leadership," *IAI Papers*, 29 Jan. 2020. https://www.iai.it/sites/default/files/iaip2005.pdf

71. Coulton, Marisa. "Canada's Carbon Pricing System Is a Model for the World." *Foreign Policy*, 29 Nov. 2021, foreignpolicy.com/2021/11/29/canada-carbon-pricing-club-theory-climate-imf. See also: Ian Parry, "Four Charts on Canada's Carbon Pollution Pricing System." *IMF*, 18 Mar. 2021, www.imf.org/en/News/Articles/2021/03/17/na031821-four-charts-on-canadas-carbon-pollution-pricing-system.

72. A carbon tax is a charge on the carbon content of fossil fuels, whereas an emission trading system allows firms to acquire allowances to cover their emissions subject to a cap on total allowances.

73. Group of Thirty. *Mainstreaming the Transition to a Net-Zero Economy*, Working Group on Climate Change and Finance, 2020.

74. Jones, Liam. "$500bn Green Issuance 2021: Social and Sustainable Acceleration: Annual Green $1tn in Sight: Market Expansion Forecasts for 2022 and 2025." *Climate Bonds Initiative*, 31 Jan. 2022, www.climatebonds.net/2022/01/500bn-green-issuance-2021-social-and-sustainable-acceleration-annual-green-1tn-sight-market.

75. Group of Thirty, 2020.

76. Chenet, Hugues, et al. "Finance, Climate-Change and Radical Uncertainty: Towards a Precautionary Approach to Financial Policy." *Ecological Economics*, vol. 183, 2021, p. 106957. *Crossref*, https://doi.org/10.1016/j.ecolecon.2021.106957.

77. Atalla, George, et al, "Six Ways That Governments Can Drive the Green Transition", *EY Denmark*, 6 Dec. 2021, www.ey.com/en_dk/government-public-sector/six-ways-that-governments-can-drive-the-green-transition.

78. European Commission, "Sustainable Europe Investment Plan European Green Deal Investment Plan", Communication to the European Parliament, the Council, the European Parliament, and Social Committee and the Committee of the Regions, 14 January 2020.

79. Zhang, Coco, and James Knightley. "Biden's Billions—a Sustainable Shift?" *ING Think*, 19 Nov. 2021, think.ing.com/articles/bidens-billions-a-sustainable-shift.

80. "Global Recovery Observatory", *Oxford University Economic Recovery Project*, recovery.smithschool.ox.ac.uk/tracking. Accessed 16 Apr. 2022.

81. Madan, Şebnem Erol, "How Can Developing Countries Get to Net Zero in a Financeable and Affordable Way?" *World Bank Blogs*, 9 Feb. 2022, blogs.worldbank.org/ppps/how-can-developing-countries-get-net-zero-financeable-and-affordable-way.

82. See IEA (2021) for a thorough discussion.

83. Hellstern, Tom, et al. "Innovating to Net Zero: An Executive's Guide to Climate Technology." *McKinsey & Company*, 28 Oct. 2021, www.mckinsey.com/business-functions/sustainability/our-insights/innovating-to-net-zero-an-executives-guide-to-climate-technology.

84. Ibid.

85. "Home", *EIT HEI Initiative*, eit-hei.eu. Accessed 16 Apr. 2022.

86. "Strengthening International Cooperation on Climate Change Research", *Climate-ADAPT*, climate-adapt.eea.europa.eu/metadata/projects/strengthening-international-cooperation-on-climate-change-research. Accessed 16 Apr. 2022.

87. Hellstern, 2021.

88. Poon, Linda, et al. "Cities Are Our Best Hope for Surviving Climate Change",

Bloomberg, 21 Apr. 2021, https://www.bloomberg.com/graphics/2021-cities-climate-solutions/.

89. *The State of Cities Climate Finance: Part 2. The Enabling Conditions for Mobilizing Urban Climate Finance.* World Bank, 2021, https://openknowledge.worldbank.org/handle/10986/35929.

    See also: *The State of City Climate Finance 2015*, Cities Climate Finance Leadership Alliance (CCFLA), 2015, https://www.ccacoalition.org/en/resources/state-city-climate-finance-2015.

90. "Urban Sustainability in Europe—Opportunities for Challenging Times." *European Environment Agency*, 14 June 2021, www.eea.europa.eu/publications/urban-sustainability-in-europe. Bulkeley, Harriet, "Managing Environmental and Energy Transitions in Cities: State of the Art & Emerging Perspectives," Background paper for an OECD/EC Workshop on 7 June 2019, https://www.oecd.org/cfe/regionaldevelopment/Bulkeley-2019-Managing-Transition-Cities.pdf

91. Singapore Ministry of National Development, "Singapore Green Plan 2030 Charts Ambitious Targets for Next 10 Years to Catalyse National Sustainability Movement", Press Release, 10 February 2021, https://www.mnd.gov.sg/newsroom/press-releases/view/singapore-green-plan-2030-charts-ambitious-targets-for-next-10-years-to-catalyse-national-sustainability-movement-1

92. See "Singapore Green Plan 2030: Key Targets" https://www.greenplan.gov.sg/key-focus-areas/key-targets#resilient-future

93. Asit Biswas, "How Singapore's water management has become a global model for how to tackle climate crisis", *The Conversation*, 24 November 2021, https://theconversation.com/how-singapores-water-management-has-become-a-global-model-for-how-to-tackle-climate-crisis-162117

94. Pharmaceutical Technology, "How Singapore is positioning itself at the forefront of aquaculture innovation," March 22, 2022, https://www.pharmaceutical-technology.com/sponsored/how-singapore-is-positioning-itself-at-the-forefront-of-aquaculture-innovation/

95. Singapore Land Transport Authority, "Singapore Honoured at Inaugural C40 & Siemens City Climate Leadership Awards for Efforts in Tackling Traffic Congestion", Press Release, 5 September 2013, https://www.lta.gov.sg/content/ltagov/en/newsroom/2013/9/2/singapore-honoured-at-inaugural-c40-siemens-city-climate-leadership-awards-for-efforts-in-tackling-traffic-congestion.html

96. The Asean Post Team, "Smart Nation: Singapore's Intelligent Transport System", *The Asean Post*, 13 April 2018, https://theaseanpost.com/article/smart-nation-singapores-intelligent-transport-system-its

97. McKinsey Global Institute (2022).

98. Schulz, Thomas. "How can we accelerate decarbonization methods in the mining and cement industry?", *World Economic Forum*, 23 Aug. 2021, www.weforum.org/agenda/2021/08/the-green-transition-needs-minerals-and-cement.

Hundertmark, Thomas, et al. "Green Growth Avenues in the Cement Ecosystem." *McKinsey & Company*, 16 Dec. 2021, www.mckinsey.com/industries/chemicals/our-insights/green-growth-avenues-in-the-cement-ecosystem.

99. For details on different industries' potential transition challenges, see McKinsey, 2022.

100. "'Bring the Problem Forward': Larry Fink on Climate Risk." *McKinsey & Company*, 21 Apr. 2020, www.mckinsey.com/business-functions/sustainability/our-insights/bring-the-problem-forward-larry-fink-on-climate-risk.

101. Lovins, 2011.

102. On this point, see Group of Thirty, 2020.

103. Leavitt, Mike, and Rich McKeown. *Finding Allies, Building Alliances: 8 Elements that Bring—and Keep—People Together*. Jossey-Boss, 2013.

104. For examples of the diversity of transition challenges, depending on industry and a country's economic structure, see: McKinsey, 2022.

105. For details on different industries' potential transition challenges, see McKinsey, 2022.

106. For an analysis of potential job disruptions, see McKinsey, 2022.

107. Allan, Bentley, et al. "Green Industrial Policy and the Global Transformation of Climate Politics." *Global Environmental Politics*, vol. 21, no. 4, 2021, pp. 1–19. *Crossref*, https://doi.org/10.1162/glep_a_00640.

108. Pradeep K. Khosla and Paul T. Beaton, Editors, *As Assessment of ARPA-E*. National Academies Press, 2017.

109. World Bank Group, "Technology Transfer and Innovation for Low-Carbon Development", 2020. https://openknowledge.worldbank.org/bitstream/handle/10986/33474/9781464815003.pdf?sequence=2&isAllowed=y

110. "Institute of International Finance." *Task Force on Scaling Voluntary Carbon Markets*, www.iif.com/tsvcm. Accessed 16 Apr. 2022.
      See also: Blaufelder, Christopher, et al. "A Blueprint for Scaling Voluntary Carbon Markets to Meet the Climate Challenge." *McKinsey & Company*, 29 Jan. 2021, www.mckinsey.com/business-functions/sustainability/our-insights/a-blueprint-for-scaling-voluntary-carbon-markets-to-meet-the-climate-challenge.

111. "A Transition in Thinking and Action—Speech by Mark Carney." *Bank of England*, 6 Apr. 2018, www.bankofengland.co.uk/speech/2018/mark-carney-speech-at-international-climate-risk-conference-for-supervisors.

112. O'Connor, Philippa, et al. "Linking executive pay to ESG goals", PWC Brief, June 2021, https://www.pwc.com/gx/en/issues/reinventing-the-future/take-on-tomorrow/download/Linking-exec-pay-ESG.pdf

113. UL operates today in over 45 countries and focuses on certifying product safety, sustainability, and security. *Underwriters Laboratories*, ul.org/about# history. Accessed 16 Apr. 2022.

114. Nordhaus, William D. "Climate Change: The Ultimate Challenge for

Economics." *Nobel Prize Lecture*, 8 Dec. 2018, www.nobelprize.org/prizes/economic-sciences/2018/nordhaus/lecture. Williams Nordhaus first proposed the idea of a "Carbon Club."

See also Nordhaus, William. "Climate Clubs: Overcoming Free-Riding in International Climate Policy." *American Economic Review*, vol. 105, no. 4, 2015, pp. 1339–70. *Crossref*, https://doi.org/10.1257/aer.15000001.

———. "The Climate Club: How to Fix a Failing Global Effort." *Foreign Affairs*, 10 Apr. 2020, www.foreignaffairs.com/articles/united-states/2020-04-10/climate-club.

———. "Why Climate Policy Has Failed: And How Governments Can Do Better." *Foreign Affairs*, 12 Oct. 2021, www.foreignaffairs.com/articles/world/2021-10-12/why-climate-policy-has-failed.

115. For analyses of "carbon clubs," their advantages and challenges, and potential mitigation steps, see: Adams, Bethan, et al. "The Carbon Club Revisited: Harnessing enterprise and trade to decarbonize the global economy," Oxford Smith School of Enterprise and the Environment, Working Paper No 22–01, 02 Feb. 2022.

Cernicky, Jan, et al. "Avoiding a Carbon Trade War: G20 Dialogue and Coordination and the European Carbon Border Adjustment Mechanism (CBAM)." *SSRN Electronic Journal*, 2021. *Crossref*, https://doi.org/10.2139/ssrn.3892398.

Doshi, Tilak. "Will U.S. Join The New Trade Protectionism Of Europe's 'Climate Club?'" *Forbes*, 5 Apr. 2021, www.forbes.com/sites/tilak-doshi/2021/04/05/belong-to-the-climate-club-or-get-penalized-the-eus-new-trade-protectionism/?sh=21e9218c896d.

Parry, Ian, et al. *Proposal for an International Carbon Price Floor Among Large Emitters*. International Monetary Fund, 2021.

"Climate Policy Leadership in an Interconnected World." *OECD*, 2020. *Crossref*, https://doi.org/10.1787/8008e7f4-en.

Tagliapietra, Simone, and Guntram Wolff. "Form a Climate Club: United States, European Union and China." *Nature*, 23 Mar. 2021, www.nature.com/articles/d41586-021-00736-2?error=cookies_not_supported&code=a3b3c6719ccf-47cd-925c-52717fa1a7ed.

Vetter, David. "As The World Heats Up, Could 'Carbon Clubs' Supercharge Climate Action?" *Forbes*, 16 Feb. 2022, www.forbes.com/sites/davidrvetter/2022/02/16/as-the-world-heats-up-could-carbon-clubs-supercharge-climate-action.

116. Adams, 2022.

3. A DIGITAL FUTURE FOR ALL

1. The World Bank, UNESCO and UNICEF (2021), "The State of the Global Education Crisis: A Path to Recovery", Washington D.C., Paris, New York: The

World Bank, UNESCO, and UNICEF, pp. 5 and 20. See also Eric A. Hanushek and Ludger Woessmann, "The Economic Impacts of Learning Losses", OECD, 2020; and Azevedo, João Pedro, Amer Hasan, Diana Goldemberg, Koen Geven, and Syedah Aroob Iqbal. 2021, "Simulating the Potential Impacts of COVID-19 School Closures on Schooling and Learning Outcomes: A Set of Global Estimates." *The World Bank Research Observer*, 36 (1): 1–40. doi:10.1093/wbro/lkab003.

2. Lécuyer, Christophe. *Making Silicon Valley: innovation and the growth of high tech, 1930–1970*. MIT Press, 2006; O'Mara, Margaret. *Cities of Knowledge: Cold War Science and the Search for the Next Silicon Valley*. Princeton University Press, 2015; O'Mara, Margaret. *The Code: Silicon Valley and the Remaking of America*, Penguin, 2019. The literature on clusters is vast. See, for instance, Porter, Michael E. "Clusters and the New Economics of Competition," *Harvard Business Review* (November–December 1998); Mercedes Delgado, Michael E. Porter, and Scott Stern, "Clusters and Entrepreneurship," *Journal of Economic Geography*, Vol. 10 (July 2010), pp. 495–518.

3. Rhett Morris, "The First Trillion-Dollar Startup," *TechCrunch*, 26 July 2014. https://consent.yahoo.com/v2/collectConsent?sessionId=3_cc-session_877b15b5–7de2–4d2e-8da1–4f20ea3322ac

4. For an annual survey of global innovation, including ranking of innovation clusters, see World Intellectual Property Organization, *Global Innovation Index 2021: Tracking Innovation through the COVID-19 Crisis*, Geneva: World Intellectual Property Organization, 2021.

5. On the role of Paul Baran in the early history of the Internet, and access to copies of his original RAND work on packet switching, see "Paul Baran and the Origins of the Internet" (March 22, 2018) available at: https://www.rand.org/about/history/baran.html

6. Robert Solow, "Manufacturing Matters," *New York Times Book Review* (July 12, 1987), p. 36.

7. Haskel, Jonathan, and Stian Westlake, *Capitalism without Capital: the rise of the intangible economy*, Princeton University Press, 2017. See also Brynjolfsson, Erik, Daniel Rock and, "Artificial Intelligence and the Modern Productivity Paradox: A Clash of Expectations and Statistics", in *Economics of Artificial Intelligence*, Agrawal, Gans, and Goldfarb (eds.), 2017; Gordon, Robert J. *The Rise and Fall of American Growth: The U.S. Standard of Living since the Civil War*. Princeton University Press, 2017; McKinsey Global Institute, *Solving the Productivity Puzzle: the Role of Demand and the Promise of Digitization*, 2018. For a summary about the debate: Edoardo Campanella, "The Real Payoff From Artificial Intelligence Is Still a Decade Off", *Foreign Policy*, 9 August 2018, https://foreignpolicy.com/2018/08/09/the-solution-to-the-productivity-puzzle-is-simple-robots-ai/

8. Stephen Roach, "Why is technology not boosting productivity", World Economic Forum, 24 June 2015, https://www.weforum.org/agenda/2015/06/why-is-technology-not-boosting-productivity

9. McKinsey Global Institute, *Digital Globalization: The New Era of Global Flows* (March 2016).

10. WIPO (2021), *World Intellectual Property Indicators 2021*, Geneva: World Intellectual Property Organization.

11. This discussion of the patterns of global digitalization in the 2010s draws upon McKinsey Global Institute, *Digital America: A Tale of Haves and the Have-Mores* (December 2015); McKinsey Global Institute, *Digital Europe: Pushing the Frontier, Capturing the Benefits* (June 2016); McKinsey Global Institute, *Digital China: Powering the Economy to Global Competitiveness* (December 2017); McKinsey Global Institute, *Twenty-five years of digitization: Ten insights into how to play it right* (May 2019). See also Dan Andrews, Chiara Criscuolo and Peter N. Gal (2015), "Frontier firms, technology diffusion and public policy: micro evidence from OECD countries", OECD Working Paper.

12. McKinsey Global Institute, *Digital India: Technology to transform a connected nation*, 27 March 2019.

13. Allen, Nathaniel. "The promises and perils of Africa's digital revolution", Brookings Institute, 11 March 2021, https://www.brookings.edu/techstream/the-promises-and-perils-of-africas-digital-revolution/

14. David Autor, David Dorn, Lawrence F Katz, Christina Patterson, John Van Reenen, "The Fall of the Labor Share and the Rise of Superstar Firms", *The Quarterly Journal of Economics*, Volume 135, Issue 2, May 2020, pp. 645–709.

15. IBM Cloud Education, "Artificial Intelligence," June 3, 2020, https://www.ibm.com/cloud/learn/what-is-artificial-intelligence

16. The development of AI technical performance across a range of activities including vision, language, learning, and advanced problem solving are tracked in the annual *Artificial Intelligence Index* reports produced by the Stanford University Institute for Human-Centered Artifical Intelligence (HAI). See https://hai.stanford.edu/ for the 2020–21 issue.

17. Ibid.

18. Ibid.

19. Marcus Blosch and Jackie Fenn, "Understanding Gartner's Hype Cycle" (August 20, 2018), available at: https://www.gartner.com/en/documents/3887767

20. The latest AI developments can be followed at Stanford University Institute for Human Centered Artificial Intelligence (HAI). See https://hai.stanford.edu/

21. The fourth industrial revolution is defined as the trend toward automation and data exchange in manufacturing technologies and processes which include cyber-physical systems, Internet of Things, cloud computing, cognitive computing and artificial intelligence. See for example, Schwab, Klaus, *The Fourth Industrial Revolution*, London: Portfolio Penguin, 2017; Brynjolffsson, Erik, and Andrew McAfee, *The Second Machine Age: Work, Progress, and Prosperity in a Time of Brilliant Technologies* (New York: Norton, 2016).

22. McKinsey, "Technology Deep Dive: DLT and blockchain", 11 June 2021, https://www.mckinsey.com/~/media/mckinsey/Business%20Functions/McKinsey%20Digital/Our%20Insights/The%20top%20trends%20in%20tech%20final/Tech%20Trends%20slides%2032%2033%2034

23. https://oecd.ai/en/data?selectedArea=ai-research&selectedVisualization=ai-research-by-institution

24. *Artificial Intelligence Index 2022*, pp. 154–155.

25. *Artificial Intelligence Index 2022*, p. 160 for summary. For original survey, see McKinsey & Company, "The State of AI 2021," (December 2021).

26. Viewed through a per capita lens, the AI Vibrancy Rankings highlight that the United States remains a global leader alongside smaller AI innovators often based in city clusters such as Israel (Tel Aviv), Singapore, Switzerland, and Australia.

27. *Artificial Intelligence Index 2022*, p. 161.

28. Galindo, L., K. Perset and F. Sheeka (2021), "An overview of national AI strategies and policies", *Going Digital Toolkit Note*, No. 14, goingdigital.oecd.org/data/notes/No14_ToolkitNote_AIStrategies.pdf

29. The major recommendations included: investing in AI research and development; fostering a digital ecosystem for AI; shaping an enabling policy environment for AI; building human capacity and preparing for labour market transformation; and international co-operation for trustworthy AI. OECD, *Recommendation of the Council on Artificial Intelligence*, OECD/LEGAL/0449, OECD-LEGAL-0449-en-2faedcefa4d54e98bd155d4f2c37b8fb

30. See https://oecd.ai/en/dashboards

31. *Artificial Intelligence Index 2022*, pp. 163–164.

32. Quotation from Amy Bernstein and Anand Raman, "The Great Decoupling: An Interview with Erik Brynjolfsson and Andrew McAfee," *Harvard Business Review*, June 2015.

33. Ye, Jason, "Using digitalization to achieve decarbonization goals", *Climate Innovation 2050*, September 2021.

34. Ibid., p. 2.

35. Espen Mehlum, Dominique Hischier and Mark Caine, "This is how AI will accelerate the energy transition", World Economic Forum, 1 September 2021, https://www.weforum.org/agenda/2021/09/this-is-how-ai-will-accelerate-the-energy-transition.

36. See United Nations' website at https://www.un.org/press/en/2021/dsgsm1579.doc.htm#:~:text=As%20the%20world%20becomes%20more,crisis%20has%20highlighted%20this%20disparity.

37. OECD, *OECD Digital Economy Outlook 2020*, Paris: OECD Publishing, 2020, https://doi.org/10.1787/bb167041-en.

38. For an assessment of 130 economies' digital network readiness, see Durra, Sumitra, and Bruno Lanvin, eds., *The Network Readiness Index: 2021* (Washington, DC: Portulans Institute, 2021).

39. See global comparisons of costs in the "Cost of Connectivity" reports by the Open Technology Institute and the New America Foundation, https://www.newamerica.org/oti/oti-collections/cost-connectivity/.

40. Chao, Becky, and Claire Park, *The Cost of Connectivity 2020*, New America and Open Technology Institute, July 2020, p. 6.

41. Federal Communications Commission, *Broadband Progress Report 2020*, https://www.fcc.gov/reports-research/reports/broadband-progress-reports/2020-broadband-deployment-report and Office for National Statistics, *Internet access—households and individuals, Great Britain: 2019*, 12 August 2019, https://www.ons.gov.uk/peoplepopulationandcommunity/householdcharacteristics/homeinternetandsocialmediausage/bulletins/internetaccesshouseholdsandindividuals/2019

42. OECD (2020), *OECD Digital Economy Outlook 2020*, OECD Publishing, Paris.

43. Kantar, "Internet Adoption in India, ICUBE 2020," June 2021; "India to have 900 million active internet users by 2025, says report," *India Times*, 3 June 2021, https://economictimes.indiatimes.com/tech/technology/india-to-have-900-million-active-internet-users-by-2025-says-report/articleshow/83200683.cms.

44. Ford, Martin. *Rise of the Robots: Technology and the Threat of a Jobless Future*. Basic Books, 2015, Ch. 3. For a broader discussion on the labor market effects of technological progress see: Frey, Carl Benedikt. *The Technology Trap: Capital, Labor, and Power in the Age of Automation*. Princeton University Press, 2019.

45. Brynjolfsson, Eric, and Andrew McAfee, *The Second Machine Age: Work, Progress, and Prosperity in a Time of Brilliant Technologies*. Norton, 2014.

46. Eric Brynjolfsson quotation from Amy Bernstein and Anand Raman, "The Great Decoupling: An Interview with Erik Brynjolfsson and Andrew McAfee," *Harvard Business Review*, June 2015.

47. Loukas Karabarbounis and Brent Neiman, "The Global Decline of the Labor Share," *The Quarterly Journal of Economics* Vol. 129, No. 1 (February 2014), pp. 61–104. See also Michael W. L. Eseby, Bart Hobjin, and Aysegul Sahin, "The Decline of the U.S. Labor Share," *Brookings Papers on Economic Activity* (Fall 2103), pp. 1–52; Mai Chi Dao, Mitali Das, Zsoka Koczan, Weicheng Lian, "Why is Labor Receiving a Smaller Share of Global Income? Theory and Empirical Evidence," *IMF Working Paper* (July 2017); OECD and ILO, "The Labor Share in G20 Economies," report prepared for the G20 Employment Working Group (February 2015).

48. McKinsey Global Institute, *Jobs Lost, Jobs Gained: Workforce Transitions in a Time of Automation* (December 2017).

49. McKinsey Global Institute, *A Future that Works: Automation, Employment, and Productivity* (January 2017), p. 5. This report also includes estimates of the automation potential by activity types for different sectors, p. 7. See also OECD, "The Future of Work", *OECD Employment Outlook 2019*.

50. David H. Autor and Brendan Price (2003), "The Changing Task Composition of the US Labor Market: An Update of Autor, Levy, and Murnane", *MIT Working Paper*, June 2013.

51. James Bessen (2015), "How Computer Automation Affects Occupations: Technology, Jobs, and Skills", Boston Univ. School of Law, Law and Economics Research Paper No. 15–49.

52. James Bessen (2015), "Toil and Technology", *Finance and Development* 52(1).

53. Zia Qureshi, "Inequality in the Digital Era", OpenMind, November 2019, https://www.bbvaopenmind.com/en/articles/inequality-in-the-digital-era/

54. Dan Andrews, Chiara Criscuolo and Peter N. Gal (2015), "Frontier firms, technology diffusion and public policy: micro evidence from OECD countries", OECD Working Paper.

55. Qureshi, 2019.

56. Edoardo Campanella, "The Revenge of the Precariat", *Project Syndicate*, 18 November 2020, https://www.project-syndicate.org/commentary/technological-innovation-and-the-need-for-low-skill-labor-by-edoardo-campanella-2020-11

57. On the value of trade problem solving and work, see Matthew B. Crawford, *Shop Class as Soul Craft: In Inquiry into the Value of Work*, New York: Penguin, 2009.

58. Dan Andrews, Chiara Criscuolo and Peter N. Gal (2015), "Frontier firms, technology diffusion and public policy: micro evidence from OECD countries", OECD Working Paper.

59. Sergei Trentev, "How Fintech Is Meeting The Needs Of The Unbanked—Now And In The Future", *Forbes*, 19 November 2021, https://www.forbes.com/sites/forbesbusinesscouncil/2021/11/19/how-fintech-is-meeting-the-needs-of-the-unbanked---now-and-in-the-future/?sh=5ca185791c20

60. Marcin Szczepański (2020), "Is data the new oil? Competition issues in the digital economy", European Parliament Research Service, PE 646.117.

61. On the small and medium-sized enterprise challenge, see Edoardo Campanella, "The Digital Revolution's Silent Majority", *Project Syndicate*, 16 April 2019, https://www.project-syndicate.org/commentary/digital-revolution-silent-majority-by-edoardo-campanella-2019-04

62. The model of the ManufacturingUSA network of 14 institutes, to support advanced manufacturing, combines federal financial government support in partnership with academic institutions and businesses to develop and promote best practices. https://www.manufacturingusa.com/pages/how-we-work

63. For information on the Fraunhofer Institutes, see https://www.fraunhofer.de/en/institutes.html. See also Dan Breznitz, "Why Germany Dominates the U.S. in Innovation", *Harvard Business Review*, 27 May 2014, https://hbr.org/2014/05/why-germany-dominates-the-u-s-in-innovation

64. https://www.academy.fraunhofer.de/en/continuing-education.html

65. The Economist, "The world's most valuable resource is no longer oil, but data", 6 May 2017, https://www.economist.com/leaders/2017/05/06/the-worlds-most-valuable-resource-is-no-longer-oil-but-data

66. Yan Carriere-Swallow and Vikram Haksar (2019), "The Economics and Implications of Data: An Integrated Perspective", IMF Working Paper, No. 19/16.

67. The same basic logic favoring scale operates with digital *creator* firms, as will be discussed in the next two sections.

68. OECD (2019), *Measuring the Digital Transformation: A Roadmap for the Future*, OECD. See also Marcin Szczepański (2020), "Is data the new oil? Competition issues in the digital economy", European Parliament Research Service, PE 646.117.

69. Google's share of desktop internet searches varies by country, ranging from 94% in India to around 80% in the United States, to less than 10% in China. See https://www.statista.com/statistics/220534/googles-share-of-search-market-in-selected-countries/

70. See, for example, the start-up Neeva at neeva.com.

71. Max Cherney, "Apple's Privacy Move Has Scrambled Social-Media Advertising. We'll Know the Real Impact Soon", *Barron's*, 22 July 2021, https://www.barrons.com/articles/apple-facebook-privacy-ad-tracking-social-media-earnings-51626886549

72. Both U.S. and European regulators have questioned Amazon's possible use of third-party data from its marketplace to inform Amazon's decisions of which of its own private label products to develop. See John Porter, "Amazon accused of EU antitrust violation over Marketplace data", *The Verge*, 10 November 2020, https://www.theverge.com/2020/11/10/21558119/amazon-european-union-antitrust-charges-competition-commission-margrethe-vestager; Dana Mattioli, "Amazon Scooped Up Data From Its Own Sellers to Launch Competing Products", *Wall Street Journal*, 23 April 2020, https://www.wsj.com/articles/amazon-scooped-up-data-from-its-own-sellers-to-launch-competing-products-11587650015; Annie Palmer, "Amazon uses data from third-party sellers to develop its own products, WSJ investigation finds", CNBC, 23 April 2020, https://www.cnbc.com/2020/04/23/wsj-amazon-uses-data-from-third-party-sellers-to-develop-its-own-products.html; Tim de Chant, "Amazon lied about using seller data, lawmakers say, urging DOJ investigation", 3 September, *Ars Technica*, https://arstechnica.com/tech-policy/2022/03/us-lawmakers-seek-criminal-probe-of-amazon-for-lying-about-use-of-seller-data/

73. Intelligencer Staff, "Why Subscriptions May Be the Wave of the Future," *New York Magazine*, 4 June 2021, https://nymag.com/intelligencer/2021/06/why-subscriptions-may-be-the-wave-of-the-future.html

74. Shoshana Zuboff, *The Age of Surveillance Capitalism: The Fight for the Future at the New Frontier of Power*, New York: Faber and Faber, 2019.

75. As reported in Aspen Italia, "The Way To Venice", Report, September 2021, file://i13pfg01.hd00.unicreditgroup.eu/C308163$/C308163.HOME/Redirected_Profile/Downloads/Report%20The%20Way%20to%20Venice.pdf

76. See details of the *Official Journal of the European Union* at https://eur-lex.europa.eu/legal-content/EN/TXT/HTML/?uri=CELEX:32016R0679&from=EN#d1e3265-1-1

77. For statement following inaugural meeting of the TTC on September 21, 2021, https://ec.europa.eu/commission/presscorner/detail/en/STATEMENT_21_4951. See also https://ec.europa.eu/commission/presscorner/detail/en/IP_21_5308

78. "United States and European Commission Joint Statement on Trans-Atlantic Data Privacy Framework", White House Press Release, 25 March 2022, https://www.whitehouse.gov/briefing-room/statements-releases/2022/03/25/united-states-and-european-commission-joint-statement-on-trans-atlantic-data-privacy-framework/

79. Camille Boullenois, "China's Data Strategy: Creating a State-led Market", European Union Institute for Security Studies, Brief 21, 6 October 2021.

80. Jared Cohen and Richard Fontaine, "Uniting the Techno Democracies", *Foreign Affairs*, November/December 2020.

81. Paola Tessari and Karolina Muti, "Strategic or critical infrastructures, a way to interfere in Europe: state of play and recommendations", European Parliament, July 2021, https://www.europarl.europa.eu/RegData/etudes/STUD/2021/653637/EXPO_STU(2021)653637_EN.pdf; Fabio Rugge (2019), "The Global Race for Technological Superiority", *ISPI-Brookings Report*, https://www.ispi-online.it/sites/default/files/pubblicazioni/ispi_cybsec_2019_web2.pdf

82. Ian Bremmer, "The Technopolar Moment: How Digital Powers Will Reshape the Global Order", *Foreign Affairs*, November/December 2021, https://www.foreignaffairs.com/articles/world/2021-10-19/ian-bremmer-big-tech-global-order.

83. Graham Allison and Eric Schmidt. "Is China Beating the U.S. to AI Supremacy?", Harvard Kennedy School Paper, August 2020.

84. Bremmer, 2021. Meng Jing and Sarah Dai, "China recruits Baidu, Alibaba and Tencent to AI 'national team'", *South China Morning Post*, 21 November 2017, https://www.scmp.com/tech/china-tech/article/2120913/china-recruits-baidu-alibaba-and-tencent-ai-national-team

85. Eric Schmidt, "The AI competition and Strategic Competition with China", *Project Syndicate*, August 2021, https://www.project-syndicate.org/commentary/ai-revolution-competition-with-china-democracy-vs-authoritarianism-by-eric-schmidt-2021-08

86. CNAS, "The Future of the Digital Order", November 2021, https://s3.us-east-1.amazonaws.com/files.cnas.org/documents/CNAS-Report-HTI-Nov-2021-finalb.pdf?mtime=20211117084510&focal=none; National Security Commission on Artificial Intelligence, Final Report, 2021, https://www.nscai.gov/wp-content/uploads/2021/03/Full-Report-Digital-1.pdf

87. *The Economist*, "The rules of tech game are changing", 27 February 2021, https://www.economist.com/leaders/2021/02/27/the-rules-of-the-tech-game-are-changing

88. Lina Khan (2017), "Amazon's Antitrust Paradox", *Yale Law Journal*, 126–710, https://www.yalelawjournal.org/pdf/e.710.Khan.805_zuvfyyeh.pdf

89. See, for instance, Nitasha Tiku, "Big Tech: Breaking US Up Will Only Help China," *Wired* (May 23, 2019): https://www.wired.com/story/big-tech-breaking-will-only-help-china/

90. Kati Suominen, "On the Rise: Europe's Competition Policy Challenges to

Technology Companies", CSIS, 26 October 2020, https://www.csis.org/analysis/rise-europes-competition-policy-challenges-technology-companies

91. U.S. Congress, House of Representatives, "Investigation of Competition In Digital Markets: Majority Staff Report And Recommendations", 2020, https://judiciary.house.gov/uploadedfiles/competition_in_digital_markets.pdf

92. Jin Waterson and Dan Milmo, "Facebook whistleblower Frances Haugen calls for urgent external regulation", *The Guardian*, 25 October 2021, https://www.theguardian.com/technology/2021/oct/25/facebook-whistleblower-frances-haugen-calls-for-urgent-external-regulation

93. Rebecca Klar, "Biden proposes funding boost for federal antitrust enforcers", 28 March 2022, *The Hill*, https://thehill.com/policy/technology/600067-biden-budget-proposes-funding-boost-for-antitrust-enforcers/

94. https://www.gov.uk/government/collections/digital-markets-unit, UK Department for Digital, Culture, Media & Sport, "Government unveils proposals to increase competition in UK digital economy", Gov.UK, 20 July 2021, https://www.gov.uk/government/news/government-unveils-proposals-to-increase-competition-in-uk-digital-economy

95. Chandler Thornton and Michelle Toh, "Australia passes new law requiring Facebook and Google to pay for news", *CNN*, 24 February 2021, https://www.cnn.com/2021/02/24/media/australia-media-legislation-facebook-intl-hnk/index.html

96. Australian Competition & Consumer Commission, "Digital Platforms", accessed 13 April 2022, https://www.accc.gov.au/focus-areas/digital-platforms#digital-platforms-inquiry

97. Japan Ministry of Economy, Trade and Industry, "Act on Improving Transparency and Fairness of Digital Platforms (TFDPA)", Accessed 13 April 2022, https://www.meti.go.jp/english/policy/mono_info_service/information_economy/digital_platforms/index.html

98. Apple, "Japan Fair Trade Commission closes App Store investigation", *Apple Newsroom*, 1 September 2021, https://www.apple.com/newsroom/2021/09/japan-fair-trade-commission-closes-app-store-investigation/

99. John Sung-wook, "KFTC chief vows to fight anti-competitive practices by platform giants", *The Korea Times*, 1 March 2022, https://www.koreatimes.co.kr/www/tech/2022/01/419_321125.html

100. Korea Federal Trade Commission, "KFTC Established Guidelines on Anticompetitive Conducts in Platform Sector", 6 January 2022, https://www.ftc.go.kr/solution/skin/doc.html?fn=23f6848cbcadf63a97f87accd6400b8ce5d2b65a537490de4adc0313932e2cc2&rs=/fileupload/data/result/BBSMSTR_000000002402/

101. Kati Suominen, "On the Rise: Europe's Competition Policy Challenges to Technology Companies", *CSIS*, 26 October 2020, https://www.csis.org/analysis/rise-europes-competition-policy-challenges-technology-companies

102. European Commission, "Digital Markets Act: Commission welcomes politi-

cal agreement on rules to ensure fair and open digital markets", 25 March 2022, https://ec.europa.eu/commission/presscorner/detail/en/ip_22_1978

103. Tom Wheeler, "U.S. regulator inaction opened the doors for the EU to step up on internet", Brookings, 29 March 2022, https://www.brookings.edu/blog/techtank/2022/03/29/u-s-regulatory-inaction-opened-the-doors-for-the-eu-to-step-up-on-internet/

104. Martin Chorzempa, "China's campaign to regulate Big Tech is more than just retaliation", Nikkei Asia, 3 August 2021, https://asia.nikkei.com/Opinion/China-s-campaign-to-regulate-Big-Tech-is-more-than-just-retaliation and Keyu Jin, "China Bets on Common Prosperity", *Project Syndicate*, 4 December 2021,https://www.project-syndicate.org/onpoint/china-common-prosperity-paradigm-shift-by-keyu-jin-2021-12

105. Mark D. Fenwick, Wulf A. Kaal, and Erik P.M. Vermeulen, "Regulation Tomorrow: What Happens When Technology Is Faster than the Law?", *American University Business Law Review*, Volume 6, Issue 3, 2017.

106. Ibid.

107. Ibid. For information on regulatory sandboxes, see for example:
    UK Financial Conduct Authority: https://www.fca.org.uk/firms/innovation/regulatory-sandbox
    Australian Securities and Investments Commission: https://asic.gov.au/for-business/innovation-hub/enhanced-regulatory-sandbox/
    Monetary Authority of Singapore: https://www.mas.gov.sg/development/fintech/regulatory-sandbox
    Also adopted by some US states: https://spn.org/blog/what-is-a-regulatory-sandbox/

108. Husain Sumra, "Best and Worst Countries for Wi-Fi Access", *Ooma Blog*, 21 July 2020, https://www.ooma.com/blog/best-worst-wifi-countries/

109. Behnam Tabrizi, Ed Lam, Kirk Girard, and Vernon Irvin, "Digital Transformation Is Not About Technology", *Harvard Business Review*, 13 March 2019, https://hbr.org/2019/03/digital-transformation-is-not-about-technology

110. See, for example, Microsoft's certification program including access to free, web-based learning modules, https://docs.microsoft.com/en-us/learn/certifications/

111. See the Lighthouse Network, World Economic Forum https://www.weforum.org/projects/global_lighthouse_network; see also https://www.weforum.org/platforms/shaping-the-future-of-production

112. See their websites at https://www.usds.gov/, https://digital.canada.ca/ and https://digitalservice4germany.org/

113. See the OECD website on this at https://www.oecd.org/digital/ieconomy/digital-security/oecd-work-on-digital-security-policy.pdf

114. Marietje Schaake, "The Lawless Realm", *Foreign Affairs*, November/December 2020; Frank Adelmann; Jennifer A. Elliott, Ibrahim Ergen, Tamas Gaidosch, Nigel Jenkinson, Tanai Khiaonarong, Anastasiia Morozova, Nadine Schwarz

and Christopher Wilson (2020), "Cyber Risk and Financial Stability: It's a Small World After All", *IMF Staff Notes*.

115. Paul See and Chaitra Chandrasekhar, "Cybersecurity is too big a job for governments or business to handle alone", World Economic Forum, 3 May 2021 and Australia eSafety Commissioner, "Placing user safety at the forefront of online service design", October 2019.

116. On the Financial Stability Board, its history, publications, and current activities, see www.fsb.org.

117. On major corporations' support for a potential G7 Data and Technology Forum along these lines, see https://www.mastercard.com/news/insights/2021/setting-principles-for-the-digital-economy-establishing-a-g7-data-and-technology-forum/

118. Jared Cohen and Richard Fontaine, "Uniting the Techno-Democracies: How to Build Digital Cooperation," *Foreign Affairs* (November/December 2020), pp. 112–122; Matthew P. Goodman, "Toward a T12: Putting Allied Technology Cooperation into Practice," *CSIS Brief* (October 13, 2021); Tom Wheeler, "U.S. regulator inaction opened the doors for the EU to step up on internet", Brookings, 29 March 2022, https://www.brookings.edu/blog/techtank/2022/03/29/u-s-regulatory-inaction-opened-the-doors-for-the-eu-to-step-up-on-internet/

119. For the 2021 G7 Digital and Technology Ministerial Declaration and supporting annexes, see https://www.gov.uk/government/publications/g7-digital-and-technology-ministerial-declaration

120. "Global AI Vibrancy Ranking", 2021, by the Stanford Institute on Human-Centered Artificial Intelligence.

121. This approach differs slightly from that proposed in Jared Cohen and Richard Fontaine, "Uniting the Techno-Democracies: How to Build Digital Cooperation," *Foreign Affairs* (November/December 2020), pp. 112–122. This approach would begin with the full G7 membership and then expand outwards.

4. TOWARD A MORE EQUITABLE FUTURE

1. Portions of this chapter draw upon Edoardo Campanella, "Inequality and the Coming Storm," *Project Syndicate*, 8 Dec. 2017, https://www.project-syndicate.org/onpoint/inequality-and-the-coming-storm-by-edoardo-campanella-2017–12
   Scheidel, Walter. *The Great Leveler: Violence and the History of Inequality from the Stone Age to the Twenty-First Century (The Princeton Economic History of the Western World, 69)*. Reprint, Princeton University Press, 2018.
   See also: Piketty, Thomas, and Goldhammer. *Capital and Ideology*. Amsterdam University Press, 2020.

2. Scheidel, 2018, p. 2.

3. Hardoon, Deborah. "Wealth: Having It All and Wanting More." *Oxfam International*, 2015. *Crossref*, https://doi.org/10.21201/2015.7955. Hardoon,

Deborah. "An Economy for the 99%: It's Time to Build a Human Economy That Benefits Everyone, Not Just the Privileged Few." *Oxfam International*, 6 Jan. 2017, oxfamilibrary.openrepository.com/handle/10546/620170.

4. Milanović, Branko, *Global Inequality: A New Approach for the Age of Globalization*, Harvard University Press, 2016.

5. Data from the World Inequality Database: WID—Wealth and Income Database. *WID—World Inequality Database*, 19 Jan. 2022, wid.world.

6. Bussolo, Maurizio, et al. *Toward a New Social Contract: Taking on Distributional Tensions in Europe and Central Asia (Europe and Central Asia Studies)*. The World Bank, 2018.

7. United Nations. *World Social Report 2020: Inequality in a Rapidly Changing World (Report On the World Social Situation)*. United Nations, 2020.

8. The Theil Index is a statistical method that allows for the decomposition in global inequality trends into within-countries and between-countries components. See: Chancel, Lucas, and Thomas Piketty. "Global Income Inequality, 1820–2020: The Persistence and Mutation of Extreme Inequality." *Journal of the European Economic Association*, vol. 19, no. 6, 2021, pp. 3025–62. *Crossref*, https://doi.org/10.1093/jeea/jvab047.

See also Bourguignon, François, and Thomas Scott-Railton. *The Globalization of Inequality*. Reprint, Princeton University Press, 2017.

9. In earlier capitalist eras, societies were broadly divided into two groups: a minority of capital owners, whose income derived from the ownership of the means of production, and a majority of workers, whose income derived from their labor. The type of income one received was closely correlated with one's position in the income distribution: capitalists at the top and workers at the bottom. In today's world of knowledge work, though, the most affluent members of capitalist societies are more likely to be endowed with human capital than with physical or financial capital. So whereas rentiers were formerly seated atop the income distribution, a large share of today's top one percent is made up of highly paid managers, physicians, and investment bankers. And this type of workers cannot sit idle and wait for rents from the capital that they own to flow into their pockets. They need to work hard to draw large salaries that are then re-invested, in large proportions, in financial assets or real estate. This marks a change from the way things worked even as late as the 1950s and 1960s, for example, when it was apt to call the richest people—who earned around three-quarters of their income from capital—a "leisure class," to use sociologist Thorstein Veblen's term. Today, elites largely work for a living like everyone else. See Milanović, Branko. *Capitalism, Alone: The Future of the System That Rules the World*. Reprint, Belknap Press: An Imprint of Harvard University Press, 2021, and Veblen, Thorstein. *The Theory of the Leisure Class: An Economic Study of Institutions*. MacMillan, 1899.

10. Koike, Yuriko. "Thomas Piketty's Japanese Tour." *Project Syndicate*, 30 Aug. 2017, www.project-syndicate.org/commentary/japanese-income-inequality-by-yuriko-koike-2015-03?barrier=accesspaylog.

11. Blanchet, Thomas and Lucas Chancel, Amory Gethin. "Why Is Europe More Equal Than the United States?" *WID—World Inequality Database*, 9 Oct. 2020, wid.world/news-article/why-is-europe-more-equal-than-the-united-states.

12. Ibid.

13. Yang, Li. "What's New about Income Inequality Data in Asia?" *WID—World Inequality Database*, Nov. 2020, https://wid.world/document/whats-new-about-income-inequality-data-in-asia/.

14. *Asia's Journey to Prosperity: Policy, Market, and Technology Over 50 Years*. Asian Development Bank, 2020.

15. Crabtree, James. *The Billionaire Raj: A Journey Through India's New Gilded Age*. Reprint, Tim Duggan Books, 2019. The data in this paragraph comes from Chancel, Lucas, et al. *World Inequality Report 2022*. Harvard University Press, 2022.

16. Chancel et al., 2022.

17. Gordon, Robert, and Ian Dew-Becker. "Controversies about the Rise of American Inequality: A Survey." *NBER*, 2008. *Crossref*, https://doi.org/10.3386/w13982.

18. Autor, David H. "Why Are There Still So Many Jobs? The History and Future of Workplace Automation." *Journal of Economic Perspectives*, vol. 29, no. 3, 2015, pp. 3–30. *Crossref*, https://doi.org/10.1257/jep. 29.3.3.

19. FP Editors. "Election 2020: America Votes." *Foreign Policy*, 2 Nov. 2020, foreignpolicy.com/projects/america-votes-2020-election-live. Saez, Emmanuel, et al. *The Triumph of Injustice: How the Rich Dodge Taxes and How to Make Them Pay*. HighBridge, a division of Recorded Books, 2019.

20. Piketty, Thomas, and Emmanuel Saez. "How Progressive Is the U.S. Federal Tax System? A Historical and International Perspective." *Journal of Economic Perspectives*, vol. 21, no. 1, 2007, pp. 3–24. *Crossref*, https://doi.org/10.1257/jep. 21.1.3.
    See also: Saez, et al., 2019.

21. Tagliapietra, Simone. "It's Time for a Green Social Contract." *Bruegel*, 12 Apr. 2021, www.bruegel.org/2021/04/its-time-for-a-green-social-contract.

22. Campanella, Edoardo. "The Bubonic Plague Killed Feudalism, but the COVID-19 Pandemic Will Only Entrench Inequality." *Foreign Policy*, 20 Aug. 2020, foreignpolicy.com/2020/08/20/bubonic-plague-pandemic-covid-19-inequality-feudalism.

23. Gallagher, Mary, and Jonathan K. Hanson. "Coalitions, Carrots, and Sticks: Economic Inequality and Authoritarian States." *PS: Political Science & Politics*, vol. 42, no. 04, 2009, pp. 667–72. *Crossref*, https://doi.org/10.1017/s1049096509990096. See also: Hanson, Jonathan K. "Loyalty and Acquiescence: Authoritarian Regimes and Inequality Outcomes." *SSRN Electronic Journal*, 2013. *Crossref*, https://doi.org/10.2139/ssrn.1642485.

24. Gandhi, Jennifer, and Adam Przeworski. "Authoritarian Institutions and the Survival of Autocrats." *Comparative Political Studies*, vol. 40, no. 11, 2007, pp. 1279–301. *Crossref*, https://doi.org/10.1177/0010414007305817.

25. Ang, Yuen Yuen. *China's Gilded Age*. Cambridge University Press, 2021.
   China's inequality is a multifaceted problem. Income disparities are due to inequality among provinces and between urban and rural areas. For example, in 2019, the income ratio between the three richest and the three poorest provinces was 4 to 1. The equivalent ratio between rich and poor states in the United States is less than 2 to 1. A person with the median urban income in China is in the global 70th percentile, while a person with the median rural income is in the 52nd percentile. Mobility restrictions are one of the main sources of inequality between rural and urban areas. See: Milanović, Branko. "China's Inequality Will Lead It to a Stark Choice: A New Oligarchy Can Be Restrained Only by the Government That Made It." *Foreign Affairs*, 11 Feb. 2021, www.foreignaffairs.com/articles/china/2021-02-11/chinas-inequality-will-lead-it-stark-choice.

26. For a detailed discussion see Piketty, 2020. See also: Lanskoy, M., and D. Myles-Primakoff. "The Rise of Kleptocracy: Power and Plunder in Putin's Russia". *Journal of Democracy*, vol. 29, no. 1, Jan. 2018, pp. 76–85.

27. The magnitude of Russia's economic disparities is hardly quantifiable as the wealth of its billionaires is hidden in screen corporations, trusts, and tax havens. Also, the Russian tax system tends to nourish inequality since there is no inheritance tax, while the income tax is strictly proportional, with a rate of just 13 percent, regardless of the size of the income being taxed. See: Piketty (2020).

28. In the most basic framework, the voter with the median income is supposed to stir the decision-making process in his favor, pushing for generous redistributive policies. See: Meltzer, Allan H., and Scott F. Richard. "A Rational Theory of the Size of Government." *Journal of Political Economy*, vol. 89, no. 5, 1981, pp. 914–27. *Crossref*, https://doi.org/10.1086/261013.

29. See: Hanson, 2013. See also: Iversen, Torben, and David Soskice. "Electoral Institutions and the Politics of Coalitions: Why Some Democracies Redistribute More Than Others." *American Political Science Review*, vol. 100, no. 2, 2006, pp. 165–81. *Crossref*, https://doi.org/10.1017/s0003055406062083.

30. The idea of meritocracy, which sprang from the liberal revolutions of the eighteenth and nineteenth centuries, is one of humanity's greatest achievements. For millennia before, individuals inherited their positions in fixed social orders. See: Wooldridge, Adrian. *The Aristocracy of Talent: How Meritocracy Made the Modern World*. Skyhorse, 2021.

31. Blanchard, Olivier, and Dani Rodrik. *Combating Inequality: Rethinking Government's Role*. The MIT Press, 2021. This book provides insights on both redistributive and pre-distributive policies. See also: Mazzucato, Mariana. *Mission Economy: A Moonshot Guide to Changing Capitalism*. Harper Business, 2021. International Monetary Fund. *Fiscal Monitor, April 2021*. International Monetary Fund, 2021.

32. McLanahan, Sara. "Diverging Destinies: How Children Are Faring under the Second Demographic Transition." *Demography*, vol. 41, no. 4, 2004, pp. 607–27. *Crossref*, https://doi.org/10.1353/dem.2004.0033.

33. "Inheritance Taxation in OECD Countries." *OECD Tax Policy Studies*, 2021. *Crossref*, https://doi.org/10.1787/e2879a7d-en.

34. Milanović, 2021.

   See also: "New Evidence That Humans Choose Their Partners through Assortative Mating." *Phys.Org*, 13 Jan. 2017, phys.org/news/2017–01-evidence-humans-partners-assortative.html.

   Reeves, Richard, and Joanna Venator. "Opposites Don't Attract: Assortative Mating and Social Mobility." *Brookings*, 29 July 2016, www.brookings.edu/blog/social-mobility-memos/2014/02/10/opposites-dont-attract-assortative-mating-and-social-mobility.

35. Aaberge, Rolf, and Jo Thori Lind and Kalle Moene. "The inequality of equal mating." *The Luxembourg Income Study Working Paper*. 15 Feb 2018, https://www.lisdatacenter.org/wp-content/uploads/files/uc2018-s502.pdf

36. Martins, V. J., Toledo Florêncio, T. M., Grillo, L. P., do Carmo P Franco, M., Martins, P. A., Clemente, A. P., Santos, C. D., de Fatima A Vieira, M., & Sawaya, A. L. (2011). "Long-lasting effects of undernutrition." *International Journal of Environmental Research and Public Health*, *8*(6), 1817–1846.

37. Dornan, Paul, and Martin Woodhead. "How Inequalities Develop through Childhood: Life course evidence from the Young Lives cohort study." *Innocenti Discussion Papers* no. 2015–01, 2015.

38. Heckman, James J. "Promoting Social Mobility." *Boston Review*, 9 Nov. 2012, bostonreview.net/forum/promoting-social-mobility-james-heckman.

39. See: McLanahan, 2004.

40. "Gender Equality in Primary and Secondary Education." *UNICEF South Asia*, www.unicef.org/rosa/what-we-do/education/gender-equality-primary-and-secondary-education. Accessed 16 Apr. 2022.

41. Asian Development Bank, 2020. For the United States, see, for instance: Reeves, Richard, and Ember Smith. "The Male College Crisis Is Not Just in Enrollment, but Completion." *Brookings*, 9 Mar. 2022, www.brookings.edu/blog/up-front/2021/10/08/the-male-college-crisis-is-not-just-in-enrollment-but-completion/#:%7E:text=In%201972%2C%20when%20the%20U.S.,1982%2C%20the%20gap%20had%20closed.

42. Demirguc-Kunt, Asli, et al. "The Global Findex Database 2017: Measuring Financial Inclusion and the Fintech Revolution." *World Bank Group*, 2018. *Crossref*, https://doi.org/10.1596/978–1–4648–1259–0.

43. Bhutta, Neil, et al. "Disparities in Wealth by Race and Ethnicity in the 2019 Survey of Consumer Finances." *FEDS Notes*, 28 Aug. 2020, www.federalreserve.gov/econres/notes/feds-notes/disparities-in-wealth-by-race-and-ethnicity-in-the-2019-survey-of-consumer-finances-20200928.htm.

44. Startz, Dick. "The Achievement Gap in Education: Racial Segregation versus Segregation by Poverty." *Brookings*, 20 Jan. 2020, www.brookings.edu/blog/brown-center-chalkboard/2020/01/20/the-achievement-gap-in-education-racial-segregation-versus-segregation-by-poverty.

45. Bradley, Steve, and Colin Green. *The Economics of Education: A Comprehensive Overview*. 2nd ed., Academic Press, 2020.

46. Harte, Emma, et al. "Education of EU Migrant Children in EU Member States." *RAND*, 2016. *Crossref*, https://doi.org/10.7249/rr1715.

47. Zacharias, Ajit, and Vamsicharan Vakulabharanam. "Caste and Wealth Inequality in India." *SSRN Electronic Journal*, 2009. *Crossref*, https://doi.org/10.2139/ssrn.1410660.

48. Chetty, Raj, and Nathaniel Hendren. "The Impacts of Neighborhoods on Intergenerational Mobility II: County-Level Estimates*." *The Quarterly Journal of Economics*, vol. 133, no. 3, 2018, pp. 1163–228. *Crossref*, https://doi.org/10.1093/qje/qjy006.

49. Leonhardt, David, Amanda Cox and Claire Cain Miller, "An Atlas of Upward Mobility Shows Paths Out of Poverty", *The New York Times*, 4 May 2015, https://www.nytimes.com/2015/05/04/upshot/an-atlas-of-upward-mobility-shows-paths-out-of-poverty.html

50. Tammaru, Tiit, et al. *Socio-Economic Segregation in European Capital Cities*. Taylor and Francis, 2019.

10. OECD. *Making Cities Work for All Data and Actions for Inclusive Growth*. Van Haren Publishing, 2016.

52. Bell, Alex, et al. "Who Becomes an Inventor in America? The Importance of Exposure to Innovation*." *The Quarterly Journal of Economics*, vol. 134, no. 2, 2018, pp. 647–713. *Crossref*, https://doi.org/10.1093/qje/qjy028.

53. Ibid.

54. Payne, Keith. *The Broken Ladder: How Inequality Affects the Way We Think, Live, and Die*. Viking, 2017.

55. Campanella, 2017.

56. International Monetary Fund, 2021. See also: Blanchard and Rodrik, 2021.

57. International Monetary Fund, 2021.

58. Winters, John. *What You Make Depends on Where You Live: College Earnings across States and Metropolitan Areas*. Thomas B. Fordham Institute, 2020.

59. Chetty, Raj, et al. "Mobility Report Cards: The Role of Colleges in Intergenerational Mobility." *NBER Working Papers*, 2017. *Crossref*, https://doi.org/10.3386/w23618.

60. Clark, Gregory, et al. *The Son Also Rises: Surnames and the History of Social Mobility (The Princeton Economic History of the Western World, 49)*. Reprint, Princeton University Press, 2015.

61. Montacute, Rebecca, and Carl Cullinane, *Access to Advantage: The influence of schools and place on admissions to top universities*, The Sutton Trust, 2018.

62. Markovits, Daniel. *The Meritocracy Trap: How America's Foundational Myth Feeds Inequality, Dismantles the Middle Class, and Devours the Elite*. Penguin Books, 2020.

63. Campanella, 2017; Chetty, et al., 2017.

64. Lim, Linda. "Commentary: Can Education Fix Inequality in Singapore? If Not, What Can?" *CNA*, 2 Jul. 2018, www.channelnewsasia.com/commentary/can-education-fix-growing-inequality-in-singapore-814696.

65. Chetty, Raj, David Grusky, et al. "The Fading American Dream: Trends in Absolute Income Mobility since 1940." *Science*, vol. 356, no. 6336, 2017, pp. 398–406. *Crossref*, https://doi.org/10.1126/science.aal4617.

66. Chetty, Raj, Nathaniel Hendren, et al. "Where Is the Land of Opportunity? The Geography of Intergenerational Mobility in the United States*." *The Quarterly Journal of Economics*, vol. 129, no. 4, 2014, pp. 1553–623. *Crossref*, https://doi.org/10.1093/qje/qju022.

See also: Krause, Richard Reeves And Eleanor. "Raj Chetty in 14 Charts: Big Findings on Opportunity and Mobility We Should All Know." *Brookings*, 11 Jan. 2018, www.brookings.edu/blog/social-mobility-memos/2018/01/11/raj-chetty-in-14-charts-big-findings-on-opportunity-and-mobility-we-should-know.

67. Smith, Alan. "How Britain's Private Schools Lost Their Grip on Oxbridge." *Financial Times*, 2 July 2021, www.ft.com/content/bbb7fe58–0908–4f8e-bb1a-081a42a045b7.

68. SCMP Editorial. "China Crackdown on Private Tutors Has to Achieve Right Results." *South China Morning Post*, 31 July 2021, www.scmp.com/comment/opinion/article/3143275/china-crackdown-private-tutors-has-achieve-right-results.

69. OECD. "*The ABC of Gender Equality in Education: Aptitude, Behaviour, Confidence.*" OECD Publishing, 2015, https://doi.org/10.1787/9789264229945-en.

70. OECD. "*The Pursuit of Gender Equality: An Uphill Battle.*" OECD Publishing, 2017.

71. "How Gender Equality in STEM Education Leads to Economic Growth." *European Institute for Gender Equality*, eige.europa.eu/gender-mainstreaming/policy-areas/economic-and-financial-affairs/economic-benefits-gender-equality/stem. Accessed 16 Apr. 2022.

72. Fuller, Joseph, and Manjari Raman. *Dismissed By Degrees*, Accenture, Grads of Life, and Harvard Business School, 2017.

73. Stockman, Farah. "Want a White-Collar Career Without College Debt? Become an Apprentice." *The New York Times*, 10 Dec. 2019, www.nytimes.com/2019/12/10/us/apprenticeships-white-collar-jobs.html.

74. Opportunity@Work and Accenture, *Reach for the STARs: Realizing the Potential of America's Hidden Talent Pool*, 2020, https://opportunityatwork.org/our-solutions/stars-insights/reach-stars-report/

75. "The Gender Gap in Employment: What's Holding Women Back?" *InfoStories*, International Labor Organization, www.ilo.org/infostories/en-GB/Stories/Employment/barriers-women#global-gap. Accessed 16 Apr. 2022.

76. Ro, Christine. "How the Salary 'ask Gap' Perpetuates Unequal Pay." *BBC Worklife*, 18 June 2021, www.bbc.com/worklife/article/20210615-how-the-salary-ask-gap-perpetuates-unequal-pay.

77. Holzer, Harry. "Why Are Employment Rates so Low among Black Men?" *Brookings*, 1 Mar. 2021, www.brookings.edu/research/why-are-employment-rates-so-low-among-black-men.

78. "*Public attitudes towards migrant workers in Japan, Malaysia, Singapore, and Thailand.*" International Labor Organization, 2019.

79. Fine, David, et al. "Inequality: A persisting challenge and its implications." McKinsey Global Institute Discussion paper, 2019.

80. Mishel, Lawrence, and Jessica Schieder, "CEO pay remains high relative to the pay of typical workers and high-wage earners." *Economic Policy Institute*, 20 Jul. 2017, https://www.epi.org/publication/ceo-pay-remains-high-relative-to-the-pay-of-typical-workers-and-high-wage-earners/.

81. Kiatpongsan, Sorapop, and Michael I. Norton. "How Much (More) Should CEOs Make? A Universal Desire for More Equal Pay." *Perspectives on Psychological Science*, vol. 9, no. 6, 2014, pp. 587–93. *Crossref*, https://doi.org/10.1177/1745691614549773.

82. Stansbury, Anna, and Lawrence Summers. "The Declining Worker Power Hypothesis: An Explanation for the Recent Evolution of the American Economy." *NBER Working Papers*, 2020. *Crossref*, https://doi.org/10.3386/w27193.

83. Song, Jae, et al. "Firming Up Inequality*." *The Quarterly Journal of Economics*, vol. 134, no. 1, 2018, pp. 1–50. *Crossref*, https://doi.org/10.1093/qje/qjy025.

84. Frick, Walter. "Corporate Inequality Is the Defining Fact of Business Today." *Harvard Business Review*, 11 May 2016, hbr.org/2016/05/corporate-inequality-is-the-defining-fact-of-business-today.

85. Bloom, Nicholas. "Corporations in the Age of Inequality." *Harvard Business Review*, 21 Mar 2017, https://hbr.org/2017/03/corporations-in-the-age-of-inequality

86. Philippon, Thomas. *The Great Reversal: How America Gave Up on Free Markets*. First Printing, Belknap Press: An Imprint of Harvard University Press, 2019.

87. Berlingieri, Giuseppe, et al. "The great divergence(s)." *OECD Science, Technology and Industry Policy Papers*, No. 39, OECD Publishing, 2017, https://doi.org/10.1787/953f3853-en.

88. Sadun, Raffaella. "Worker Representation on Boards Won't Work Without Trust", *Harvard Business Review*, 17 Aug 2018, https://hbr.org/2018/08/worker-representation-on-boards-wont-work-without-trust. Rogers, Joel, and Wolfgang Streeck. *Works Councils*. Amsterdam University Press, 2009.

89. Christensen, Julian, et al. "Human Capital and Administrative Burden: The Role of Cognitive Resources in Citizen–State Interactions." *Public Administration Review*, vol. 80, no. 1, 2019, pp. 127–36. *Crossref*, https://doi.org/10.1111/puar.13134.

90. Jin, Keyu. "China Bets on Common Prosperity." *Project Syndicate*, 4 Dec. 2021, www.project-syndicate.org/onpoint/china-common-prosperity-paradigm-shift-by-keyu-jin-2021–12?barrier=accesspaylog.

91. In the United States, for example, around 40 percent of families with low incomes used their Child Tax Credit payments to cover education costs, such as school books and supplies, tuition, after-school programs, and transportation to and from school.

    Zippel, Claire. "9 in 10 Families With Low Incomes Are Using Child Tax Credits to Pay for Necessities, Education." *Center on Budget and Policy Priorities*,

21 Oct. 2021, https://www.cbpp.org/blog/9-in-10-families-with-low-incomes-are-using-child-tax-credits-to-pay-for-necessities-education

92. See: https://parentsasteachers.org/

93. Rodgers, Daniel. *Atlantic Crossings: Social Politics in a Progressive Age*. Belknap Press: An Imprint of Harvard University Press, 2000.

94. "The Future of Jobs Report, 2016." World Economic Forum, 2016, https://reports.weforum.org/future-of-jobs-2016/chapter-1-the-future-of-jobs-and-skills/#view/fn-1

95. Nietzel, Michael. "Arizona State University Announces Effort To Educate 100 Million Students Worldwide." *Forbes*, 21 Jan. 2022, www.forbes.com/sites/michaeltnietzel/2022/01/21/arizona-state-university-announces-effort-to-educate-100-million-students-worldwide/?sh=3baf00330c92.

96. Crow, Michael M., and Dabars, William A. *The Fifth Wave: The Evolution of American Higher Education*. The Johns Hopkins University Press, 2020.

97. Nietzel, Michael. "Arizona State University Announces Effort To Educate 100 Million Students Worldwide." *Forbes*, 21 Jan. 2022, www.forbes.com/sites/michaeltnietzel/2022/01/21/arizona-state-university-announces-effort-to-educate-100-million-students-worldwide/?sh=3baf00330c92.

Belkin, Douglas. "Arizona State University Looks to Enroll 100 Million More Students by 2030," *Wall Street Journal*, 20 Jan. 2022, https://www.wsj.com/articles/arizona-state-university-looks-to-enroll-100-million-more-students-by-2030–11642674604, https://thunderbird.asu.edu/lifelong-learning/100-million-learners

98. https://thunderbird.asu.edu/global-entrepreneurship-innovation-bootcamp-english

99. "Spending in the Global Workplace Training Industry 2007–2020." *Statista*, 11 Jan. 2022, www.statista.com/statistics/738399/size-of-the-global-workplace-training-market.

In the United States, companies with more than 100 employees already spend more than $80 billion per year on training. https://pubs.royle.com/publication/?m=20617&i=678873&p=24m).

100. Sen, Amartya. *Development as Freedom*. Van Haren Publishing, 1999.

Summers, Lawrence H. "Investing in All the People." *World Bank Policy Research Working Paper*, May 1992, https://documents1.worldbank.org/curated/en/434361468739196605/pdf/multi-page.pdf.

101. Strauss, Karsten. "More Evidence That Company Diversity Leads To Better Profits." *Forbes*, 25 Jan. 2018, www.forbes.com/sites/karstenstrauss/2018/01/25/more-evidence-that-company-diversity-leads-to-better-profits/?sh=4012c18c1bc7.

102. On broken ladders, see: "Women in the Workplace 2021." *McKinsey & Company*, 2021, www.mckinsey.com/featured-insights/diversity-and-inclusion/women-in-the-workplace.

103. "Women Sue Idaho Over Expensive Hair Branding License Rules," *Idaho State*

Journal, 13 Mar, 2022, https://www.idahostatejournal.com/news/local/women-sue-idaho-over-expensive-hair-braiding-license-rules/article_bb581d3c-911a-59a7–9be5–45f76f74059f.html.

104. "Thousands Of State Jobs No Longer Require A College Degree Under Maryland Initiative." *CBS Baltimore*, 15 Mar. 2022, baltimore.cbslocal.com/2022/03/15/thousands-of-state-jobs-no-longer-require-a-college-degree-under-maryland-initiative.

105. Carapezza, Kirk. "No College, No Problem. Some Employers Drop Degree Requirements to Diversify Staffs," *NPR*, 29 Apr. 2021, https://www.npr.org/2021/04/29/990274681/no-college-no-problem-some-employers-drop-degree-requirements-to-diversify-staff.

106. Stansbury and Summers, 2020. In the United States, for example, private sector unionization has declined from a peak close to 35 percent in the 1950s to around 5 percent in recent years.

107. Between 2000 and 2020 (or latest reported data), only four OECD countries saw increased unionization rates: Chile, Costa Rica, Iceland, and Korea. The other 34 countries reported declines. For OECD data, see: "Trade Union Dataset." *OECD*, stats.oecd.org/Index.aspx?DataSetCode=TUD#. Accessed 16 Apr. 2022.

108. For an example of more "people-centric" models of management, see: Chapman, Bob, and Raj Sisodia. *Everybody Matters: The Extraordinary Power of Caring for Your People Like Family*. Portfolio, 2015.

109. Thaler, Richard, and Cass Sunstein. *Nudge: Improving Decisions About Health, Wealth, and Happiness*. Revised&Expanded, Penguin Books, 2009.

On the US experience, see: Sunstein, Cass. *Simpler: The Future of Government*. Illustrated, Simon and Schuster, 2014.

On the UK experience, see: Halpern, David. *Inside the Nudge Unit: How Small Changes Can Make a Big Difference*. Reprint, WH Allen, 2016.

110. For examples of innovations in use of data to inform government policy and management, see the compilations and annual reports of the nonprofit *Results for America*. results4america.org/about-us.

111. "The Economics and Politics of Market Concentration." *NBER*, www.nber.org/reporter/2019number4/economics-and-politics-market-concentration. Accessed 16 Apr. 2022.

Covarrubias, Matias, et al."From Good to Bad Concentration? US Industries over the Past 30 Years," NBER Chapters, in: NBER Macroeconomics Annual 2019, volume 34, pages 1–46, National Bureau of Economic Research, 2019.

Wu, Tim. *The Curse of Bigness: Antitrust in the New Gilded Age*. Columbia Global Reports, 2018.

112. EIG Editor. "The Case for Non-Compete Reform: How the Workforce Mobility Act Would Support Workers and Spur Entrepreneurship." *Economic Innovation Group*, 25 Feb. 2021, eig.org/news/the-case-for-non-compete-reform#:%7E:text=%20Accordingly%2C%20the%20empirical%20

research%20documents%20significant%20negative,for%20underrepre-sented%20entrepreneurs%3A%20The%20threat%20of…%20More%20.

See also: Wiens, Jason, and Chris Jackson. "Rethinking Non-Competes: Unlock Talent to Seed Growth." *Kauffman Foundation*, 16 July 2014, www.kauffman.org/resources/entrepreneurship-policy-digest/rethinking-non-competes-unlock-talent-to-seed-growth.

113. "New York City Enacts Law Requiring Salary Disclosures on Job Postings." *Morgan Lewis*, www.morganlewis.com/pubs/2022/01/new-york-city-enacts-law-requiring-salary-disclosures-on-job-postings. Accessed 16 Apr. 2022.

114. Bessembinder, Hendrik (Hank). "Wealth Creation in the U.S. Public Stock Markets 1926 to 2019." *SSRN Electronic Journal*, 2020. *Crossref*, https://doi.org/10.2139/ssrn.3537838.

Bernstein, Jared. "Why Aren't There More? Assessing Barriers to ESOP Creation." *ESCA Report*, Jan 2021.

115. "France—An Update on Mandatory and Optional Profit-Sharing Schemes." *Lexology*, 7 June 2019, www.lexology.com/library/detail.aspx?g=453c69e4-c618-42cf-b5f6-b184cffcc005.

"When Workers Are Owners." *The Economist*, 20 Aug. 2015, www.economist.com/business/2015/08/20/when-workers-are-owners.

Gottfried, Miriam. "Private-Equity Giants Back New Nonprofit Promoting Employee Ownership." *WSJ*, 5 Apr. 2022, www.wsj.com/articles/private-equity-giants-back-new-nonprofit-promoting-employee-ownership-11649151000.

116. OECD Tax Policy Studies, *The Role and Design of Net Wealth Taxes in the OECD*. OECD, 2018.
See also: Piketty (2020).

117. OECD Tax Policy Studies, *The Role and Design of Net Wealth Taxes in the OECD*. OECD, 2018.

118. Alstadsæter, Annette, et al. "Tax Evasion and Inequality." *American Economic Review*, vol. 109, no. 6, 2019, pp. 2073–103. *Crossref*, https://doi.org/10.1257/aer.20172043.

119. Herd, Pamela, and Donald Moynihan. *Administrative Burden: Policymaking by Other Means*. 1st ed., Russell Sage Foundation, 2019.

120. For a modern reform approach inspired by the Apollo program, see Mazzucato, 2021.

5. TOWARD A NEW SPIRIT OF CAPITALISM

1. A 2018 survey across the G7 countries revealed that "82 percent of low-income individuals and 69 percent of middle-income individuals believe their own wealth has decreased or stagnated in the past few years." A different survey of OECD countries showed more than 60 percent of those surveyed said their country would be worse off for future generations.

Fine, David, et al. "Inequality: A Persisting Challenge and Its Implications." *McKinsey & Company*, 26 June 2019, www.mckinsey.com/industries/public-and-social-sector/our-insights/inequality-a-persisting-challenge-and-its-implications.

2. Ipsos' "What Worries the World" series of polls covers 28 countries, including all members of the G7. For example, in September 2019 61 percent on average reported they felt their country was on the wrong track. For the G7, the results were Italy (83 percent), Great Britain (77 percent), France (74 percent), Germany (69 percent), Japan (62 percent), the United States (60 percent), and Canada (58 percent). The most positive countries were China, Saudi Arabia, and India. Atkinson, Simon, et al. "What Worries the World—September 2019." *Ipsos*, 12 Nov. 2019, www.ipsos.com/en/what-worries-world-september-2019.

3. Weber, Max. *The Protestant Ethic and the Spirit of Capitalism (Norton Critical Editions)*. First, W. W. Norton and Company, 2008.

4. In June 2021, majorities in all G7 countries reported feeling that their countries had become more divided during the COVID-19 pandemic.

Devlin, Kat, et al. "People in Advanced Economies Say Their Society Is More Divided Than Before Pandemic." *Pew Research Center's Global Attitudes Project*, 23 June 2021, www.pewresearch.org/global/2021/06/23/people-in-advanced-economies-say-their-society-is-more-divided-than-before-pandemic.

INDEX

INDEX

INDEX

INDEX

INDEX

Industrial Internet of Things (IIoT), 42–3
Industrial Revolution
  First, 3, 14, 18–19, 27, 35, 93, 140
  Second, 93
  Fourth, 41, 42, 84
inequality, 6, 7, 11–12, 14, 23, 26, 31, 35, 121–60, 164, 165
  administrative burden and, 157–8
  assortative mating and, 133–4
  authoritarianism and, 126, 130–32, 147
  childhood and, 133–6, 147–9
  data and analytics, 153–4
  democracy and, 126, 130–32
  digital revolution and, 79, 89–94, *89*, 111–12
  domestic, *124*, 125
  education and, 134, 136–41, 149–52, 165
  gender inequality, 134, 139, 141
  green transition and, 47–8, 71, 129
  incomes, 7, 142–6, *143*, 152–3
  inherited wealth and, 133, 157
  labor market and, 141–6
  legacy barriers, 146, 151
  market concentration and, 154, 166
  mental health and, 136
  merit-based, 132
  race and, 135
  redistributive policies, 130–31, 132–3
  social status and, 136
  status-based, 132
  taxation and, 156–7
  transparency and, 154–5
  women and 134, 139, 141–2, 150, 151, 155
inflation, 129, 162, 165
Infrastructure Investment and Jobs Act (US, 2021), 58
inherited wealth, 133, 157
innovation, 59–61, 98–9, 113–14
Institute of International Finance, 72
Intel, 80
intellectual property, 17, *25*, 49, 59
interactions, 28
Intergovernmental Panel on Climate Change (IPCC), 38, 39
International Energy Agency (IEA), 43, 44
International Labor Organization (ILO), 134, 141, 142
International Monetary Fund (IMF), 22, 49, 116, 136
international standard setting, 55
International Telecommunication Union, 103
Internet, 24, 70, 79, 81
  access to, 79, 89–91, *89*, 111–12
  broadband, 90, 112
  cyber-security, 116–17
  Industrial Internet of Things (IIoT), 42–3, 84
  online shopping, 24, 97, 100, 106
  splinternets, 103
  streaming services, 84, 106
InvestEU, 58
investments, 27–8
  climate change, 67–71
  digital revolution, 110–14

INDEX

INDEX

INDEX